Corporate
Acquisitions

Gulf Publishing Company
Book Division
Houston, London, Paris, Tokyo

Corporate
Acquisitions

Gordon Bing

Corporate Acquisitions

Library of Congress
Catalog Card Number

ISBN 0-87201-009-0

Library of Congress Cataloging
in Publication Data

Bing, Gordon.
  Corporate acquisitions.

  Includes index.
  1. Business enterprises—Purchasing. 2. Consolidation and merger of corporation. I. Title.
HD2741.B55   658.1'6   80-22386
ISBN 0-87201-009-0

Contents

Preface

This book is for individuals who wish to learn how to either acquire one substantial business or to establish a continuous program of multiple takeovers that would last indefinitely. It describes what must be accomplished and how to do it step by step in sufficient detail for the average business person to follow. Accompanying the description of necessary steps is a commentary to provide greater understanding of all acquisition activity. Seldom are acquisitions easy, and people are often misled by news articles announcing and summarizing them. Even experienced executives tend to forget all that was involved and the hundreds of hours of effort by many people with diverse skills and backgrounds that preceded the press releases. A very long and difficult path was traveled after someone decided to acquire a business before a company was located and acquired. There is nothing mysterious about the acquisition process and a business genius is not required for its implementation, but there are many aspects, details, and a few complexities that must be accommodated if success is to result.

While the book will give a seller considerable insight into the acquisition process, it is written primarily for buyers, from the buyers' point of view, and with unabashed sympathy for them. Buyers need all the help they can get because too often they discover belatedly they bought something other than what they expected. They are also victims of a double standard. The business press and country club locker rooms are full of stories of shareholders who sold their companies only to find the shares they received deteriorated in value or they could not continue to manage their companies in a manner compatible with the personalities and policies of the new owners. Seldom, if ever, are unfortunate buyers discussed sympathetically. They are usually portrayed as predatory villains receiving their just rewards, or at best, as business fools if the acquisition does not go well. If it is a success, the buyers are "shrewd." The old dictum "let the buyer beware" applies totally, and a buyer can expect little sympathy if an acquisition proves unprofitable regardless of the reasons.

The buyer's shares may deteriorate because of the performance of the acquisition; the management of the acquisition may become lazy and hopelessly independent as nouveau riche; the acquired company's assets may have been misrepresented; the market may begin to decline; the products may be mature to a point of near obsolescence; once docile competitors become voracious; labor relations explode; government regulations change or are suddenly enforced; litigation over "dead" issues commence; warranty claims abound; and key employees leave—to mention a few of the possibilities. While these events are occurring and adversely affecting the business, the former shareholders are enjoying the benefits of the cash or stock they received from the buyer. The buyer is left to struggle as best he can with the business and all its problems. If the acquisition proves to be more profitable than anyone anticipated, then the sellers complain they sold for too low a price.

This book describes a systematic proven approach to acquisitions for those who are serious buyers. It is of little use, and possibly an embarrassment, to executives who only want to be on record as having an acquisition program or those who hope good acquisitions will just walk in their door. It is helpful in evaluating how serious a company is about acquisitions by comparing what has been done and what is being done with what needs to be done. Desirable acquisition candidates are not likely to approach the buyer asking to be acquired, and in the absence of an acquisition program it is even more improbable that the company, once approached, would know how to evaluate and acquire. The systematic approach is for those who are willing to devote the time and effort to get the job done. It is for those who recognize that a commitment to making acquisitions requires an expensive investment before one dollar or share is delivered to a seller, but it is an investment with the potential for huge returns.

The systematic approach presented in this book constitutes a description of things to be done, checklists of factors to consider, ideas to be explored, and alternatives that may have been overlooked. It is a basic program for a buyer to use as a starting point to develop his own program, because a buyer must tailor his program to fit his company, industry, and objectives. It would be a mistake to treat this as a canned program, not requiring modification by each buyer, but the basic approach and principles do have a universal applicability. Buyers may decide to shorten or eliminate parts of the program, but the result can only be a lessening of the odds that the buyer will acquire the best company available and not make costly mistakes.

This book is indirectly a plea for the use of competent professionals, primarily lawyers and accountants. Emphasis is on competence and recognition that not all professionals possess the same ability. A buyer or seller who uses second-rate professionals in a complex acquisition transaction commits a fundamental error. Professionals cannot be avoided in an acquisition program, so the buyer should use the best available to the best advantage. Government regulations and accounting rules change frequently and only a professional active daily in the field can hope to maintain fully up-to-date knowledge. There are also grey areas without clear rules where only superior judgment will suffice. The technical aspects of law and accounting are not covered here, but the book does describe the activities and decisions of a buyer in the acquisition process that are governed or influenced by legal, tax, or accounting rules. One objective of the book is to describe what the buyer can and should do himself and when he should call upon professionals.

The acquisition process is a very human affair and what individuals should do or how others may react must continually be under consideration. Only in a legal sense do companies buy companies and recognition of this fact is one of the keys to making successful acquisitions. Individuals in the buying and selling organizations are not solely motivated by the most rational or lofty type of business thinking. Business decisions are frequently influenced by factors other than pure economic ones and while this may be disillusioning or appear cynical, it is a condition that practitioners in the field daily confront. How a transaction will economically and psychologically affect the decision-makers of the buying and selling organizations will determine whether or not there will be a transaction.

The described systematic approach is applicable primarily to the friendly acquisition of established corporations or businesses. It will be helpful as a reference book for those who wish to acquire a small "mom and pop" type business, but the program is for those about to acquire businesses that are well established and have grown to some size. The book will provide little help for those looking for guidance on how to engage in hostile takeover battles, because the author believes most are misguided and wrong for a buyer from an economic and social point of view. Unfriendly acquisitions are primarily conducted by buyers with short-term personal objectives and strong stomachs.

In the book the terms "buyer" and "seller" are commonly used. These terms are convenient and accurate in describing the parties regardless of what type of acquisition or merger is being contemplated. In any transaction some organization or person eventually ends up in control and is considered to be the buyer. Buyer and seller are also applicable to individuals because they make the necessary decisions and are the participants. The use of masculine pronouns throughout the book is not to deny the substantial participation and contribution of women in the business world.

Gordon Bing
September 1980

1.
Acquisition Objectives and Policies

Every generation of executives and entrepreneurs rediscovers the potential advantages of acquiring businesses instead of starting them from scratch. After their discovery they proceed to reinvent methods and techniques for use in their acquisition programs, which in all probability were used hundreds of times before. Acquisitions and mergers have been a regular part of business activity at least since the Industrial Revolution, and while a few of the rules may have changed and will continue to change, the basic elements and procedures remain the same. If a house is to be built, there still must be a foundation, walls, and a roof. If a company is to be acquired, the buyer and seller must somehow communicate, evaluate each other, agree upon a price, and the type of currency or other consideration before shaking hands.

Not only do the basic aspects of acquisitions remain the same but upon review of the statistics of the number of acquisitions made in proportion to the size of the economy, or the number of corporations, we find little change here too. There are variations from year to year and decade to decade, but, when the entire period of the last 100 years is examined, the inescapable conclusion is that acquisition activity has continually existed and the number of acquisitions in relation to the size of the economy remains relatively constant. A hundred years ago, just like today, owners grew old, wanted to cash out, had reverses they could not cope with, needed working capital and experienced most of the conditions owners do today that cause business sales. Aggressive buyers seeking economic gain, power and status were looking for opportunities then as they do today. While the game remains the same, the individual players come and go. However, the players' motivations, which may on the surface be diverse and have varying degrees of importance, all stem from fundamental human characteristics that do not change.

1

A sophisticated buyer with established realistic objectives can greatly improve his chances of obtaining his goals in the shortest practical time with minimum expense. To do so, he must learn from others, understand the acquisition process, modify proven techniques to fit his own situation rather than continually "reinvent the wheel," and emphasize the psychological and economic needs of the participants in planning his actions. Innovation and imagination are always valuable in an acquisition program, but time need not be lost while they are being applied to situations, conditions, and problems for which ample data and successful tested techniques and solutions are readily available. Better methods and techniques are welcome but it is impossible to know they are superior if the others are unknown and unavailable for comparison.

High Risks

The business system has as one of its fundamental concepts, risk taking. Executives tout themselves as risk-takers and entrepreneurs, yet their basic task is to avoid or minimize risks. Managers are expected to make decisions that produce results favorable to the enterprise. It is their job to gather sufficient information and have the judgment for their decisions to be nearly risk-free and under no condition contain a large element of risk. Studies of all types, forecasts, financial analysis, and opinion gathering from varied sources are all part of the process to avoid making decisions involving unnecessary risks. Because managers avoid risk and do not deliberately make decisions which, at the time, with the information available, and under the circumstances, they believe are bad, one must ask why do so many decisions turn out poorly. It is because the greatest risks in any enterprise are associated with the level of competence of the managers involved and the number of variables they must evaluate in their decisions.

A measure of the risk elements in any type of business activity is how often do the executive decisions produce unexpected results. Using this standard, it is obvious that buying businesses is an extremely high risk activity. It is a rare buyer who can claim that even one of his acquisitions performed exactly as he forecast in his preacquisition studies. They either do much better or much worse, but seldom as forecast. Unfortunately, a large percentage of acquisitions turn out to be failures rather than successes for the buyers; as evidenced by numerous statistical studies, the very active market in divestitures, and the number of liquidations.

In view of management's normal aversion to risk and the high risk nature of acquisitions, the question also arises as to why do so many individuals and corporations want to make acquisitions. Nearly all corporate senior executives proclaim they are interested in making acquisitions, at least, if the "right thing" came along and fell in their lap; some because they actually do want to buy companies, and some only because they believe such proclamations are expected of them, like statements on quality and equal employment rights. One of several answers to the question of why would anyone want to make acquisitions is the great economic benefit to the buyer if all turns out well. Another reason is that acquisitions are often made primarily for noneconomic reasons associated with the personal desires of the decision-making participants. Furthermore, a buyer can not resist believing he is smarter than others and will do a superior job of selecting, evaluating, negotiating, and managing thus reducing his risk to a neglible factor. A buyer may feel he can afford a mistake now and then if the majority of his acquisitions turn out well, but this rationale will not prevent recriminations once an acquired company turns sour.

Buyers should be realistic and face up to the fact that while they can do a great deal to improve their chances of success in making acquisitions, they are still engaged in an extremely high-risk activity.

Buyers and Sellers Are Only Human

In the press we read that Corporation A has acquired Corporation B, which in a legal sense is quite accurate. However, from a practical standpoint, acquisitions are made by people and not corporations. If a buyer is to have any degree of success, he will have to continually organize his approach around how people act and react. Usually, he needs to be concerned most with the attitude of very few on the seller's side and most commonly, one key individual. In an acquisition only one or two people on each side have any real decision-making authority although thousands of shareholders and employees may be affected by their decisions. How the proposed transaction will personally affect the decision-makers will be the critical issue in the negotiations, although it may not be discussed in that light.

Often great discretion is exercised to avoid any direct discussion of the personal benefits of a transaction, but both parties know very well what the key issues are that must be accommodated if there is to be a transaction. The seller's decision-makers will expect the buyer to structure his sales presentation and proposal to buy in a manner that will be attractive to them and show how they will benefit. Under no conditions should they be worse off upon selling. To expect a decision-making executive to support an acquisition that may be highly beneficial to others, but not him, is unrealistic.

The strategy of any acquisition will center around how best to contact and influence the decision-makers. The buyer will attempt to persuade the seller's decision-makers that a sale is in their interest and the price is generous under current market conditions. The seller almost always has the advantage of knowing more about his business and industry than the buyer and will work to convince the key members of the buying organization of the business's values and potential that may not be readily apparent.

Realism Is Essential

A high degree of realism and sophistication is essential for those active in making acquisitions becasue they must operate in a changing framework of rules and no rules. This is a complex activity where there are many peripheral values and procedures but none exist for the basic issues that must be resolved in every acquisition. As a result, most acquisition activity must be conducted and decisions made in an amoral environment where there are no rules of right and wrong. There is no definition of a "fair price," and society has not attempted to set standards that would enable a buyer and seller to readily calculate a price. Each is on his own to negotiate as best he can. Society has not fully established what, if any, are the obligations of selling share-holders to loyal employees who labored for years to help build the enterprise. There are some regulations protecting minority share-holders but few govern a majority shareholder's obligations to minority holders in a sale situation. The minority usually have only unpleasant alternatives if they do not follow the pattern set by the majority holders. Outside of antitrust regulations, which are subject to varying interpretations, society does not set rules on what is a good or bad acquisition.

The lack of basic rules has created a vacuum filled with superficial rules, procedures, and gamesmanship. Price arguments tend to center around price earnings ratios, discounted future earnings forecasts, book values, forecasted return on investment, and any other criteria the participants can think of to help justify their position. At some point in an acquisition negotiation, the selling shareholders will express great concern over the welfare of their companies' employees and the buyer's representatives will make appropriate remarks on how all employees will be well treated and prosper under their ownership. With that formality over, they will proceed to make whatever deal they can in their own self-interest. This is not to say that in most cases concern for employee welfare is not genuine, but economic self-interest seems to have a higher priority.

Fairness to minority holders receives its share of lip service and the minimum attention required to induce them to follow the wishes of the majority. Most majority holders who have played a major role in building a company have little compassion for minority holders who benefitted from their efforts, but contributed nothing other than their money. Minority holders are largely considered a nuisance to be manipulated rather than an important decision-making group. Minority holders frequently are all too happy to see a sale because they no longer are fond of the majority holders and view sale as the reasonable way out of their investment.

Buyers and sellers both look at a transaction in terms of how it will benefit them personally and their respective businesses with effects upon the communities where they are located, the industry or economy being of secondary interest. There is always ample fanfare by the participants as to how desirable an acquisition is for everyone, and their powers of rationalization are quite remarkable. Public pronouncements indicate an awareness that there may be obligations to other segments of society which are not legal obligations or clearly defined, but do exist. Satisfaction of these nebulous broader obligations seldom have a priority over self-interest in the minds of the buyer's and seller's decision-makers.

Establish Objectives

A prospective buyer should ask himself and decide prior to starting an acquisition effort exactly what he wants to achieve and why, and determine if these objectives could be more easily accomplished by other means. The objectives once established should be communicated to all key management people in the buyer's organization to provide a foundation for a coherent program. Rational objectives, communicated to all involved, are essential if a systematic program is to be carried out that will elicit enthusiastic internal support. The better defined the objectives, the easier will be the acquisition task, but clear objectives do not necessarily make a good program. They only make possible an effective program.

Most companies have not thought out goals as carefully as they should, and as a result, spend too much time looking at companies they will never buy. Without objectives, they are precluded from a systematic program to identify and pursue companies that would be logical additions to their business. Waiting for attractive companies to "walk in the door" can be a long and tedious wait. Purchasing numerous companies that do not tie together with realistic objectives, existing markets, or operations can produce an unmanageable mixture. Creating objectives to rationalize the acquisition of a company that unexpectedly becomes available is putting the cart before the horse.

The overall logical objective of acquisitions is to maintain or increase profits, and a buyer must conduct his program consistent with this standard regardless of the reasons for buying. However, this is more of a standard or policy than a specific objective, although a few companies have it as their only objective. It is too broad to use as an objective only, but it is applicable in all cases. Objectives must be specific to be useful, such as: secure at least 20% of the high priced market in the office furniture industry, acquire a foundry that can supply 75% of present casting requirements, or acquire a company with $10-20,000,000 in sales and a product that can be marketed by the buyer's existing sales organization.

Objectives, company policies, and reasons for buying are often difficult to distinguish between one another and an effort to do so can become a fruitless exercise in semantics. It does not matter greatly what the guidelines or goals are called as long as they are precise enough to provide a framework within which an acquisition program can be efficiently conducted. The objective to acquire a furniture manufacturer with 20% of the high-priced market could also satisfy the policy (which might be considered an objective) of acquiring a company in furniture manufacturing that has a 15% pre-tax return on sales. It could also satisfy the buyer's chief executive's real reason for buying, which is that he is overworked, needs relaxation, and wants a company located in an area where he can fly in the company plane on Fridays to review its operation and ski nearby during the weekend. Clever sellers will do their cause no harm by showing a buyer the major recreational opportunities in the area where his business is located.

Established formal business objectives often conceal the real reasons for buying, which may be socially unacceptable but nevertheless exist. Society seems to recognize that most business executives work very hard and long hours and they deserve extra and unusual compensation, but the tax regulations and unreasonable shareholders with their strike suit attorneys make it difficult.

Reasons to Buy

There are two general categories of reasons for making acquisitions. In some instances a particular reason may fall in either category (some could argue for one category or the other), but this is not of great importance. The establishment of categories is primarily to provide insight into the acquisition process and enable a prospective buyer to find reasons for doing what he was going to do anyway and provide comfort for buyers who may believe their self-interest motives are unique. In any acquisition there usually are several reasons from both categories to buy, and their importance can vary from very little to the only reason for buying. These two categories of reasons are *business/institutional* and *management/shareholder*.

Business/Institutional Reasons

These reasons support acquisitions that directly benefit the buyer's business with benefits, one would hope, coming to the mangement and shareholders indirectly as a result of greater corporate earnings. Acquisitions of this type are expected to provide growth, increase earnings, and may solve internal problems of the buyer. These socially acceptable reasons are made public and tend to be acceptable to respective sellers. They are discussed openly and sound splendid in annual reports, policy statements, and press releases. An acquisition based on business/institutional reasons often has synergistic potential and, at a minimum, the business acquired is expected to perform at least as well under new ownership. Both the acquirer and the acquired expect to be stronger as a result of the transaction.

The following list of business/institutional reasons is undoubtedly incomplete, but it contains the common reasons publicly proclaimed why Company A acquired Company B:

1. Complete or extend an existing product line.
2. Acquire distribution and a broader market.
3. Better control material supply.
4. Secure key personnel.
5. Secure needed technology or patents.
6. Replace products in a declining market.
7. Secure manufacturing facilities or develop products for idle facilities.
8. Secure a place to move an existing product line.
9. Combine operations with a similar company and solve overwhelming economic problems.
10. Use nonproductive assets to acquire other businesses.
11. Develop a concept that would provide a "unique" service or product.
12. Increase purchasing power.

13. The price was low because of the seller's need to sell and the buyer had little or no risk.
14. Add strength to weak areas of the acquired such as add needed capital, and greatly increase earnings.

Management/Shareholder Reasons

These reasons are the main motivational factors for individuals and center around how they will benefit personally regardless of any undesirable short- or long-term effects on either the acquired or acquirer's business. Acquisitions for management/shareholder reasons are often predatory and do not fit with acquirer's other businesses. The acquired company's chances of prospering are not greater once acquired. These reasons are seldom discussed or made public and may not even be mentioned in the buying organization, but the participants know they exist. Examples of the management/shareholders reasons are:

1. Executive status; the larger the company, the more important are its executives.
2. Executive compensation; compensation levels do correlate with company size.
3. Find a position for relatives of key shareholders or the chief executive officer.
4. Buy blocks of stock for "investment" purposes, which will be sold at a profit to increase buyer's share and executive option values.
5. Raise the value of buyer's stock by acquiring companies in industries currently in favor with Wall Street.
6. Cover up poor management of existing companies by acquiring new.
7. Move capital from one country to another.
8. Liquidate the acquired at a profit that will be non-recurring.
9. Real, imagined, or contrived inside information that a company is about to boom.
10. Conglomerating—propping up an earnings record by acquiring sellers having low price/earnings ratio stock (PE) with the buyer's high PE stock.
11. Acquire companies because other companies acquire companies. (A sort of "keeping up with the Joneses" approach.)
12. The "swan song"; an aging executive wants a big acquisition to wind up his career.

13. "Can't say no"; a key executive is infatuated with an acquisition and the board feels it can't refuse to go along, despite misgivings.
14. A key executive committed the company to buy and the board does not want to make him appear unsupported.
15. Keep acquisition executives busy and justify their presence.
16. Spend excess cash and make buyer less attractive for takeover and preserve incumbent management.
17. Make the buyer's company less desirable or more difficult to be acquired and protect management.
18. Career building; it looks good on an executive's resume to have made acquisitions.
19. Asset stripping; under the guise of "superior management," liquidate or sell and lease back assets of acquired to finance buyer and executives and then resell remains of the business.
20. Travel; executives often like to travel to distant cities and countries and acquisitions provide the excuse.
21. Entertainment; an acquisition in an area that offers skiing, hunting, nightlife, or other activities favored by the chief executive officer may have unusual appeal.
22. Publicity; making frequent acquisitions or one big acquisition is a way for an executive to receive public recognition.
23. Acquisitions in the media or entertainment fields are a means for the chief executive officer and his wife to associate with celebrities.
24. The collectors; the psychological desire to collect companies like some collect postage stamps or antiques.

These management/shareholder reasons for acquiring should never be underestimated in importance, and in every acquisition their presence can be suspected to some degree, regardless of any public pronouncements. A wise planning or acquisition executive will recommend companies for acquisition that accommodate the CEO's desires, whims, and preferences. The ultimate political acquisition may be the leading industry either in the CEO's hometown or the town where he went to college.

The business reasons to buy should be made known to all those in the buyer's organization who will participate in making acquisitions, as well as the key members of management. When approaching a prospect, one of the first things to explain is why the acquisition would make sense for the buyer and how it would fit into his overall program. These business reasons to acquire will normally imply to a seller how his business will be stronger if sold.

It is not easy for a company to decide what it wants to accomplish and the nature of its objectives. Often, bitter controversy surrounds the determination of corporate objectives. Objectives to be reached through acquisition should be evaluated before finalization to see if there are more sensible alternatives.

Acquisition Alternatives

Because making acquisitions is such a common activity of the business world and has an air of grand adventure about it, there is a tendency to rush into an acquisition program before evaluating the alternatives. Acquisition programs are costly, time consuming, and have no certainty of success, let alone financial success with a company once acquired. Therefore, after a company's objectives are established, a study should be made to see how best they may be successfully achieved. The study should include an estimate of the cost, time, and probability for making an acquisition that would satisfy the objectives and then evaluate and compare the following basic alternatives.

Do nothing. Just how important are the objectives? Are they worth any effort? Do these objectives present a solution to a problem that will solve itself in time? Could the objectives be reached with normal management effort.

Internal growth. Could a business be started up easier than acquired? Could facilities be constructed, new products developed, or marketing expanded cheaper and easier than by acquisition? What would be the cost of starting up as opposed to acquisition?

Internal amputation. Rather than take drastic steps to save an ailing operation, why not shut it down or divest? Could the capital employed in a sick business be better deployed elsewhere?

Joint venture. Would a joint venture be a better solution? The joint venture need not be a start-up situation, because it could involve purchasing a minority or 50% interest in an existing company. Anyone considering a joint venture should also evaluate their own talent for working with partners they may not be able to control, because many find cooperation rather than total control difficult to accept.

Licensing. Companies strong in distribution in search of technology and products should compare the cost of licensing with acquisition. In fields of rapid technological change licensing often is a better solution. Businesses with technology to promote may be able to do so more profitably, in less time, and with less risk through licensing than to acquire a company with idle manufacturing space or underutilized distribution.

Management agreements. An increasingly popular alternative in international business is a combination of agreements, which may specify management rights and responsibility, board seats, licensing or distribution, along with the acquisition of a minority position. In some cases only an investment into the company is made in the form of a loan and the conditions of the loan specify the term of the total agreement.

"Do it anyway." If the main reason is for the personal benefit of management or key shareholders, possibly the perquisites could be given without all the expense of an acquisition. Salary increases, trips abroad, and entertainment cost will be much less than an acquisition. No one may be looking and no one may care and the perquisite may be well deserved and quite justified.

The Plan and the Planners

For efficient execution of an acquisition plan, it is necessary to first determine by some means what businesses the buyer wants to be in, and this selection process is usually referred to as strategic planning. Planning has always existed in some form in business, but during the past decade there has emerged an abundance of literature on strategic planning and today it is fair to say planning is in vogue.

No one questions the desirability of planning, but the results are often controversial and the activity still considered by most a luxury that is dispensable in difficult times. The young man whose coat is on fire can hardly be expected to be thinking of who he will dance with next. Plans and planning can consist of as little as an unexplained, unequivocal statement by the CEO or controlling shareholder describing precisely the type of business he wants to acquire all the way up to the creation of an elaborate staff of planners, prophets, soothsayers, and second-guessers who generate reams of reports, expense, and often little else.

Most companies are somewhere in between. The CEO's plan of "this is the industry I want to be in," which may be based on a hunch or very careful personal study and thought, may prove to be an excellent selection, and so too may be the accepted recommendations of the professional planners; or both may eventually prove to be terrible mistakes. However, industry selections as a result of in-depth studies will probably produce the better selections because they do tend to bring into the open the known parts, problems, and opinions for rational evaluation.

Despite all the difficulties and often poor results, a management must assume the odds for success are better if an endeavor is intelligently planned and the known variables accommodated instead of relying on whims and chance. Sometimes it is possible to have the best of both worlds because recommendations based on formal studies are always more welcome and readily accepted if they match the decision-makers preconceived ideas. The purpose of many studies is supportive rather than creative.

Planning, Full of Uncertainty

Planning is a hazardous occupation because it involves predicting the future, and major events that negate the best of plans persist in occurring. All one has to do is look back at the past ten years and ask who predicted the oil embargo of 1973, the changes in electronic technology, the energy crisis, the political instability in countries thought to be stable such as Iran, Proposition 13, the rate of inflation, the Mount St. Helens volcano, or prime interest rates of 20%, to mention a few of the surprises. A five-year business plan based on any of these events occurring in the fourth or fifth year would never have been accepted by any board of directors. There is every reason to believe there will again be many future events of great magnitude that no one could forecast today without being thought a fool or at best a peculiar curiosity. Even events that are considered a certainty by reasonable men, such as a great California earthquake, are ignored by most in planning because it is too horrible to contemplate and does not fit into our preferred future.

The whims and changing attitudes of consumers are particularly difficult to measure and predict as evidenced by the many new product failures, as well as a few that exceeded everyone's expectations. There is no better example than the U.S. automobile industry, which has access to every sophisticated technique of forecasting, market studies, and planning, yet consistently has model failures and massive errors in production forecasts. Regardless of the uncertainties and problems, there is almost universal agreement that planning is essential for any business enterprise. The odds are good that the results will be better if they are intelligently planned rather than achieved by "muddling through." Every CEO must claim he has a plan although he may choose not to disclose it, and it may be at best a vague idea in the back of his mind. There usually is some plan no matter how cursory or inadequate and invariable plans are for success, not failure. Executives do not deliberately botch up companies, as it may appear at times to their detractors. Failures are the results of plans gone wrong and not the results of plans.

Scope of Planning

While it is generally agreed that planning is desirable, there is far less agreement as to the extent or nature of planning, responsibility of the planners, who should do the planning and where does planning fit into a business organization's overall structure and activities. Obviously, the size of an organization and its attitude towards growth will set some practical limits on this function. A small business cannot afford a General Electric type planning staff and a company more concerned with immediate survival than rapid expansion is unlikely to devote any time or expense to long-range planning.

When business size and growth objectives are equal, there are still great differences in the planning functions and no one approach is accepted as the best. Perhaps the unpredictable future, which unjustly discredits the planners from whom the impossible is expected, is a basic cause of the variations.

Another cause is the extreme differences in the planners' stature and capabilities, which are reflected by their positions in the corporate hierarchies. Planners are convenient scapegoats readily given the blame for faulty recommendations, while executives claim credit for making decisions that proved to be wise, which were based on planners' studies—studies quickly forgotten by everyone but the originators. These conditions lead to turnover and more attempts to find better means of peering into the future.

Industry Selection

To initiate an acquisition program it is not as important how the strategic planning is conducted as it is to decide in which industry the buyer desires to make an acquisition. Industry selection is the next most important decision to be made after the decision to commence an acquisition program. This decision is of such fundamental importance that it should involve the key decision makers in the buyer's organization. It is impossible for a management to be effective in all industries, although a few executives still resist the notion. The concept that a good professional manager familiar with so-called management skills and techniques could run any business in any industry with ease was pretty well discredited by the end of the 1960's. Industry knowledge is important and it takes time to absorb information and gain experience, and an executive can not learn them all in one lifetime. By selecting the industry in which to acquire, the buyer reduces the prospects to a number that can be identified and further evaluated against the buyer's criteria. The prospect list then becomes a manageable list from which to work and a source of further information of leads on the selected industry.

"Industry" is a broad term that should be defined as narrowly as possible. The narrower it is defined, the shorter will be the list of potential prospects that can be readily identified and evaluated. As an example, "natural resources" may be considered an industry but it is far too broad. An industry within it would be mining—again quite broad. An industry within mining would be lead mining, which would be precise enough. Another three-tiered example would be capital equipment—heavy machinery—paper machinery. In selecting an appropriate industry the buyer should develop background information on the broader categories as well. In the above examples the buyer may find there are no paper machinery companies he could acquire and he may wish to study other types of heavy machinery.

The best approach is to decide on the industry first and then the companies within it rather than the reverse. An industry study and selection may have been precipitated by information that a certain company within the industry was available, but without full knowledge of the industry, it cannot be determined if the available company is the one to buy. Chances are it is not. Industry selection presupposes that within every industry there is some company that can be acquired at some future time at some price. This usually is the case but the evaluation of the companies within the industry may disclose that none are practical prospects for the buyer and the buyer must select another industry or discontinue his acquisition efforts. He is, at this stage, disappointed and a bit wiser but will no longer spend time contemplating an industry he cannot enter.

Setting Realistic Acquisition Policies

Companies within an industry selected should be evaluated against the buyer's policies covering the characteristics of prospects, price considerations, and the buyer's current capabilities. These predetermined policies should be carefully constructed and correlate with the buyer's overall objectives. The comparison of prospect characteristics to the buyer's policy standards is a key element in shortening the prospect list and reducing the amount of detailed evaluation of contacted prospects willing to negotiate. However, they should not be so stringent and unrealistic that the buyer can only seek the perfect company, which does not exist. Searching for the Holy Grail is romantic and exciting but no one has been successful to date.

The policies should also not be so broad, minimal, or weak as to be useless. The policy standards for companies to be acquired can be higher than the buyer's company's performance and often should be, but they must be realistic. For example: a cash-only buyer who set as a policy a prohibition on acquiring goodwill (an amount in excess of book value) but also had a policy where the prospects must have had three years of at least 20% annual sales and earnings growth would never buy anything. Acquisition policies should not be so rigidly applied that they automatically preclude every unforeseen or unanticipated opportunity that does not exactly fit, but by forcing more careful evaluation of those prospects falling outside of the policy guidelines, they should screen out all but the truly outstanding ones.

Evaluating the Degree of Compliance

If a buyer has developed comprehensive policies covering most key areas, it is unlikely a prospect will fully comply. However, those areas of non-compliance should receive special attention and lack of compliance in one area should require superior compensatory factors in other areas for the prospect to be attractive. Standards serve as alarms signalling areas requiring corrective action to be taken after an acquisition is made. Such corrective action should be planned prior to closing the transaction. Of course, regardless how bad an acquisition may be and inconsistent with established policies, a determined buyer can rationalize the reasons for buying it. Conversely, no matter how good an acquisition may be and how fully it complies with all policies, a buyer can always find a way to talk himself out of it.

In setting policy the buyer should remember that the greater diversification he tries the greater will be his chances of failure. Diversification is essentially buying a business in an industry about which the buyer is ignorant. The policies should be set with an awareness that success in making profitable acquisitions is more probable if selection is limited to companies of a size with which the buyer is accustomed and in an industry similar to the buyer's present business and overall knowledge, rather than in some totally unrelated industry that some prophet proclaims to be on the verge of spectacular growth.

Policy Development

Every buyer must develop his own policy guidelines and the policies must cover the business of the prospect prior to acquisition and the forecasted performance under the buyer's ownership. The following is a list of subjects that most buyers should consider appropriate for policy development:

1. Return on investment and price considerations.
   a. The minimum return acceptable on the buyer's investment with return and investment accurately defined.
   b. Price-earnings ratio (PE) which must be defined.
   c. Time to recover total investment, investment must be defined.
   d. Length of time, if any, investment may decrease earnings per common share (dilutible) before increased earnings eliminate the condition.
   e. Type of currency, stock, cash, etc.
   f. Minimum earnings per share contribution of prospect once acquired.
2. Present financial condition of prospect including acceptable key ratios and minimum net worth.
3. Minimum percent pre-tax income to sales.
4. Type of product or service.
5. Minimum sales.
6. Minimum after-tax income.
7. Location of business that is acceptable including policy on international businesses.
8. Type of marketing.
9. Management characteristics and probability of retention.
10. Type of facilities and present capacity.
11. Ethnic and racial considerations.
12. Present percent of market share.
13. Financial history; define trends sought, if any.
14. Willingness to buy a turnaround situation.
15. Willingness to add working capital or cash for capital improvement.
16. Amount of debt the prospect may have.
17. Minimum growth potential.
18. Amount of goodwill, if any, to be acquired.

Policy guidelines on these subjects will permit screening of prospects to a point where very few will be rejected by the board of directors.

In writing the policies a buyer can make them strict or loose by the degree to which he chooses to define the terms. A balance has to be struck between such precise definitions that few prospects could ever comply and so loose that anyone could qualify. For example, the following short policy statement of "Return on investment must be

20%" is virtually meaningless unless most of the following questions are also clarified:

1. Is the investment the buyer's or the seller's?
2. How is investment defined?
3. How is stock valued?
4. Are future cash additions to the company to be counted as investment?
5. Must actual cash be returned to the buyer to be considered "return"?
6. What time period are we to measure "return" in?
7. Is return before or after tax?
8. Will synergistic profits in other businesses of the buyer be counted as "return"?

The same type of questions also apply to the subject of price-earnings ratios. A policy statement of "The acquired must have a PE ratio of not more than 10" is again meaningless. What period of time is to be used in calculating the ratio? How is price defined? How are earnings defined? Policies must be carefully constructed because of the lack of precise business definitions for terms commonly used and the willingness of people to use the terms without considering their meaning. Investment, price, earnings, proprietary, taxes, and revenues are all basic business terms that fit into a nebulous category. It would be wise for a buyer to write his policies in concise form for ready reference but also develop a series of commentaries on each to define and clarify terms, a kind of concordance.

Policies also must be constructed to reflect the capabilities of the buyer. A buyer with only $1,000,000 cash to spend and little credit can hardly set a minimum level of pre-tax profits on a prospect's current earnings at $500,000. A buyer with serious internal shortages of management cannot look at turnarounds. A buyer must engage in a good deal of introspection and self-evaluation before he establishes acquisition policies that are realistic for him. See chapter 2 for more information on buyer's capabilities.

Acquisition Policy Approval

Policies also must be approved at the top decision-making level and be applied by someone with respect in the organization. If the policies are submitted to the board of directors for approval, then the board can be expected to measure submitted acquisitions against the policies. They will expect to have acquisitions submitted that comply with their approved policies and a complete explanation of any deviations. Whoever develops the policies for board approval should not forget that he may be developing standards for himself. The more demanding and precise are the policies, the greater will be the difficulty in finding acceptable prospects.

Having policies approved by a senior executive of stature within the organization who reflects the thinking of the board, rather than the board itself, is another approach worth considering. If the policies are not approved by the board, the board will not be placed in the position of having to monitor their own policies. However, any policies that are not respected or administered by individuals who have little stature will probably be ignored and constitute nothing more than vague guidelines. If there are no formally approved policy guidelines and none are wanted either to retain total flexibility or because no agreement can be reached, then whoever is responsible for making acquisitions would do well to develop his own private policies based on his best judgement as to what the board of directors will accept and what makes good business sense for the buyer. Without policies of some sort, there can be no screening of prospects.

2.
Buyer's Capabilities

A buyer's objectives will remain as dreams if he does not possess the capabilities to seek out, pursue, buy, and absorb acquisitions. Somewhere in the buyer's organization there must be a mechanism, no matter how informal, for having discussions with sellers and making acquisition decisions. For example, a currency of some sort acceptable to sellers must be available for exchange if a transaction is to be completed. The currencies used are a wide variety of different mediums of real or questionable value ranging from cash or quality stock to only an assumption of liabilities with often the quality of the currency matching the quality of the business acquired. Cash or a sound equity issue will be demanded by sellers of superior companies because they know they need not settle for less.

Sellers of companies with erratic earnings histories and uncertain potential may have to sell for stock with its value largely to be determined by future events or promissory notes of little promise. The highly leveraged transactions that occasionally surface in the business press are still relatively rare and usually involve buyers long in nerve and short in net worth and companies heavy in assets and problems. Buyers waste a great amount of time and money when they attempt to seek out acquisitions of quality and pay with "funny money" or expect someone to carry their questionable notes in exchange for control. Of course, if the buyer is looking only for sick companies and turnaround situations, almost anything goes.

Perhaps the most important capability a buyer must possess is the ability to manage and provide for all the needs of a company once acquired. Nearly all buyers prefer to acquire companies with "good" management that require little or no attention, but the best of managements expect some policy decisions from their shareholders and demand a great deal of time and attention if the acquired is to be

19

integrated into the buyer's organization. Regardless of how well managed the acquired may appear, sooner or later the buyer will be faced with devoting time to any business. A wise buyer will carefully assess his own capabilities and match those with his aspirations to avoid becoming overextended.

A Buyer's Limits

A very rough guideline to use in deciding the limits of a buyer's acquisition capability is that his limits will be exceeded whenever his present position and other operations will be adversely affected and jeopardized by an unsuccessful acquisition. Dilution of earnings, inadequate capital in existing business, diversion of management, the necessity to liquidate assets to retire debt and loss of control, to name a few, are all possible results of acquisitions that fail or an overextended acquisition program. There is little merit in a buyer losing what he has by taking on the risks associated with a new acquisition. How much a buyer can afford to lose and at what point a buyer is imperiling his present position varies greatly with each buyer and is always difficult to determine.

Such determinations involve substantial business judgment with often the buyer a poor judge of adverse consequences because he is convinced of the wisdom of making a particular acquisition and believes it to be such a sure thing that it could not possibly go sour. Thousands upon thousands of acquisitions have preceded the buyer's and in all the buyers must have been convinced they were making excellent business moves. The fact that over half turned out otherwise should be evidence enough for a buyer to spend some time contemplating the effects if the acquisition does not turn out as expected. The buyer must ask himself, what happens if it does fail? If the buyer is not convinced an acquisition has a very high probability of success, he should not buy and the subject of the buyer's capability will be irrelevant.

Unfortunately, blind enthusiasm or some personal considerations all too frequently rule the day if we judge by financial results. Perhaps, some deals are for love as they surely are not for money because often there is no obvious economic justification for one of the participants. Regardless, as in most romances, outsiders never know all the facts or motives of the parties. One has to assume either the buyer or the seller has rationalized some economic benefit and the other looks at it as a deal too good to pass up.

It may be that a buyer's capacity to acquire can only be accurately determined on a retrospective basis, but historical reviews are usually of little value because the buyer has limited history to evaluate. The "no adverse effect upon current position" concept has to be defined to mean severe effects that would cause a buyer to radically change his overall business, or existing operations would be jeopardized. Obviously, any acquisition that is a financial failure will have some adverse effect, but the buyer need only be concerned if the effect is severe. Otherwise, he would never make an acquisition.

The Seller's Viewpoint of the Buyer's Capability

Buyers must remember that sellers will be applying the same yardstick to them and if they believe a buyer's existing business will become overextended as a result of the acquisition, they will not readily agree to sell and most likely will not even discuss the possibility. A seller will be evaluating a prospective purchaser from the first day he learns of the buyer's interest and capability is an area of intense initial study because without the capability to acquire a company of the size and type of the seller, there is no point in further discussions.

Buyers who devote their time during the acquisition process to evaluation of the seller and neglect to satisfy the seller's concerns about the buyer's financial and management strength are not likely to close the transaction. A buyer's executives' egotistical views of their own talents and optimistic business forecasts are usually in themselves inadequate to convince a seller. If the seller does not immediately see the buyer would be overextended by the acquisition, he will certainly consult with his lawyers and accountants who are more critical of immodest claims, and they will educate the seller as to the true conditions. It is not only their professional responsibility to do so, but they are highly motivated because if the acquisition is completed, they probably will lose a client and income. Regardless, a small minority of the transactions each year prove gullibility and greed have no bounds, but a solid acquisition program cannot be built on either of these very human defects.

Introspection by the Buyer

A buyer, to determine his capability to acquire, should attempt a systematic appraisal of his present status. For nearly all executives the company most difficult to objectively evaluate is their own. They are too close, too involved, and too much saddled with past decisions and uncertain forecasts to make totally dispassionate judgments. Any manager can easily develop an overly critical and unbalanced view of his company because the nature of a manager's job is that he spend most of his time on what is wrong rather than what is right.

However, some evaluation is necessary and because the buyer's executives will make and live with their acquisition decisions, they are the best to evaluate their capacity to acquire, regardless of their limitations. This all is a highly subjective exercise because a buyer's capacity to acquire can only be estimated in advance. These capacity estimates must be used as a basis for making acquisition policy decisions that will screen out automatically prospects with characteristics that exceed the policy limits. The extremes to be covered by policy statements will be outer limits, such as the maximum amount of cash to be used in a purchase, maximum number of shares of stock to be issued, amount of debt to be assumed, and conditions of companies to be reviewed as prospects. These would be used in early screening of prospects.

In deciding if a specific acquisition can be afforded, the buyer has to again decide what he can afford in light of current conditions and the condition of the prospect. What actually happens, either formally or informally, is a two-step approach. In step one, which occurs before a specific acquisition is evaluated, the buyer rules out prices and businesses that are clearly beyond his means. In step two, a specific acquisition opportunity is evaluated in light of current conditions.

A good way for a buyer to begin to assess his capacity to acquire is to conduct the same type of evaluation of himself that he should do of a prospect. Appendix 1 is an approach to systematic evaluation of a seller that the buyer could use to determine his present condition and outlook. Conducting a formal evaluation of himself will provide valuable experience as well as insight into the evaluation process. It will identify problems and opportunities that will affect forecasts of future earnings and balance sheet conditions. The use of an acquisition evaluation method can give a buyer a view of his business different from what is received in periodic budget or profit plan reviews. A buyer's capability to buy must be based upon his condition at the time an acquisition is likely to occur so major anticipated changes must be taken into account. In the evaluation the standards that will be applied to acquisition candidates should be applied to the buyer. This can highlight problems in the buyer's business or bring about a change in the standards.

Basic questions will emerge in this evaluation exercise that should be given particular weight. What is the outlook for the buyer's present business activity? What capital expenditures are required in the future and how will they be financed? If the buyer is forecast or found to be saddled with serious problems, such as a declining share of the market, greatly increased capital expenditures, and management gaps or weaknesses then he has conditions that may make an acquisition program impractical. The buyer and his management people will best devote their time and energy to solving existing business problems before expanding through acquisition. This comprehensive evaluation process will produce a list of strong points as well as weaknesses that should be helpful in giving a balanced view of the buyer's condition. Most managers tend to forget their businesses' strengths because they are so heavily focused on the problems.

Type of Payment Affects Capability

Because a buyer's capacity to buy is a direct function of the type of currency he will use in an acquisition, he should consider all types and select those that are suitable. As a part of setting his basic acquisition policies, he should decide upon which he would be willing to use in order of preference and those he would not use under any conditions. The more common types of currency used singularly or in combinations are listed below as a reminder of possibilities to consider. Each has its advantages and own dimensions in estimating a buyer's capacity to buy.

1. Cash
2. Common stock
3. Common stock — less than full voting rights or nonvoting
4. Preferred stock
   a. nonvoting
   b. voting
   c. cumulative
   d. convertible
5. Debentures
   a. senior
   b. subordinated
   c. convertible
   d. with warrants
6. Warrants
7. Promissory notes
   a. guaranteed by buyer
   b. unguaranteed or secured
   c. guaranteed by third party
   d. partially guaranteed by buyer
   e. secured by assets of buyer
   f. secured by assets of the prospect acquired
8. Assumption of liabilities
9. Earnout — contingency payments

10. Employment or consulting agreements
11. Management Contracts

With the exception of cash and debt instruments with third party guarantees, a buyer's currency is only as strong as the buyer. Each has its own characteristics for penalizing a buyer if the acquisition sours, ranging from cash lost forever at the most severe end of the scale to earnout obligations that are worthless in the absence of earnings. The type of payment or consideration used is also subject to external influences such as changing tax laws and conditions in the economy. A buyer should discuss with his financial and tax advisors the merits and disadvantages of each as they apply to his situation.

A buyer's capability to acquire varies with the type of consideration contemplated to be used in a transaction. For most buyers payment in cash would be most restrictive in ability to pay. The least restrictive, with almost no limit on price would be unsecured promissory notes. The capability to pay cash will be readily determined by the amount of excess cash the buyer possesses combined with the amount of cash he can borrow. The capability when lesser quality consideration is acceptable to a seller is limited only in theory by the willingness of the buyer and the gullibility of the seller.

However, to be realistic, a buyer should assume sellers will only accept consideration of a type and quality that can eventually be converted into cash and will not deteriorate in value prior to that time. If securities are issued, the seller must be convinced the buyer will remain in business and eventually the securities can be sold for cash at a value equal or greater than their valuation when accepted. The more readily marketable, the more desirable they will be.

The buyer's ability to retire debt instruments will determine their value to a seller and the seller's perception of the certainty or lack of certainty to convert the debt instruments to cash will govern their acceptability. A reputable buyer will not issue debt if he has doubts about his ability to retire it, because default would jeopardize what he already has. Sellers have been known to make many imprudent decisions in their haste to sell by accepting low quality currency, but a buyer cannot build a successful acquisition program or organization that will survive if he expects to base it upon issuance of paper only a fool would accept.

Low quality consideration is usually seen in the acquisition of companies that have serious problems by companies that are relatively new, or also have major problems and an appetite for growth beyond their means. On occasion, a reputable buyer will acquire a sick company using a type of consideration (usually unsecured promissory notes) that the seller accepts knowing full well the notes will only be retired upon the recovery of the company under the buyer's direction and ownership, and if recovery does not occur, the seller receives nothing.

Earnings Dilution

A practical limit on a buyer is the necessity to avoid dilution of per share earnings. Dilution occurs when the cost either in debt service or loss of present earnings on the money paid for the acquisition exceeds earnings of the acquired or earnings per share of new stock issued to acquire is less than earnings per share of previously issued old stock. Earnings per share is the single most important criterion used in the measurement of a business organization's progress and any decision that causes earnings per share to decline will be heavily criticized and rightly so. In rare instances decisions that have a negative effect on earnings may be rationalized as being necessary to build a solid base for growth or to clean up a prior management's sins, but these are extraordinary and very controversial conditions unrelated to acquisition decisions.

Other measures of a company's condition, such as current and debt-equity ratios, are important, and the effect an acquisition will have upon them will be studied, but they are inconsequential compared to the attention given to effects on per share earnings. Managements evaluating an acquisition, shareholders, and outside investors should (and most do) look first to see what impact an acquisition will have on earnings per share.

Financial projections that indicate acquisition of a company will have an adverse effect upon a buyer's per share earnings should tell the buyer the price is too high and beyond his capability. The buyer must then secure a price reduction, restructure the transaction, use a different type of consideration, or walk away. He cannot proceed with the acquisition without peril if dilution is anticipated. Shareholders and investors will look at current earnings of the seller in calculating the possibility of dilution and tend to place limited weight on forecasts although an exceptionally strong and obvious case may be made for the seller's potential.

Buyers are often so optimistic about the future of their existing business or the potential of an acquisition that they enter into acquisition agreements containing provisions that could produce future dilution. These terms are to be avoided by every prudent buyer. Provisions for the repurchase by the buyer of stock issued to the seller, provisions setting a floor on the price of the stock issued, and unlimited contingency payments based on the future earnings of the acquired are all dangerous for a buyer and create the possibility for unexpected dilution. During a negotiation in which a buyer's stock has shown a steady upward trend and the seller looks like a near perfect company, it is easy for a buyer to agree to provisions with dilution potential because it seems so improbable that they will ever become applicable and by acquiesing to such terms, the deal can proceed. This euphoria should be guarded against by the buyer.

In a later chapter on pricing it will be explained that price should be determined on a combination basis of suitable return on investment and what a buyer can afford to pay based on his financial condition. One buyer may be able to pay more than another without overpaying, but overpayment must be considered to have occurred whenever dilution results. Overpayment is largely a function of the buyer's capability and not directly related to whatever may be considered a fair price for the acquired. If the buyer has available a high PE common stock to use as currency, he can pay more for a company than if he uses cash. A buyer with a low PE common stock could pay more if he used cash instead of his stock. A buyer who persuades a seller to accept long-term, low interest, limited security notes would have a totally different capacity before overpaying.

Determining Financial Limits

Another test of capability is to determine how much money the buyer could borrow to make an acquisition. This is done by going to several banks or insurance carriers and explaining that an acquisition program that includes some borrowing is being contemplated and ask how much they will loan an the basis of the buyer's present financial condition. A request could even be made for a standby loan commitment, which banks commonly make at a rate of 1/2% to 1% if the buyer was nearly certain he would need the money. The size of the loan commitment available will indicate cash financing capability. Some lenders will give a larger loan than others, although both have the same information on a company. There is no uniformly accepted method of evaluating a balance sheet and income statement for loan purposes so various results are to be expected.

The loan officers may also have totally different perceptions of an industry and markets as a result of prior experiences. A lender who made a loan to a company that became a problem is going to look at loan applications from companies in the same industry on a cautious and critical basis as opposed to companies in industries in which the lender has had good experience. Other factors unrelated to the quality of the borrower, such as the lender's desire to make loans, money available, and loss experience all affect loan decisions and make loan shopping a necessity to determine the approximate maximum amount that can be borrowed. The quality and value of a company to be acquired may eventually affect the maximum loan range because the lenders will conduct their own evaluation of the prospect.

A buyer with former bankers in his organization could have them make estimates of maximum borrowing capability that would be accurate enough for preliminary needs. This would avoid disclosing plans to lenders who could then become persistent in trying to make the loan. The internal former bankers who estimate the maximum loan could be called upon to assist in securing the loan.

Collateral

Collateral is important but a buyer's capacity to borrow or issue debt instruments will primarily be evaluated on the basis of the probability of repayment in accordance with the agreed schedule. Responsible lenders do not enter into a loan with the expectation of recovering their principal through liquidation of collateral. The threat of foreclosure and liquidation is often more important to the safety of a loan for a lender than the actual carrying out of the foreclosure because of their inspirational effects upon management.

While a buyer should expect to service and eventually retire any debt incurred in making an acquisition from earnings of the acquired, the buyer's present financial condition and outlook will remain a controlling factor in decisions on the amounts to be loaned. An aggressive buyer cannot expect to limit his acquisitions to highly leveraged transactions with unguaranteed borrowings.

Excessive Debts

At some point a buyer's debt instruments will begin to lose credibility if holders or contemplated holders begin to have doubts about the ability to repay. The volume of debt instruments issued may be such that the credibility of the buyer becomes suspect. The point at which credibility deteriorates varies with each debtor and external factors, such as the condition of an industry or the overall economy. Debt instruments tend to become limiting and often contain provisions prohibiting the creating of more debt. Lenders, through control of the amount of indebtedness, have an additional means of protecting themselves. A buyer should review his outstanding loan agreements for provisions limiting new debt. He may find his capacity to borrow has already been determined in prior loan negotiations.

Dealing with Lenders

The source of borrowings must be considered in estimating capacity. It is all very well and necessary to calculate in theory the amount a buyer can borrow, but this will remain theory unless there is a logical identified lender. The closer the buyer is to the time of drawing down funds, the more he needs to be certain the prospective lenders will lend. Earlier conversations with lenders may now be void because of changing monetary conditions.

The most common problems center around a lender's approval system and the conditions that a lender may demand that were not covered when the general concept was first discussed. Lending institutions have procedures for reviewing and approving loan commitments that are necessary for their protection, but are easy for a buyer to forget. General discussions with a loan officer should be kept in perspective and never be considered as commitments.

A first-level loan officer's job is to evaluate, process, and recommend loans within his insitution, but most important, he should sell loans and encourage suitable loan applications. He often has the authority of a showroom automobile salesman and works in much the same manner, dealing directly with customers, generating loan applications for review by a higher authority (usually a loan committee) that often does not approve at all or without the attachment of new conditions. The loan may be approved in the amount requested, but the conditions of the loan are so onerous that the loan is unacceptable to the buyer. Many borrowers have been shocked to find their loan officer has little authority and his preliminary estimates of willingness to lend have been modified by new conditions, which make earlier acquisition capacity calculations void.

Maintaining Management Control

Another type of capacity to acquire is determined by the capability of dissatisfied new shareholders to throw the buyer's present management out. Shares of common stock issued in an acquisition have the same rights as shares presently controlled or voted by management, and the new holders may not remain docile or sympathetic to the buyer's management. Reverse acquisitions occur when the buyer issues so much stock to the seller that the seller controls the buyer. Sometimes this is the intent of the parties, but it can occur inadvertently. A buyer must review the present ownership of its shares and calculate how many shares can be issued to a new shareholder or group of shareholders before they become the dominant shareholders. If the seller is privately held with only a handful of shareholders, it is reasonable to assume the seller shareholders could be rallied to vote as a block if they become disenchanted with the buyer. This is a condition that few buyer managements are willing to permit.

After an acquisition in which the buyer's outstanding shares were widely held, control could move easily to former holders of the seller's shares if they now owned a large enough block. A management with indifferent shareholders today who take little or no interest in the company cannot assume they will remain secure if they make a sizable but unsuccessful acquisition for stock. Today's docile holders may team up with the new holders to unseat the management.

Often, a buyer's chief executive will minimize this problem in the belief that either the problem is unlikely to occur or his own performance is so outstanding that shareholders will never challenge him. A vigorous acquisition program will be allowed to progress to the stage where negotiations commence until it is realized that completion of the acquisition will not only bring in a fine new company, but a new largest single shareholder. The reality of the potential for loss of control is usually enough to terminate the negotiations. A reluctance exists with some buyers to establish formal acquisition criteria that flatly prohibit the consideration of any acquisition which, if completed, would jeopardize the control position of the buyer's existing management. It is not a sign of weakness for the buyer to take a position that he will not turn over the control of his company to others.

Control can also be lost in transactions that do not involve exchanges of common stock. The issuance of debt instruments or preferred stock that contain provisions permitting the election of directors in the event of default or missed dividends may seem innocuous at the time, but adverse business results could bring these rights to life.

Management Depth and Competence

The capacity of the buyer's management to acquire and absorb new acquisitions is another area for study. There are no precise measures as to what is a buyer's managerial capacity, but there are many existing symptoms that should signal a "go slow" approach. Buying new companies will not conceal existing operational failures and most probably will exacerbate old problems as well as bring in a host of new ones demanding solutions. For a buyer to evaluate the capacity of his management to take on new acquisitions he should look at the condition of his present operations and determine how the management spends its time. If the buyer has loss or marginal operations requiring a disproportionate share of senior management's time and this condition is expected to continue for an indefinite period, it may be best for the buyer to delay his acquisition program. Loss or marginal operations constitute measurable unsatisfactory conditions requiring immediate management attention, and regardless of who or what caused the poor performance, it is the buyer's management's job to solve the problems and turnaround the business.

A CEO's affection or preference for his management or key managers may blind him from conducting an objective evaluation of his managerial capacity, but financial reports are tangible and will eventually disclose poor performance. The causes of poor financial performance are varied, but all are problems requiring management attention. Declining share of market, capital requirements, quality defects, shortage of personnel, lack of financial control, underutilization of capacity, and governmental regulation conflicts are all major conditions whose existence should cause a buyer to lower his estimate of his managerial capacity to acquire.

A very fine management team may be unable to take on a major acquisition even if all the business is profitable and relatively free of problems. Internal growth programs may be too demanding or they just may be working too close to capacity to take on major new responsibilities.

Experience as a Factor of Capacity

If the buyer is a private investor or investment group, it must consider how much experience it has in running a company of the type it wishes to acquire and, equally important, how much time does it have to devote to management of a company. It is naive to assume a major investment can be made in a company and then all one has to do forever is attend an occasional board meeting and collect dividends, no matter how good the management may appear. A buyer will acquire on the basis of a forecast that justifies his investment, but he also is prudent if he has contingency plans should the investment sour. Any such plan will involve management input.

The availability of management time and expertise should influence a buyer's policy relative to the condition and similarity of the company(ies) to be acquired. If the buyer limits his acquisitions to well-managed, profitable companies, then he does not need a "surplus" of management talent standing by to handle problems. Conversely, turnaround situations may represent bargain acquisitions but they also represent large requirements for management time and talent.

Some buyers have had great success in reviving losing companies and have developed the necessary management skills, but real ability in this area is scarce. A buyer contemplating the acquisition of a losing company should ask himself what experience exists in his organization for handling turnaround situations. If there is none, he had better forget the whole idea. Losing companies seldom return to profitability quickly, and when one hears of a quick revival, it is wise to assume the turnaround is more a result of accounting ingenuity than an operational miracle. Even those companies experienced in taking over sick companies are often dismayed to find the company in worse shape than anticipated and the recovery period more extensive and expensive than planned.

Diversification Requires Extra Management

Diversification moves usually sound impressive to the public and tend to give the impression the buyer is aggressive and forward thinking.

However, by its very nature diversification means the buyer is buying a company in an industry with which he is not familiar. The more diverse the acquisition, the less he knows and the more he will have to learn. It is the author's opinion that the most common reason for unsuccessful acquisitions is a buyer making a diversification move and then attempting to impose standards, policies, and techniques that do not fit. This quickly brings about a breakdown in the relations between the buyer and the acquired, which leads the buyer to conclude that he needs new management in the acquired company.

Some buyers have a policy of automatically changing management of a company once acquired and not even attempting to work with the acquired managers. Others have a policy of not changing managers, but in practice they always become dissatisfied and do make changes. In either case, the buyer is not holding on to key assets for which he paid. Unless the new managers come from the buyer's organization, there will be an adjustment period during which the buyer and the acquired company will have to adjust to the new manager and he to them. During this period, operations are likely to decline even further.

As a general rule, a buyer needs management capacity to acquire in proportion to the diversification being attempted. A buyer who owns retail stores and acquires other similar stores can get along with less capacity than if he begins to buy suppliers. A buyer who manufactures garden tools needs more capacity to acquire a furniture company than a company manufacturing garden rakes. High production type managements will have difficulty in understanding job shop (metal fabrication) or personal service type operations (engineering companies). Differences in marketing approaches are also endless areas of controversy. Any buyer should evaluate his management capacity with extra care if he is contemplating diversification moves.

Buyer Organizational Problems

Acquisitions tend to disrupt the status quo within the buyer's management organization. Before the acquisition is made, considerable study and effort usually is required and the results of the studies and conclusions are often very controversial. A buyer may not be ready for this condition and the disrupting conflicts. Few acquisitions are ever made in which someone in the buying organization does not question the wisdom of an acquisition. The opposition may be open and hostile or subtle and restrained in the probably correct belief that vigorous opposition would be detrimental to their careers. A CEO enthused about an acquisition is more likely to consider those opposed as having doubtful loyalty and low intelligence instead of being vigilant executives advocating and protecting the buyer's best interests.

Organization Status

The status quo in a management organization can be disrupted by the decision of to whom shall responsibility for an acquisition be assigned. Executive status and compensation are directly affected by the size of the organization for which he is responsible. A material acquisition assigned to an executive constitutes a vote of confidence and enhancement of his prestige. Failure to assign an acquisition to a logical executive is an open insult. Therefore, when an acquisition program is contemplated, the buyer must give early thought as to where new companies will be placed in the organization structure. This becomes a particularly troublesome question in a larger organization where the group to which an acquisition should be assigned is not performing well. In practice, acquisitions are seldom assigned to groups or divisions that are doing poorly on the assumption (probably quite correct) that present management is not capable of taking on any more responsibility. Should it be considered inadvisable to assign an acquisition to a logical group or to an unwilling or incapable but appropriate executive, then a decision must be made balancing the advantages of the acquisition against the problems caused by creating an unwieldly organization structure. The buyer will usually be better off to forget or delay the acquisition and concentrate on first improving his current organization.

Differences of opinion between directors or senior managers and the line managers who must look after a company once acquired are not unusual. The executives on top are looking at a broad picture and set of objectives that can more quickly be achieved through acquisitions. The line managers know their careers will be best served by successfully managing their present operations and if they have their hands full, they will not be enthusiastic about taking on more companies.

It is not likely a line manager will declare he has all he can handle and actively oppose an acquisition program sponsored by senior management, but this will not change the basic lack of capacity to absorb acquisitions or prevent the line managers from being overly critical of specific prospects in an effort to discourage consummation. There is no more certain way to cause an acquisition to fail than to assign it to an executive who recommended against it or did not want it. Senior management will have to make a careful evaluation as to the ability and true attitude of the executive to whom they are contemplating assigning an acquisition.

Organizational Assistance and Conflicts

While an acquired company's president will normally report directly to an executive of the buyer, other executives of the buyer will be in contact with the acquired. Staff executives can be as helpful or detrimental to new acquisitions as the line manager with full responsibility. Their attitudes, talents, and limitations must also be included in evaluating a buyer's managerial capacity. In nearly all acquired companies it is necessary to change the accounting system for it to become compatible with the new parent's and this takes time and manpower. New legal assistance, marketing programs, and manufacturing help, to name a few areas, also require expertise and time that can be provided by staff personnel. Most acquisitions are sold to some degree on the basis of operational or financial benefits that the buyer will bring to the acquired company and the buyer should have the capability equal to his promises.

Other questions regarding the buyer's managerial capacity exist. Are there key executives so set in their ways and cantankerous that few within the present organization can get along with them? Managers of an acquired company would be discouraged or run off by such people. Is the present management team of the buyer such a closed clique that an acquired company's management would always feel on the outside? One attraction for selling to some companies is the opportunity for managerial advancement in a larger organization. Who will run the acquired company if its present management fails? Failure is always a possibility. What is the overall level of morale within the buyer's management? A management discouraged by operational problems, controversial policies, and disorganized organization structures, or racked with internal politics will have great difficulty implementing an acquisition program.

Number of Acquisitions

A final basic question for buyers with an ambitious acquisition program is how many companies can be acquired and absorbed. The record of companies who have made a large number of acquisitions in a short time is largely one of euphoria during the acquisition phase followed by severe indigestion. Few, if any companies, have been able to make five or more acquisitions a year for any period of time and successfully assimilate them into their organization. For most buyers, five would be too many to ever attempt and most buyers would be pleased with one or two good acquisitions a year. Rapid buying not only brings on difficult assimilation problems, but hasty evaluations and excessive prices are usually involved, which provide a poor foundation. The fallout from rapid acquisitions is divestiture programs. It is now fashionable for executives to claim they are engaged in "asset management," which all too often is a euphemism for disposing of hastily purchased and mismanaged acquisitions.

Buyer Attractiveness

A buyer should attempt to determine how he appears to others. Regardless of a buyer's grand perceptions of himself, rationalizations, and desire to make acquisitions, his success in doing so will largely be determined by a potential seller's perception of him. It does not matter half as much what the facts are as what the sellers believe the facts to be. A buyer will find it difficult to secure an objective view of how he appears to others but an effort should be made. The results may indicate the entire business community thinks well of him and this is an ideal time to acquire, or the program should be shelved indefinitely while remedial measures are taken to change his image.

Financial Appearance

The buyer's financial condition and outlook will be of paramount importance. A strong profit picture and balance sheet make an acquisition program possible and their importance is such that other undesirable attributes may be overlooked. Sellers of profitable companies are not inclined to become involved with nonprofitable companies. Low or no earnings by a buyer may be explainable as a temporary condition but explanation will be impossible if the sellers will not even discuss acquisition with a financially weak buyer. Too many sellers have been duped by buyers claiming to be on the verge of turning around their earning status. Sellers want to be able to proudly tell their friends when they do sell that they have sold to an outstanding company rather than be embarrassed by having to explain why they sold to such a group.

Sellers are often bothered by some guilt feelings when they do sell even to the best of buyers, so they will avoid selling to a buyer for whom they must apologize. The score card of business is the financial report and sellers want to see the buyer have the record of a winner. A strong financial statement of the buyer also makes it possible to borrow funds, issue acceptable debt instruments, and provide a foundation that will influence the value of the buyer's stock.

Assimilation Success

The buyer's record in making and assimilating other acquisitions will be closely scrutinized by intelligent sellers. One of the wisest things a seller can do is contact owners of companies who have sold to the buyer. From them he can learn first hand what really happens to a company once acquired by the buyer, as well as gain valuable insight that will be helpful in negotiations. Second only in importance to a buyer's financial performance is his success with other acquired companies. A buyer able to point to previously acquired companies that still have their management and assets intact and have grown and prospered under his ownership is in an ideal position. The ability to introduce prospective sellers to happy sellers of prior acquisitions is a major asset to an acquisition program. Buyers who have a record with a high percentage of acquisition failures as evidenced by poor financial results, management turnover, declining market share, and an active divestiture program will find it difficult to acquire new companies. Such a buyer had best not try until he improves his operational competence because, even if able to find a willing seller, he probably will again convert a profitable company into a loser.

Asset Stripping

A reputation for asset stripping, which consists of selling off assets declared to be surplus or not producing a satisfactory return, is always controversial. To most people this looks like an activity conducted by clever financial operators after a fast buck who are usually glib but have miniscule operational competence. After the major assets are sold from the business the business itself is offered for sale, and if the entire operation is performed in a short enough time, operational skills are not necessary. It is remarkable how those engaged in this activity can rationalize the process as being economically beneficial to society. It is certainly beneficial to the practitioners because their objective is to recover more through separate sales of pieces than they paid for the whole. No one has been able to stay in this game for any length of time because their reputation drives away willing sellers. However, they may not have to be in the game very long to accumulate enough wealth to live very well indeed.

A new variation of asset stripping is highly publicized groups attempting to take over companies openly arguing that the shareholders will receive more for their shares in a liquidation than in the market. It remains to be seen if they will have much success.

Public Image

A buyer may have an owner or CEO who is frequently in the press taking controversial positions or advocating and practicing bizarre management methods. Lavish spending, excessive salaries, and disputes with the government are other activities that do not help a buyer's image. The buyer's executives who take these unconventional public positions are convinced of their wisdom and reasonableness and have difficulty in believing their behavior could adversely affect an acquisition program. The ideal CEO for a buyer is the hard-working executive and family man who has compassion for his subordinates, uses conventional but up-to-date management techniques, is seen in the press in non-controversial activities, and has fostered growth and prosperity in the business under his direction. Any significant variation from this will make an acquisition program more difficult.

Buyers should recognize that a double standard of morality exists in the public's mind for business. One standard is for large established companies and another much more severe standard for new ambitious firms. The older large firms can be convicted of wrongdoing by every type of government agency but there is little public outcry or interest, let alone effect on their business. Smaller, new firms that are accused of or do violate government regulations have their reputations damaged, their business decline, and acquisition programs made ineffective. There is an element of injustice in all this, but that is how the system works. Buyers who are established and have names readily recognized by the public have a better chance with sellers than unknowns. The old companies have prestige and status, which may be totally underserved and exist solely because they have survived so long, but they do have an advantage their younger competitors should recognize and must work harder to overcome.

Bad buyers attract bad sellers. A buyer with a mediocre financial picture, an ineffective management, a poor reputation, government trouble, or possessing other warts is not going to find the best companies willing to sell to him. More likely a substandard buyer will find only companies with severe problems willing to sell. While most buyers prefer to buy companies that are better than they are in terms of financial ratios, market share, and other indices, they cannot expect companies greatly superior to sell to them. Sellers like to use their areas of superior performance in bargaining for a higher price, but if there is too much difference in relative performance, it is most unlikely a sale will occur. The sellers are justly proud of a well-managed business in excellent shape and are not about to turn it over to second-raters.

Geographical Considerations

An evaluation of capacity to acquire must consider geographical factors. The further an acquisition prospect is located from the buyer, the more expensive in time and money will be the acquisition before and after closing. This fact makes it necessary for a buyer to exclude from consideration progressively larger companies the further they are located from him. A buyer can estimate his costs and from those costs calculate minimum size companies that can be economically attractive. Local acquisitions in the community of the buyer obviously require less time and travel expense than the more distant. Furthermore, a buyer familiar with his community is less likely to buy undisclosed problems, when the acquisition is in his own territory. In international acquisitions where the buyer has very heavy travel expenses before and after the acquisition, he is faced with buying in an unfamiliar and often hostile environment.

A buyer must carefully study what he wants to accomplish and his capacity to acquire and then set realistic limits on the geographical area in which to seek out prospects. Another complicating factor is each state has slightly different laws affecting acquisition and the laws of each country are extremely varied. Laws in each country are so different that a buyer must have expert local professional assistance before he discusses in detail with the seller any contemplated international transaction.

Operational Policies and Philosophies

Once contact with sellers commence, it will be essential for the buyer to compare his policies on key aspects of his business with those of the seller. The buyer may not have his policies or overall business philosophy neatly written. Some may even be characterized as attitudes rather than firm policies and their degree of importance or depth of conviction have yet to be tested. A buyer will do well to formalize as many of his policies as possible before contacting prospects. Prospects falling outside the policies who are unable or unwilling to readily conform should not be pursued. A buyer should not forget that the policies followed by a seller are ones he believes to be best for his business and others will probably be considered inappropriate or detrimental.

From the first contact with a prospect many key policy areas will be addressed and answers must be ready. The buyer should be probing to learn if a seller's business can be integrated into his policy framework. The capacity of a buyer to absorb companies with business philosophies and policies widely different from his is a matter for serious study that requires exceptional business judgment.

Are the financial objectives of the buyer and seller compatible? Does the seller believe the buyer's objectives for return on investment and pre-tax profit on sales to be reasonable and obtainable? If the seller does not, then the buyer must be able to show the seller how he will operate the business differently or what new ingredients he will add that will make the goals possible.

Is the seller union or nonunion? This may not be an issue with an employer with existing union contracts but an employer with few or none may not want anymore for fears that in some cases are unfounded but in others very real. Regardless, this can prevent many transactions from going ahead. Conflicting attitudes toward organized labor are some of the most difficult to reconcile.

Does the seller have fringe benefit plans more generous than the buyer? For companies with uniform fringe benefit programs spread throughout multiple operations, integration of a new company into the existing plans may be impossible.

What is the buyers attitude towards community relations, charitable contributions, political activity, social programs, and other external activities? Some business executives are very strong advocates of participation and others believe in as little involvement as possible. Sellers who have been very active in their community will reluctantly cease such activity.

Does the seller have salary levels and a salary program that are much higher or lower than the buyer's or that contain substantial incentive provisions? Tampering with established salary programs is a sure way to demoralize employees and a buyer must recognize the dangers if he plans to change the seller's programs after acquisition.

What is the seller's approach to marketing, distribution, and pricing? Are the seller's and buyer's concepts on marketing approach compatible or will serious differences exist? Will the buyer believe his ideas are so superior that he will force changes on the seller?

Is the seller's debt structure compatible with that of the buyers? There may exist provisions in one or the others debt instruments that make any talk of acquisition a waste of time. One party may have a policy of leasing capital equipment whenever possible while the other advocates only outright purchase, and this could cause conflicts.

Acquisition Costs

Later chapters describe the activities and associated costs other than price in seeking out and acquiring companies. These costs are formidable and cannot be neglected in considering the cost of an acquisition. Usually, a buyer fails to include in his cost of an acquisition the costs of maintaining a program. These could be greater than the prices paid if few acquisitions were completed or only small businesses were purchased. A buyer must estimate the cost of his contemplated program and ask himself if he can afford the effort and if results justify the expense.

Professional Advice

A buyer must have competent professional advisors to make acquisitions. Not only are attorneys and accountants required, but also tax experts, finance specialists, engineers, various consultants, and market research specialists may be called in for advice on special situations. However, in all transactions an attorney and an accountant will be necessary. Professionals are needed for their technical advice and to expand the capability of a buyer to his full potential. Their experience in acquisitions can provide a buyer with approaches and ideas of which the buyer himself would never think. Their solutions may be well known or extremely innovative, but for the buyer they are what he needs.

Methods of structuring, financing, treatment of taxes, and booking of a transaction are areas where major savings and advantages can be achieved if the buyer has superior professional advice. The more experienced and capable the buyer's professionals, the greater will be his capability to acquire. A wise buyer will identify and arrange for the services of the best professionals he can locate at the start of his acquisition program in order for them to be available as needed.

Stock Registration Requirements

A buyer who is a public company must decide if it is prepared to register stock given in an acquisition transaction. Unregistered or lettered stock, as it is often referred to, cannot readily be sold except in private transactions causing the owner to have little liquidity, and if he can find a buyer, the stock will be sold at a substantial discount from the quoted market price for the registered. A buyer will severely restrict his capability to acquire if he is unwilling to give registered stock because sellers will rarely accept unregistered stock in exchange for the shares of a quality company. From practical and legal standpoints a public company buyer who decides to engage in an ambitious acquisition program must be prepared to use registered stock if he plans to buy with stock and his only decisions will center around how and when to register. A buyer with a modest acquisition program has a more difficult decision because registration may be impractical for him.

To register stock, filings, which are voluminous, time consuming, and very costly to produce, must be made with the Securities and Exchange Commission. The cost is so great that on a cost basis alone it is prohibitive for small acquisitions. The cost is so high because of the extreme accuracy required, the depth of information, and the time requirements of the professionals necessary to do a registration.

The regulations for registering stock change from time to time and the subject of what is involved and the alternatives should be discussed at length between the buyer and his attorney. This is a very complex subject area with vast ramifications for the buyer that can only be adequately covered in discussions with a top professional familiar with the buyer's situation.

Contemplating Failure

In estimating capacity to buy an effort should be made to estimate capacity to absorb the losses of an acquisition that fails. The cost of failure can be very high and includes more than the difference between price paid and the amount recovered in a liquidation or divestiture sale. There are the costs of making the acquisition, cost of diverted executive time, the loss of alternate investment income, and the operating losses prior to divestiture. There is no way to precisely estimate these sums in advance and seldom will financial records fully capture the costs after the fact. However, some rough estimates are possible and will be useful to a buyer in estimating his possible losses.

A buyer may have difficulty in visualizing a "What if everything goes wrong" scenario because he is convinced all will go well or he would not buy. Regardless, he will find the effort worthwhile and possibly sobering.

Does the Buyer Truly Have the Capacity to Acquire?

All of the factors covered in this chapter go into determining a buyer's capacity to buy. For most buyers there develops a theoretical or maximum capacity to acquire and a more important informal capacity consisting of what the buyer would really do in a given situation. The closer the two are together, the more realistic, efficient, and less costly will be the program.

Some buyers put on the brave front that they can raise any amount of cash, will issue any number of shares, and can manage any business in any industry better than anyone. They believe it is a sign of weakness to indicate to subordinates and the public a lack of unlimited capability, but they are only being unrealistic and no one is fooled. A little of this bravado exists in most buyers and is to some degree desirable, but it must be kept within bounds. A buyer needs to present to sellers a strong impression that he is able to do what he says he can do. A careful study of his capacity to buy will help prevent promises that are difficult or impossible to keep.

3.
Elements of
an Acquisition Program

It is one thing to decide to acquire companies and quite another to go out and do it. The executive hours, professional time, and expenses required to make acquisitions are formidable with their full extent often never known. If companies are to be bought with minimum peril to the buyer, there are certain tasks and activities that must be accomplished either with formal assignments of responsibility or on an informal, less organized basis.

Most buyers have a combination of formal and informal systems for making acquisitions that continue to evolve with the experience from each acquisition and as changes occur in the buyer's organization and business. Systems that are too formal tend to become inflexible and slow, and the participants become more concerned with procedure than accomplishment. Highly informal systems are inefficient, confusing to most involved, and more readily permit mistakes through oversight. Such a system may allow great speed in processing and negotiating an acquisition, but it does not encourage broad evaluation discussions within the buyer's organization, which would bring out opposing views and give a more balanced picture. Each buyer must develop his own system for seeking out and buying companies, but whether it is a highly formal or predominantly informal system, it will have, in some form, the same essential elements.

The best system for processing of acquisitions by a buyer is one in which a fairly formal written procedure exists that is followed as much as is practical. Superimposed upon the formal procedure is an available informal system to be used whenever greater speed is required, preliminary decisions and approvals are necessary to structure a possible transaction, or when a quick survey of buyer executive attitudes regarding a new prospect is needed to determine the course of action. For a program to be successful speed and flexibility are often essential, because desirable prospects do not remain available indefinitely. Frequently there is not time to process an acquisition through long lines of authority on its journey to the CEO and board of directors. However, a buyer must guard against his shorter informal system becoming the only one utilized because of its convenience. Not all acquisitions need to be on a rush basis for fear of losing them.

Skill and luck do play a role in any acquisition program, but the results will largely be in proportion to the ability of the participants and the time and effort spent. Assuming a reasonable level of competence on the part of the buyer's executives and an environment within the buyer's organization conducive to making acquisitions, the more people assigned to the program, the more acquisitions will be made. The greater the man-hours available and committed, the more research can be accomplished, contacts with prospects made, evaluations conducted, and negotiations completed. Experience and enthusiastic efforts by an intelligent buyer organization will also improve their skills and create more "lucky" situations. A minimal acquisition program requires a substantial effort and expense to complete all the basic elements that cannot be bypassed without damaging or terminating the program. Any program greater than minimal size will require proportionately more time and expense.

An understanding of the basic elements in making acquisitions is necessary to plan a sensible program. Each of the elements is an identifiable function that must be provided for by the buyer. To plan and execute each element a buyer must ask himself such questions as: Who do I have to assign to perform each function? What does this element involve in my organization? What will be the cost? Can I staff from my existing organization? To what degree should I use outside professionals? Answers to all these questions should be found before the program commences so it can be planned and everyone informed of how the program is to function. The basic elements are as follows:

1. Major decision-making
2. Management and planning
3. Industry and prospect data accumulation
4. Contact and selling prospects
5. Evaluation
6. Negotiations
7. Financing
8. Documentation and closing
9. Transition

Major Decision-Making

Acquisition decisions are among the most important executives will be called upon to make during their business careers. The associated investment, commitments, and impact made upon a business organization are unequalled in their potential for causing profitable growth or failure of the business. A system must be established whereby decisions are promptly made by an individual or group with access to all available information and a complete understanding of the present condition and goals of the buyer.

A private investor will make final decisions and his authority will be unchallenged. He has no individual but himself to blame if his decisions are based on inadequate information, he procrastinates and loses an opportunity, or he uses poor judgment. However, most buyers are corporations with organizations reporting to a chief executive officer or board of directors, and a number of people are involved in the decision-making. Legally, the board of directors will be required to make the final buyer decision through their review and approval authority. However, the board's action may vary from disinterested routine acceptance of decisions made by others to intense scrutiny with approval by no means certain. Present trends toward forcing more responsibility upon directors are causing acquisitions to be reviewed more fully and carefully. Board members are also more likely to contact or be contacted by executives of the buyer's organization other than the CEO for opinions.

While legal final approval rests with the board, in most companies the CEO makes the major decisions on acquisitions and his decisions are submitted to the board for approval and cannot be readily rejected without repudiation of the CEO. Should rejection occur frequently or, in some cases, even once, there will either be a new CEO or new board members. Whether it is the board, the CEO, or a special appointed committee, such as an executive committee, that is responsible for major decisions, someone or some group must be prepared to do so on a prompt basis. Promptness requires accessibility and an environment for the open discussions necessary to make intelligent decisions.

Major decisions are not limited to approval, rejection or setting prices. Overall acquisitions policy, objectives, timing, staffing, terms, and assignments of responsibility are areas requiring major decisions. Vast differences in opinion exist between buyers in defining what are major or minor decisions but from a practical standpoint a major decision is best defined as one a buyer considers to be major. The degree of delegation of decision-making within an organization will be influenced by the competence and record for wise decisions of subordinates, and this too will affect a buyer's definition of major and minor.

If all appropriate policy decisions are made and a mechanism exists within the buyer's organization for selection and review of prospects for policy compliance as the program progresses, there should rarely be an acquisition rejected by the board of directors. Rejection by the board indicates either failure to communicate to executives the organization's policies and objectives or a lack of discipline on the part of the executives. Both are unacceptable conditions creating a waste of the buyer's two most important assets, time and money. An acquisition prospect that has been courted and a transaction fully negotiated subject only to board approval constitutes, upon board rejection, a humiliating experience for the buyer's executives and the elimination of all chances of recovering the time and expense wasted. It also reflects poorly upon the buyer's overall program and reputation.

Management and Planning

The collection of industry data, information on specific prospects, evaluation of data, coordination of acquisition activity with plans and objectives of the buyer's enterprise, arranging of financing, setting of priorities, directing of personnel involved, the employment of professionals, motivation of personnel, expediting of approvals, evaluation of prospects, preparation of strategic and tactical plans, and securing support for projects are all parts of an acquisition program that must be managed by someone. In a small operation it can be one man managing himself, but in a larger program a staff of people could be involved. Regardless of a buyer's size, someone must be in charge and responsible for acquisitions or little can be expected to happen. Whoever is responsible must be an open advocate of making acquisitions and serve as a ramrod to accomplish the necessary activities. Acquisitions are outside of the usual day-to-day business activity of most buyer's executives and requires extra effort, which is only forthcoming upon request.

Seldom are all essential acquisition functions under the direct management of one individual. The executive who is assigned responsibility for the acquisition program must persuade, cajole, or coax his counterparts to provide the necessary missing services. An acquisition program is a complex affair involving a variety of activities and people who must be closely coordinated and managed if success is to result. For smaller buyers where acquisition management is considered a part-time job, not much of anything is likely to happen, until the activity demands full-time attention.

The management structure and quality of management of an acquisition program are key factors that must be taken into account by any buyer if he is to succeed. The executive responsible must be senior and should report directly to the CEO. To bury this key position under several levels of management is to bury the entire program. The individual must be exceptionally able to be effective internally and with sellers. This is not a position for the semi-retired or the likeable executive who failed somewhere else in the buyer's organization.

Industry and Prospect Data Accumulation

The gathering of data on the industries of interest or on new industries as possible areas in which to expand is an important part of a program. Industry data is the background information necessary to understand the position and relative success of a known prospect as well as valuable in determining the identity of other prospects. It is essential in forecasting the future market and potential for a prospect under consideration. From industry data logical prospects can be identified if none are known.

Prospect identification and the securing of information about a prospect prior to contacting is an early step in any buyer's program. The buyer must take all the available information on a prospect and decide if it appears to fit with established policies and objectives. If it does, then contact can proceed, but if not, the subject should be rejected.

Even in situations where the seller first contacts the buyer, a process of industry review and evaluation of data supplied by the seller and other available sources occurs and a preliminary decision is made on whether or not discussions should commence or proceed beyond the introductory meeting. Information gathering is a continuous part of any acquisition program and can be conducted on a casual, as needed basis or on a broad systematic scale. The odds will favor the buyer who has a well-planned systematic program for gathering, organizing, and using the accumulated information.

Contacting and Persuading Prospects

Contact must be made with prospects in a manner that presents the buyer in the best light, creates interest in the seller, and moves discussions to a conclusion. There are discussions prior to price negotiations. These may be lengthy and continue over a period of years involving much persuasion and entertaining or just occasional meetings to maintain contact until such time as the seller is ready or the seller eliminates known obstacles to selling. The contact may be brief and lead promptly into price negotiations, as is the case when the seller must sell or has decided to sell as promptly as possible. Even in quick sales, some persuasion activity is necessary, because even the most anxious seller will be reluctant to sell to a buyer he dislikes. An offensive buyer cannot expect any price concessions or terms more favorable than what the seller considers absolutely essential to bring about the deal.

Evaluation

Not only must a prospect be studied and systematically evaluated, but also the entire industry, economy, environment and socioeconomic and political climate in which it conducts its business. In-depth studies are not guarantees that an acquisition will prove successful, but the odds on success increase immensely if comprehensive studies of all relative factors have been made and no significant factors have been discovered that show success to be improbable. A buyer cannot expect a seller to volunteer information about the present and anticipated problems of the business, but he can expect the truth when asked. Few sellers will lie about the condition of their business, but most believe it to be an obligation of the buyer to ask the right questions and the seller is not responsible for volunteering detrimental information.

Prospect evaluation begins prior to the first contact when a decision based on limited available data is reviewed to decide if a first meeting is warranted. The first meeting and each subsequent meeting brings out more information and interim evaluations, usually on an informal basis, to decide if a next step is in order. Once agreement seems probable, a formal and comprehensive study of the business is in order and this includes all aspects of the business. A final evaluation may be conducted just prior to closing to verify that material changes have not occurred in the company since the first agreement was reached or the complete formal study was conducted. Within a few months, a business can easily change very much for the better or worse.

Evaluation implies someone in the buyer's organization is responsible for reviewing all the information collected. The job of gathering and assembling all necessary information is formidable, and considerable time is required for review. Busy executives tend to only read portions of the data they believe most important, such as financial summaries or forecasts, and assume the rest has been checked by others. The buyer must establish a system for the careful evaluation of all data collected, which has safeguards to assure the evaluation of all collected data and a balanced conclusion is reached.

Negotiations

Exactly when becoming acquainted, selling, and building rapport ceases in the acquisition process and formal negotiations commence is far from clear. Negotiations may also go on simultaneously with other activities of the parties who may or may not be a part of the acquisition process. Negotiations may be so subtle that even the participants do not realize they have begun.

If in the first exploratory meeting a buyer declares that he only uses his stock in acquisitions and the potential seller agrees to continue discussions in another meeting, this can be considered as negotiations and acceptance of a point. Seldom are acquisitions negotiations the formal variety where groups of executives and their attorneys sit around a large table and negotiate price. Basic issues and terms are usually settled by the parties in small meetings in an office, during a private lunch or dinner, and even over the telephone after a number of meetings have occurred to narrow the issues. Negotiations is the process of defining and narrowing the issues and reaching agreement upon a basis that both parties find acceptable. The form of negotiations and the participants vary with every transaction.

Financing

At some point the buyer must be prepared to fulfill the obligation he has assumed and pay the seller. Seldom will this be as simple as someone writing a check from an ample account.

If stock is used, certificates must be secured, exchanges notified, and all regulations complied with. The secretaries' records must be modified and cash flow projections revised to reflect added dividend payments.

Sales involving debt instruments being issued to sellers must be planned in such a way that interest and repayment can be accomplished.

Cash transactions usually involve large sums whose disbursement must be planned. Someone must assemble the funds from various accounts or arrange for borrowings. In some cases a substantial amount of work must be accomplished to borrow the cash even for the most credit worthy buyers. This all takes time and planning.

Leveraged transactions in which the seller's assets are used as collateral for loans to pay the sellers are the most complex and often require the most imagination and include a variety of debt instruments. The ability to structure and arrange financing may easily be the most important part of transaction. The buyer and seller often want to complete the sale but the problem is how to arrange the financing. Because no one is familiar with all money sources and financing techniques, a buyer who needs financing should contact various appropriate professionals. Bankers and investment bankers are readily accessible and the buyer's public accountants and attorneys should be able to recommend less conspicuous experts in acquisition financing.

Documentation and Closing

Definitive acquisition agreements and all their related documents and exhibits containing all the terms and conditions agreed upon by the parties must be prepared and executed. The execution is usually considered the closing, but it is not uncommon for signing to be first with the actual transfer of ownership at a later date after certain specified events occur, such as board of director or shareholder approval, transfer of funds, or delivery of stock shares. Acquisition agreements with all the related documents and exhibits are voluminous and usually non-attorneys are astounded by the quantity of paper.

Closings can be anything from acrimonious meetings to celebrations, but common to almost all is the exhaustion of the participants. Carefully drafted documents that accurately reflect the agreements of the parties and a smoothly run, well-organized closing are most likely to occur if competent experienced attorneys are involved.

Transition

When it appears agreement between the buyer and seller is probable, some transitional activities often begin without the parties recognizing them as such. Both parties begin thinking in terms of how it will be after the acquisition and act accordingly. The seller may delay major decisions and ask the buyer his opinion on important moves such as capital expenditures or employment levels, and the buyer may begin placing business with the seller. Care must be exercised by the buyer not to begin making decisions for the seller prior to closing, because he could set himself up for a lawsuit if the decisions proved imprudent and the transaction did not go through.

Transition or integration of the seller into the buyer's organization on a well-planned and harmonious basis is critical to the success of any acquisition program. Few buyers seem well prepared for this all-important function. Immediately after the closing of an acquisition, there is a tendency for a psychological letdown because all the great effort of making the acquisition is over and the tension ended. The buyer's and seller's executives may be physically exhausted and need a long rest before starting a program of integration. However, it should start as soon as possible at a time when the seller's employees expect changes and they have unjustified dark fears that need to be removed.

Too many buyers' transition programs consist solely of assigning responsibility for the newly acquired to an executive and ordering a massive change in the acquired's accounting system to make it conform to the buyer's. All the other promises and plans made by the buyer during the selling stage often are lost or forgotten after closing, but this should not be.

For a buyer to maximize the return on his investment, he must have prepared in advance of closing a step-by-step detailed plan for integrating the newly acquired into the buyer's organization so that immediately upon closing the transitional process commences. Special periodic reviews should be conducted to make certain the transition is progressing as planned and unforeseen problems are being resolved. Any acquired company expects changes to occur and the buyer need not be reluctant to step in and do what is necessary.

Staffing

An understanding of the basic elements described above and their application to the buyer's business makes it possible for the buyer to decide upon the staff needed. Staff decisions will be influenced by the number and type of acquisitions to be made, cost, time to complete, availability of personnel with necessary skills, and the buyer's determination to make acquisitions. Outside professionals, primarily attorneys and accountants, should be used as required for each acquisition situation but their level of usage will be governed by the number of willing sellers the buyer agrees to acquire. Only the largest of companies maintain an internal staff of personnel capable of handling all aspects of making acquisitions; most buyers must call on outside assistance from time to time.

Buyers who are individual investors without a hired staff will share performance of all the necessary elements with their professional advisors. Some rely heavily on competent business brokers who seek out prospects and assist throughout the transactions. Such buyers are able to acquire very few companies in a period of time, but most are only interested in making one or two.

Many corporate buyers have only one executive on a part or full-time basis handling their acquisition program, performing all functions except those professional jobs for which he has no training or background. One executive cannot accomplish very much and few acquisitions can be expected with such a limited commitment. Sometimes a one-person department is partially misleading because substantial assistance is available from other departments of the buyer's organization. However, such a fragmented acquisition effort will be unwieldly with continued competition for the time of personnel and is not a fully satisfactory approach.

If a buyer is truly serious about making acquisitions, he will not attempt it as a part-time assignment for one employee, and the size of the staff assigned will indicate the degree of seriousness.

Number of Acquisitions Staff Can Handle

The number of acquisitions that can be completed in a given time is a direct function of the amount of manpower assigned and the priority acquisition activity is given. A large staff will not guarantee a large number of acquisitions but a small or part-time staff will certainly make only very few possible. This is not to imply that competence and ingenuity are not critical factors in staffing, but the man-hours must be available to get the job done. Because a buyer can only absorb so many new companies in a period of time, it is important for the staff size to be appropriate for the number of companies to be acquired. Limiting the staff responsible for acquisitions to one full-time person will usually limit acquisitions to one, possibly two, per year. An exception would be where small repetitive acquisitions are made such as retail outlets or small service organizations. Another exception would be an imprudent buyer who conducts little investigation, pays more than what is reasonable for companies and relies primarily on finders, brokers, and investment bankers for identification of prospects. Such a buyer could acquire a good many companies in a brief time, but can expect many operational and financial problems shortly thereafter.

For a buyer to select the personnel responsible for acquisitions, he must consider the skills and background required. The executive who will make the major decisions is already there and his ability is not a factor because he cannot be changed or bypassed. Usually, there is no outward doubts in his mind about his judgment regardless of the private thoughts of the rest of the organization about his ability. Top business skills are required by the executive responsible for administering, managing, and coordinating the program. An equal level of ability is required by the negotiator of the transaction and for many buyers the executives in charge of the program and the negotiator are the same person. Those managing and negotiating must have the ability to understand the entire acquisition process and their activities cannot be broken down into components. The market study, prospect identification, data gathering, and evaluation of prospects are activities that lend themselves to specialization and a business educated person can be trained within a few months. In between the two groups are those skills necessary for contacting and persuading prospects to sell their companies. This activity requires not only extensive business knowledge but also personality traits favorable to a selling effort.

Divisional or Group Roles

Staff planning must involve decisions regarding the role, if any, of divisions, groups, or subsidiaries below the parent level. The parent company will always retain final decision-making authority, but it is common for operating units to have some responsibility for identification and contact with prospects. Less common is for operating units to have negotiating responsibility because they seldom have the required experience and the parent organization is reluctant to delegate any authority in this key area.

Involvement and responsibility for acquisitions in operating units in most larger companies varies from year to year depending on personalities, success achieved, internal politics, and the attitude of the head of the operating units. There are many opportunities for conflict between parent and operating unit acquisition personnel and the relationship can rapidly become counterproductive. Although the parent has the final word on acquisitions because of status and approval authority, the operating units can always find reasons not to submit any sellers for approval and to reject any acquisitions that the parent tries to force upon them. A parent management would be foolish to force upon an operating unit an unwanted or unapproved acquisition.

Acquisitions Require an Advocate

Staffing involves organization and assignment of responsibilities. It should be clear who does exactly what. The head of the acquisition program must be an able proponent of acquisitions in general and be willing to unequivocally advocate the purchase of businesses he considers desirable as well as openly oppose those he believes to be unwise. He must be willing to stand up and be counted. In a business organization there usually are those uninterested in acquisitions or careful to avoid recommending anything for fear of damage to their careers if the acquisition turns out bad. Someone must be the open advocate of an acquisition or nothing will happen. Should an acquisition turn out well, there will be no shortage of executives claiming credit for the decision to buy.

Acquisition Expenses

There is a tendency to look at the cost of an acquisition as the price paid, but this is far from the case. The cost of acquisition personnel, outside professionals, diversion of management time, and other expenses required are formidable with their full extent often unknown. Accounting systems are seldom capable of capturing completely all the direct and indirect costs associated with an acquisition program, because much of the expense falls into various general and administrative accounts where records are lacking in detail or do not exist at all.

Time spent by executives on acquisitions but not assigned full-time is rarely booked as an acquisition expense. The corporate department responsible for acquisitions usually has an awareness of the magnitude of the costs, but it is not always in their best interest to encourage the development of complete accurate cost data because this might expose the program to overly cost conscious critics. Cost criticism could be unreasonable because the period of time in which acquisition benefits fall is not the period in which the costs of acquiring are incurred. Acquisition effort associated with a given acquisition by its very nature precedes any profits that will be enjoyed by the buyer. If the buyer is engaged in a continuous program, then a nearly impossible task exists in attempting to allocate costs to specific acquisitions.

Earnings or losses of newly acquired companies usually occur under management direction other than that of the acquisition technicians further compounding cost versus income responsibility. This permits acquisition executives to argue they never made a bad acquisition but some good companies may have been acquired and fouled up afterwards. This line of reasoning is not readily accepted by operating managers. Efforts to place acquisition programs on a profit and loss basis are largely impractical and a needless diversion of effort.

Regardless of the problems and inadequacies of accounting systems, useful cost estimates can be made that will give some indication of the costs to be anticipated. These estimates will also demonstrate that the price paid to sellers is only a portion of the cost and the smaller the acquisition, the smaller will be the price portion of the total cost. In smaller acquisitions the cost to acquire can easily eliminate any economic justification for the transaction. Because of this fact alone, a buyer should set as an early policy the minimum size business that he will consider as a prospect.

Personnel Costs and Requirements

Costs of full-time employees assigned to the acquisition program can readily be estimated. The salaries and fringe costs of current employees are known items because they come from payroll records. If it is a start-up situation, then hiring costs plus competitive wage data can be used in the estimates. Should no competitive data be available, the cost of personnel in the buyer's organization who hold positions with status comparable to the positions to be filled will serve as adequate guidelines for estimating purposes.

A fairly standard acquisition department with an objective of two to four acquisitions per year would have three full-time employees consisting of a manager, an assistant, and a secretary. The manager should be on the vice-presidential level not only because of the importance of the position, but because of the status required to deal effectively with sellers and the necessity to command attention in the buyer's organization to get things done. An assistant who could make some first contacts with prospects, conduct research, and participate in evaluations would be at a level comparable to a level one step above a first-line supervisor. The secretary, who would also perform research activity, would be at the executive secretarial level.

Part-time Staff Costs

Cost of employees assigned only part-time to acquisitions are more difficult to estimate. One must assume in any cost estimate that time spent on acquisition activity is time that could have been spent productively in other areas of the buyer's business. Another assumption that should be made is that acquisition time is not noncompensated overtime hours or extra effort time that has no cost. Both assumptions can be challenged and may not be entirely true, but failure to accept them will produce even more misleading cost estimates. Part-time acquisition employees most commonly would be senior executives who have responsibilities for functions other than acquisitions. They could be directing an acquisition program managed and staffed by full-time employees or they may constitute the buyer's sole commitment to acquisitions. In the latter case, this is not much of a commitment and little can be expected to be accomplished.

Other employees may be used part-time on a project-by-project basis. In-house attorneys are asked legal questions as they come up and may be expected to either directly handle or assist in negotiations, document drafting, government filings, and legal audits; or hire outside attorneys to do so but retain responsibility for review and expediting their work. Accounting personnel advise on structuring the transaction, conduct evaluations, assist in developing forecasts, and become involved in the transition phase to bring the seller's financial and accounting systems into conformity with the buyer's. Other executives of the buyer may participate in studying a prospect and evaluating its desirability. Marketing, manufacturing, purchasing, engineering, maintenance personnel may all be called upon to review their respective areas of interest. This all takes time and some rough cost estimates are appropriate. Because most of these employees would already be on a buyer's payroll, their cost can readily be estimated once the amount of anticipated time they will spend on acquisitions is agreed upon.

Departmental Costs

An acquisition program has costs other than wages and professional fees that can be very significant. Travel expenses will probably be the largest of these items if the program is national or international in scope. The buyer's executives must meet with sellers at the seller's offices to be most effective and to do so incurs travel expense. These costs can be estimated by determining the number of trips contemplated and multiplying this number by the estimated cost of an average trip. It is unlikely that there will be many average trips in terms of distances and duration, but use of a theoretical average for cost forecasts should be satisfactory.

Facility costs for space, furniture, utilities, publications, telephone, mailing, duplications, and other office services can add up to a substantial cost factor. In the absence of historical data, these can be difficult items to estimate. If the buyer has a regional or district sales office of comparable size to a new acquisition department, he could use the cost data from the sales office as a guide to estimating costs.

Legal Costs

For any buyer the extent of outside legal fees for acquisition activity will be determined by a number of factors including in-house legal capacity, quality of attorneys employed, type of transactions, location of prospects, complexity of transactions, and skill of buyer's personnel in organizing legal work and conducting negotiations. A buyer can do much to hold down his outside costs but in too many cases, there is little effort made to do so because of close personal relationships that have developed between the buyer's executives and their outside attorneys. Building of close friendships and providing personal favors is a proven technique for attorneys to sell their services.

Strong in-house legal talent can do the most to control or reduce outside legal fees. Whatever work is done on the inside automatically reduces the outside needs. Legal work placed by in-house attorneys with outside firms can be better monitored and controlled because those placing the work should know its value and the time needed to complete. They also can review work for competency and reject shabby work. However, in-house attorneys are costly and if not fully utilized, more costly than outside attorneys. A buyer must study the amount of legal services he will require and conduct periodic reviews to determine if full time in-house attorneys are justified.

The quality of legal work done outside is a factor in cost considerations. Usually the best attorneys are more expensive per hour but they are faster and more competent so the cost is not much more and usually less than if the buyer used second rate talent. Selection of a good attorney can be accomplished by asking for the background of the attorney, checking with others who used him, and by not hesitating to change attorneys if he fails to perform. Refusal to pay for shabby legal work coupled with a quick willingness to change attorneys may appear to be a hard-nosed approach, but in time the buyer will have the type and quality attorneys he needs.

Factors Affecting Legal Fees

The type of transaction determines the amount of legal work. A simple purchase of unencumbered assets is at the low end of the scale and a merger of two public international companies would probably be most costly. Attorney fees are based on hours required, complexity of work, and usually clients ability to pay although the latter is not supposed to enter into the fee calculation. A simple purchase of assets involves little time or skill and could be handled by a relatively junior attorney. Merging two public international companies would require hundreds of hours of legal work and challenge the talents and imagination of the most senior attorneys. Between these two extremes are an infinite variety of transactions with great variation in time and skill required.

The size of a transaction is not always indicative of the legal requirements and cost. Other factors such as diversity and condition of operations being acquired, number of shareholders, structure of transaction, extent of liabilities, international aspects, and sophistication of the buyers and sellers will influence time and skill requirements more than size. Attorneys are required in acquisitions not only to draw up the contracts, but to conduct legal audits of the prospect, provide advice on how to structure the transaction, participate in negotiations, evaluate liabilities such as open litigation, and assist in the overall evaluation of the prospect.

A buyer's ability to organize his need for legal services coupled with a basic understanding of the laws and regulations affecting acquisitions will help control legal expense. A buyer should know enough of the rules that he does not have to confer with his attorney on every trivial issue. Legal services should not be requested for acquisitions that have a low probability of ever being finalized. The buyer should know what legal work is required and assign the work to his inside or outside attorneys along with specific guidelines describing what is wanted and when it is required.

Because of all the variables in any given situation, it is impossible to indicate here what the legal fees in any acquisition will be, but it can be stated that they will be formidable but controllable. Control starts with defining what is to be done and requesting an estimate of the cost from the attorneys before work commences. It is quite reasonable to discuss fees in advance and preliminary discussions are welcomed by responsible attorneys.

A buyer should avoid agreeing to pay the legal fees of a seller. The buyer can argue that if he paid for the seller's attorney, the attorney would have a conflict of interest and lack full independence. Another practical reason is that seller's attorneys know in all probability they are losing a client if the acquisition is completed and they tend to submit bills for exhorbitant fees.

Accounting Fees

Accounting fees are even more variable than legal fees and can range from nothing to hundreds of thousands of dollars. A simple purchase of assets by a private investor may not require any accounting expense, because the buyer could have done his own evaluation and an audit is unnecessary. The only accounting involved would be booking the assets into a new business organization. The other extreme would be the merger through a pooling of two international public companies that had not submitted registration statements during the past four or five years. A public company merging through a pooling with a large private company would have about the same maximum requirements for accounting service. Each transaction has its own accounting requirements, but who does the work and the total cost will be influenced by the capabilities and availability of the buyer's personnel and the condition of the company's records.

In-house accounting can do much to reduce the use of outside accountants, but only the larger corporate buyers would have the staff

able to step into an acquisition situation. Outside auditors are often
called upon for acquisition studies because the buyer has no one else to
turn to. Staffing for the accounting portion of evaluations is largely a
case of availability of personnel with in-house personnel having an
edge in performance because they have a better understanding of the
buyer's areas of concern and emphasis. A buyer who has a strong
internal auditing department would find this to be an ideal group to
conduct acquisition evaluations.

In many transactions the final price or even whether or not a deal
goes ahead is subject to an audit. Here outside professionals are
usually used because they are considered neutral observers, although
they are not totally. However, the parties must carefully negotiate
with the accountants the accounting principles that are to be followed
in an audit or the results will be of little value. As an example, one of
the most difficult items to value is inventory and unless the buyer and
seller have agreed upon precise definitions for evaluation of obsoles-
cense, excess quantities and scrap as well as overhead application, the
audit will be only a source of more controversy.

If registration statements are needed, outside public accounting
firms must be utilized and hundreds of hours of accounting service will
be required. The size of the transaction, condition of the financial
records, condition of the companies, and when the last registration
statement was done all play a role in determining the amount of time
and cost required. Registration statements are so costly that they are
not economically feasible for a small acquisition.

Accountants are also used in tax planning, advice on structuring a
transaction, advice on recording or entering on to the buyer's books
the acquired, and by some, directly in negotiations. These are all areas
where professionals of the highest competence and experience are
required who are more commonly found in the large public accounting
firms.

Because of the diverse nature of accounting services, both in
quantity and level of competence required, a buyer should discuss
costs in advance with the accountant he expects to have perform the
work. The more precise the buyer is in defining the scope of the work,
the more accurate will be the cost estimate. Defining the scope of work
also forces a buyer to review and separate what he needs from what it
would only be nice to have.

Consultant Costs

Often, special consultants are called upon in acquisitions to assist in
evaluations or to settle disputes over values. Consultants with techni-

cal specialties, actuaries, appraisers, and market research experts are the most common. It is impossible to anticipate the need for these experts in advance, because they only are called upon when the condition of a prospect is such that expert advice is required. There is no way to know before contacting a prospect if expert assistance is needed and, consequently, it is not possible to accurately forecast the cost.

Other than appraisers, most consultant work is on a per diem plus expenses basis. The more prominent or nationally recognized the consultant, the more will be his fee. A user of consulting services should avoid confusing prominence with competence and recognize that a big name is not a guarantee of outstanding work. However, in disputes between consultants, credentials are given weight in evaluating the respective arguments. Whenever consultants are employed, their fees should be discussed in advance and the scope of their assignment clearly defined.

Investment Bankers, Brokers, and Finders

While the fees in most cases are negotiable, a buyer who elects to use any of these intermediaries will be wise to agree to pay the full fee requested, which usually is the so-called Lehman Formula of an amount equal to 5% of the first million dollars, 4% of the second million, 3% of the third, 2% of the fourth and 1% of all consideration paid or committed over $4 million. In very large transactions the percentages may be reduced somewhat, as in the largest transaction in 1979 when the percentage was only one-fourth of one percent of the total consideration, but that fee exceeded $14 million and probably is the largest fee ever paid.

The fee percentages may seem high to some buyers, but there is great competition for good acquisitions and plenty of buyers willing to pay full fees. The result is the able intermediaries only take the quality acquisitions to buyers who pay full fees and those unwilling to pay full fees see nothing at all or prospects of low quality. A buyer who is actively soliciting acquisitions from intermediaries but is unwilling to pay full fees has nothing to complain about if he is disappointed with the prospects he sees. A buyer intent on making a number of acquisitions can conduct a very effective in-house search program for far less money than he can use intermediaries to locate prospects.

Indirect Costs

Indirect costs of making acquisitions, which are seldom fully recorded or even recognized, fall into the two general categories of management diversion and costs of deals that do not happen. For most buyers acquisition activity constitutes an exciting challenge for the executives involved but time spent in evaluating and making acquisitions is time diverted from running the existing business or pursuing internal growth. Executives often enter into their business plans the profits of businesses yet to be acquired and treat these results as a certainty. This practice can lead to faulty forecasts because no acquisition is certain until closing occurs and profits from projected acquisitions are even more speculative.

If a buyer buys every company he has an opportunity to buy, he is not evaluating and must be paying too much. Of course, few buyers are so indiscriminate and reckless with their money. For any buyer the percentage of companies acquired compared to those looked over will be very small, but the cost of shopping comes high.

If an acquisition falls through at the last moment, the expenses will be nearly the same as if the acquisition occurred. Buyers have a tendency to forget the cost of shopping and unconsummated transactions, but these are very real expenses in any program. In budgeting for the cost of an acquisition program, allowance should be made for adequate shopping and a substantial number of transactions that come close but are never completed.

Selection and Use of Professionals

Buyers should not only select the very best professionals to assist them, but they should also urge sellers to employ professionals of the highest competence. Because acquisitions are complex affairs with high stakes that often require a number of professionals other than legal and accounting, it is foolish for either party to use inexperienced professionals. In the long run, the more expensive professionals may be the least expensive to use.

Selection of professionals is not a simple task. Experience, intelligence, imagination, reputation, availability, and willingness to work diligently are critical factors in deciding upon the qualifications of a professional. These are far more important than credentials such as schools attended or memberships in professional societies, but their presence is more difficult to detect. Questioning a professional about experience, asking clients of the professional for recommendations, and willingness to discontinue the professional's service if unsatisfactory are the best approaches to selection. Care also should be taken to choose professionals on the basis of who actually will work on the assigned project. A big name firm that has great prestige and an outstanding reputation and many superb professionals also has members who are aged and slipping, new and inexperienced, all with various levels of competence.

In selecting a professional the specific person who will work on the project is more important than the firm with which he is associated. Large firms often have senior partners of real stature or public prominence who serve as extraordinary salesmen and perform little work for clients and delegate the work to subordinates. A client would do well to avoid being awed by such stars and insist on learning the caliber of those assigned to perform the work. Not infrequently the juniors assigned to perform are better than the star who has not written a clause or added a column of numbers since his hair turned grey.

Another factor in selecting professionals is whether they have time to work on the project. The best professionals are in demand and very busy individuals. Therefore, the exact scope of the assignment and time to complete must be openly discussed. Once the scope of the work and overall situation is described, the professional should be able to estimate the time required better than the buyer. Turning down work offered by a responsible client is extremely difficult for a professional but at times this should be done. The client should discuss the subject of available time openly and on occasion he, rather than the professional, may have to decide the professional is just too busy and the risk of delays too great and take his business to another.

Each party selects and normally pays for his own professionals and consequently has little influence in theory over the selection of the other's professionals. However, the buyer has a real interest in the seller's choices and will be prudent to advise the seller in a very tactful manner to select the best. Few elements can be more detrimental to a transaction than an inexperienced, bungling accountant or attorney attempting to represent a seller in a way that prevents the acquisition and preserves the account. Such a charge of professional self-interest is impossible to prove but most executives experienced in acquisitions have encountered performances that have no other logical explanation. Incompetence and ineptness can appear without any devious motives, so a buyer should not be too quick to assume the worst.

The buyer should also respect competent and diligent legal work by the seller's attorney for what it is and not challenge the professionals integrity just because he is troublesome and does not let the buyer get away with things he should not.

A seller may have built up a close relationship with an attorney or accountant who was excellent on day-to-day corporate affairs but has no background in acquisitions. The seller may be reluctant to make a change because he believes he would insult an old friend by going elsewhere and this may very well be the case. Equally possible, the professional may welcome the chance to avoid the responsibility for work with which he knows he has limited competence.

A buyer may believe he has an advantage if he has top professionals and the seller's are of low quality, but as the negotiations progress, he will find this condition is not to his advantage because his professionals will spend most of their time educating the sellers and attempting to overcome foolish positions. If a seller insists on using inexperienced professionals, there is little the buyer can do if he is determined to buy the company except bear with the problems and resign himself to the necessity of great patience.

Types of Professionals

The following list of professionals and their role in acquisitions can serve as a checklist for buyers in planning their program. Only attorneys would be present in every transaction and rarely would a transaction involve all the professionals.

Attorneys. They participate in evaluations of the prospect, conduct legal audits and are often involved in the negotiations. Preparation of contracts, filings, and most documentation necessary to complete a legally binding transaction are also normal parts of their activity. They advise their client on structuring the transaction, tax matters, government regulations, and propriety of seller's positions. Attorneys may represent the buyer before government agencies seeking necessary approvals.

Accountants. A wide range of services in all the fields of accounting, finance, and taxation are secured from accountants. They conduct or participate in evaluations, value businesses, evaluate financial positions, conduct audits, advise on structuring and taxation, prepare reports for government agencies, and advise on recording the acquired company's financial statements.

Actuaries. Costs of fringe benefit plans are high and often not fully evident. Actuaries calculate present and future costs of existing or proposed pension programs. They also calculate the cost to integrate fringe benefits programs, such as group insurance, of the buyer and seller if such is the buyer's policy.

Technical Consultants. These specialized experts evaluate conditions, assets, and people, which can only be done by experts with years of specialized training and experience. The physical condition of buildings, key equipment and facilities, or products sold are areas for an engineer's attention. Evaluation of threatened or actual warranty claims are common. Industrial psychologists, whose use remains very controversial, attempt to appraise the ability and mental characteristics of executives. Market research specialists probe to learn the present attitude of customers, estimate market potential, and struggle with their role as prophets. Private investigators may even be used to investigate rumors and allegations of impropriety on the part of the seller's executives or to verify statements by the seller. Insurance experts may be needed to evaluate present coverage and the nature and extent of prospects insurable risks.

Appraisers. They come at all levels of competence and integrity. Appraising is a subjective activity and the conclusion of an appraiser is only an opinion with which others may agree or disagree. Appraisers may evaluate an entire business or only an individual asset and often are able to present excellent arguments, supported by voluminous documentation for their conclusions. Regardless of how convincing an appraisal may appear, chances are another appraiser possessing equally impressive credentials could be located to make a convincing presentation for a very different conclusion. Sophisticated buyers and sellers both know that if they look hard enough, they can find an appraiser with the "right" answer. As a general rule, buyers should not use appraisers unless they are certain the results will help their case and they should not accept a seller's appraisal unless it has a valuation they can accept. Two basic questions about any appraisal are: Who commissioned it and why?

Investment Bankers. They conduct research to identify prospects, make initial contacts to determine interest, arrange introduction of principles, prepare evaluations, participate in negotiations, arrange financing, advise on technical and legal aspects of a contemplated transaction, and conduct stock solicitations. While there are a large number of investment bankers, only a handful are active in the larger, highly publicized acquisitions and they tend to monopolize this business. These large firms usually have little interest in smaller transactions under $5 million in price. The stature of some of the large firms and the highly publicized feats of their senior partners gives them opportunities few others enjoy. The smaller firms are willing to take on assisting in almost any size transaction if they believe the transaction can be accomplished in a short time. Investment bankers have their critics who claim conflicts of interest, doubtful confidentiality and exhorbitant fees for the services performed. Of course, all such charges are denied by the investment bankers.

One role of investment bankers that should receive more critical attention is their valuation studies. Directors and executives of buyers or sellers authorize large sums to be paid for such studies by investment bankers that either set or justify a particular price to partially absolve themselves of responsibility and for use as a defense in possible shareholder suits. These studies are windfall projects for the investment bankers because they command large fees and can easily be conducted in a short time by MBA's with little experience under the part-time direction or review of a senior partner. Most buyers could conduct their own studies with their own employees and have as good a job of valuation, but they would not have a study under the authoritative cover of a big name investment banker. Conclusions of valuation studies are only opinions and clearly stated as such, and only the future performance of the evaluated company will determine if the conclusion was reasonable. As opinions, they are not fact. It is unfortunate that fears of criticism and litigation are so prevalent, and somewhat justified, that such outside studies and valuations are thought necessary. The judgment of a responsible buyer can prove to be as valid as anyone's without resorting to the expense of an outside study.

In no area of the investment banking activity is there greater potential for conflicts of interest than in valuation studies. Because most companies can be acquired at some price if it is high enough, a study that supports a very high price and enables a buyer to rationalize the price also makes possible the transaction and the collection of the investment banker's success fee. The very high price levels of the late 1970's were encouraged and promoted by the investment bankers who had much to gain from the prices and were not responsible for the buyer's actual return on investment. It will be interesting to see how all the multi-hundred million dollar deals at 12 to 20 times current earnings are faring in the near future. Some have already proven to be disasters.

Brokers and Finders. These are firms or individuals who locate buyers and sellers and hope to match them up for a fee. Most are one- or two-person operations and few survive in the business for any length of time. Those that do survive are often very able and have developed a following of buyers and sellers because they bring the parties together, provide financial advice, help arrange financing, and assist throughout the transaction. There are no licensing requirements to become a broker or finder or any other qualifications that a person must have to declare himself a business broker, so there is total ease of entry into the business. However, the economic realities are harsh and most who attempt to enter the business are unsuccessful.

Because of the high dropout rate, a buyer who chooses to use brokers should select only those who have succeeded as evidenced by their record and the length of time they have been in business. It will also be well for a buyer to review a broker's references and request a list of transactions the broker initiated.

Brokers can be very helpful in evaluating a buyer's objectives and capabilities. If a buyer is unrealistic and there is, in the opinion of the broker, a low probability of success, most responsible brokers will explain why the buyer is impractical and decline to work on the project unless the buyer revises his thinking. Successful brokers usually have more buyer clients available than sellers and they will not waste their limited time on those they consider to be out of step. Brokers want to work with buyers who are realistic and decisive, and have learned their survival is dependent upon their ability to ignore buyers who are only shopping or will only buy companies they can "steal."

Use of Inside vs. Outside Professionals

The question and often controversy over using professionals engaged on an as-needed basis from outside the buyer's organization as opposed to employing full-time professionals may never be settled, but the areas for dispute can be greatly narrowed. If a buyer has no staff of professionals and only contemplates one or two acquisitions, then employing full-time attorneys or accountants for the acquisition program is unrealistic. In addition to the number of acquisitions anticipated, the duration of the program to acquire is a major factor. It is difficult to employ top people at any level if they do not believe their job will last indefinitely. The basic condition of having enough work to keep a professional occupied for a substantial length of time must exist or there is no reason to consider employing full-time professionals as opposed to using outsiders. If the basic conditions do exist, then a buyer should consider the following arguments for using inside professionals:

1. They cost less.
2. They will work more diligently at their tasks because the careers are more directly affected.
3. The buyer will not have to compete with other clients for their time.
4. The more work they do for the buyer, the more they will understand the buyer's wishes. Buyers can avoid training outsiders and seek to build their own organizations.
5. Acquisition work is a great training activity for able professionals aspiring to general management.
6. A permanent acquisition team will become more effective and produce better quality acquisitions.
7. Full-time employees are more readily accepted by sellers. They can speak more authoritatively.

A buyer must also consider the arguments for using outside professionals:

1. Serving many clients, their experience tends to be more varied.
2. A major law or accounting firm has more specialists to draw upon as needed.
3. Even very active acquisition programs tend to have erratic work loads creating demands or shortfalls that can best be handled by outsiders.
4. Outsiders tend to be more objective and often can play the role of neutral observer when differences arise.
5. Outsiders can more readily be terminated either because they are not needed or for cause.
6. No acquisition program goes on forever.
7. Professionals associated with prestigious firms tend to give credibility to a buyer.
8. Inside professionals are often diverted to activities other than acquisitions and are not available when needed.

Regardless of the pro and con arguments that all have a high degree of validity, many buyers will make their decision on the factors of the competency and attitude of existing in-house professionals. If the inside professionals are well respected and want to handle acquisition work, they can usually have it and build staffs as the work load increases. However, if the CEO or controlling shareholder has an extremely close relationship with key members of a legal or accounting firm, no amount of logic or astronomical professional fees will convince him to build a team of in-house professionals.

Time Factors

Acquisitions are not quickly made and a buyer must be prepared for an extended program. If there ever was an activity where the observation "everything takes longer than planned" applies, it's acquisitions. Even when all goes well, it is usually a long drawn out affair. Some acquisitions can be accomplished in a few months, but this is not common. Others drag on for years with on-again, off-again meetings and negotiations before a closing or failure occurs. Every acquisition is different but the following time estimates are realistic for a buyer to use in his planning:

Major decision-making	1-2 months
Management and planning	1-2 months

Industry and prospect data accumulation	2-3 months
Contact and selling prospects	1-2 months
Evaluation	1 month
Negotiations	1-2 months
Documentation and closing	1-3 months

Many of the above elements will overlap and run concurrently; for example, evaluation normally continues during the documentation phase. Negotiations of the definitive agreement may continue to closing. Major decisions and management are always needed. A buyer who reaches a decision to attempt to buy a company with whom he has had no prior contact should consider himself extremely fortunate if he has acquired the target company six months later and still satisfied if he made the acquisition within a year.

Role of the CEO

Even if the personnel are assembled, the professionals employed or standing by, and financing accomplished, nothing much will happen unless the buyer who is an individual or the CEO of a corporation plays a continual and very active role. Devine pronouncement from on high of "let there be acquisitions" will, in themselves, hardly get the job done.

The CEO must create the environment where acquisitions have a high priority in time and resources. Decisions must be made promptly. Access to the CEO must be readily available to those involved in the program. The CEO must meet important sellers. The CEO should be the most determined and enthusiastic backer of the program and his interest and participation should set a standard for everyone. With all the elements coordinated and headed by an enthusiastic executive, an acquisition program will succeed.

4.
Mistakes and
the Ideal Company

After a buyer has sorted out his objectives, determined his capability to acquire, and has an understanding of what is involved to make an acquisition, he is nearly ready to start his program. The last steps should include a review of external factors beyond the control of the buyer and a brief study of why acquisitions failed for others. Of course, few buyers enter into acquisitions expecting to make the same mistakes others have made or believing unsurmountable negative conditions exist, but a review of the common causes of failure may encourage a buyer to pause and reconsider before making an acquisition investment. A final step is the realistic determination of what would be the ideal acquisition and ideal method of purchase. The ideal company probably will never be discovered but the exercise will be helpful in setting priorities, clarifying objectives, and avoiding foolish "grailing" of the sort engaged in by the knights described in Mark Twain's King Arthur's court.

External Factors that Affect Acquisitions

Overall economic, political, and social factors create an environment that may tend to encourage or discourage acquisition activities. These are factors over which a buyer has virtually no control, so he must use them to his advantage, ignore them at his peril, achieve an accommodation, or, in some cases, abandon plans to acquire. Their existence must be recognized and faced by a buyer if he is to have a rational investment program. A buyer should make a priority of keeping well informed and be prepared to devote whatever time is necessary to study external factors.

Economic Conditions

The overall condition of the economy has a substantial influence on the players in the acquisition game. Primarily, current conditions but also expectations for the future effect businessmen's decisions on buying and selling. Economic prophets are as unreliable as the ecclesiastical variety but economists have the advantage in that they are more plentiful and vocal. Select whatever one wants to believe will happen to the economy and with little effort an economist can be found to support the opinion. Because economic forecasts are so unreliable, most business decisions tend to be made on the basis of the conditions as they exist today, and this may well be the most prudent course to follow. A manufacturer with a low backlog and declining order rate is unlikely to start building inventory no matter how many economists forecast a boom around the corner. A retailer enjoying record sales levels will keep his shelves full regardless of any gloomy economic predictions. It is current business conditions that most affect the attitude and decisions of business executives.

An owner is usually thinking of selling his company when his profits are high and the economy is at a strong level, reasoning buyers will be optimistic and willing to pay top prices. Buyers often do forget that any company they acquire will be owned in good times and bad and their return on investment calculations may not reflect this fact.

The buyers tend to believe their best time to make acquisitions is when the economy is low and pessimism abounds because, obviously, they should then be able to buy at the lowest prices. However, waiting until hard times to make acquisitions is too long a wait for most buyers, and the low point of a recession will not be known anyway until it is past. Although economic activity levels greatly influence pricing and willingness to sell, a buyer should not hold back from acquiring or rush to acquire because of forecasts of economic activity levels or current levels. He can and should base his decisions on the fact that neither boom nor recession times will continue forever. If a buyer at any time can make an attractive acquisition, he should do so without too much regard for the predictions of the economic prophets.

Governmental Attitudes

Government attitudes must be carefully watched to anticipate policy changes. In the United States the government will challenge acquisitions with antitrust implications. Obvious violations of anti-trust regulations will cancel an acquisition, but there is a large grey area of what is proper or improper and enforcement depends upon the attitude and zeal of the government officials in office. The growing opposition to large acquisitions may reach a point where legislation is enacted. Present proposals in this area would only affect the largest of transactions. Taxes, tariffs, environmental rules, and any other areas of governmental interest are all subject to changes which could make a contemplated acquisition more attractive or totally undesirable.

International Factors

If a buyer contemplates an international acquisition program, then he must become familiar with the laws, regulations, and procedures of every country in which he hopes to acquire a business. There are extreme differences in the rules between other countries and the U.S. and a program based on U.S. rules just will not be applicable in other countries. The regulations in other countries also change from time to time creating a real problem for an active buyer to remain current in his understanding of the economic and regulatory environment. Therefore, terrorism, political stability, relations with neighboring nations as well as the United States are other factors that can affect acquisitions and to which the buyer must be alert. These are all areas of controversy with evaluation leading to accurate forecasts most difficult. A buyer contemplating international acquisitions must seek out knowledgeable professionals in the countries involved for their advice to avoid the more obvious mistakes. The large international accounting firms are a good place to look for such professionals.

Stock Market Effects

The stock market is an external factor that affects acquisition activity in a number of ways. While it is an imperfect barometer of business optimism or pessimism, it is the best one available and is generally accepted. Its gyrations do reflect the thinking of thousands of investors every day so it cannot be totally ignored. The observation that individual market investors are largely fools but the collective results of the market show great wisdom may have some merit.

The market plays a major role in pricing. It sets the price for the buyer's shares if he plans to use them as currency. It roughly indicates the volume of shares that the market could absorb in a period of time if a buyer issued marketable shares. The market performance of the buyer's shares over a period of years reflects the success or failure of the company as seen by investors and the sellers. A strong overall rise in value during the past few years is impressive to sellers. The market establishes price-earnings ratios that some buyers use as guidelines in price negotiations. PE's for entire industries, competitors, or the market as a whole are used selectively by buyers and sellers to support their positions in price negotiations.

Sellers who are public companies have their minimum share value set by the current market price. The question becomes how much premium over the current market price is a buyer prepared to pay to gain control. It is ironic that the price to acquire control is always a premium over market but there is no way the sellers could all sell their shares on the open market without driving the price into the ground. Because the market sets the value of the buyer's shares, it indirectly determines whether or not a buyer can use his stock in acquisitions or must use cash or some other nonequity form of payment. Most buyers with low PE ratios find it impossible to use stock in acquisitions. Even in transactions involving nonpublic companies, the market is always in the background influencing the parties to a degree greater than they realize.

Political Events

Political conditions and events may occur that preclude or influence acquisition activities. Cataclysmic international events such as war, boycotts, changes in governments, and embargos can either bring a complete halt to acquisitions or greatly discourage them because of the uncertainty created. The overthrow of the Shah of Iran brought an end to many acquisition discussions in the U.S. by Iranian nationals and cancelled all joint venture negotiations in Iran by foreign nationals. Terrorism in Central and South America is also a significant deterrent to investment. Lesser events such as tariff restrictions, tax policies, monetary policies, pro-labor legislation, and antibusiness postures by the government or aspiring politicians all can affect acquisitions. For example, legislated worker participation in the boards of directors of German companies is a frightening concept to most American business executives. A political climate favorable to business is necessary to encourage business activity including acquisitions. Particularly conducive to acquisition activity is political and social stability where business people believe they know what the rules will be tomorrow as well as today.

Causes of Failure

There are many reasons why acquisitions turn out to be unsuccessful for the buyer. In individual cases there often is a combination of reasons for failure and frequently great differences of opinion exist as to their validity or importance. On occasion the true reasons will never be known and sometimes they are known but never discussed because it may be politically imprudent to discuss the shortcomings or poor decisions of key executives.

No list of human folly is ever complete but acquisition failures have been studied enough to identify the common causes. Failure can mean very different things to different people and would lend itself to a variety of definitions in attempting to define an unsuccessful acquisition. One reasonable approach would be to compare an evaluation of the results with the objectives and expectations of the buyer when the business was acquired. Even this may be fallacious in cases where a company was acquired for one reason (example: to gain distribution) that did not materialize but its profits exceeded all forecasts for an unsuspected reason (example: it had a little known product for which great volume developed totally unexpectedly). Another approach would be a straight economic one in which the acquired company's contribution to earnings per share is the measure but this yardstick often does not include all costs or all benefits from ownership. An acquisition may also be producing a profit well below that forecast but still is a good return on the investment and better than other investments of the buyer. Perhaps, failure may best be defined as simply an acquisition the buyer wishes he had not made.

The list is not in any order of importance because only one or two of the causes will be applicable to an individual buyer, and any cause is important enough to bring about a failure. For a buyer, the most important causes of failure are the ones applicable to him.

Improbable Events

Acquisitions fail for reasons that neither the buyer or seller anticipated or could have been expected to anticipate. Improbable events totally beyond the control of the buyer do occur from time to time and adversely affect businesses. Natural disasters, wars, boycotts, changes in governments, revolutions, trade embargos, fires, the sudden emergence of new superior competing products, changes in consumer tastes, new government regulations, technological changes, changes in monetary policy, extreme changes in raw material costs, product failures, and labor disputes are all events that have occurred with adverse consequences to the businesses affected. While it is possible for a buyer to develop lists of cataclysmic but highly improbable events that could occur, it is pointless to do so. A buyer concerned over events that are unlikely will end up buying no businesses and may as well forget an acquisition program. Regardless, there is a business risk of this improbable category that a buyer must be prepared to face if he is in business.

Acquired Is Different From Buyer's Expectation

The buyer may find he owns a company quite different from the one he thought he had acquired. Most buyers conduct their evaluations of acquisition candidates on a basis where they do not show the results and conclusions to the sellers and ask for their verification. Usually these studies are withheld from the sellers for fear of giving the seller second thoughts on the price previously agreed upon, or because the study contains information critical of the seller of possibly remedial plans by the buyer to improve the seller's business, which if known by the seller, might cause the seller to back out of the deal.

Buyers tend to spend so much time informing the sellers of their own virtues and the advantages of being acquired that they never learn enough about the prospect. In hostile takeovers the buyers know even less about the acquired and its problems, because they will not have access to the prospect's top management for discussions of their views of the business. Former employees, disgruntled employees, published data, and opinions of analysts can all contribute information, but there is no substitute for candid discussions with top management. Sellers are under no obligation to patiently explain to a buyer that his concept of the business and its potential are all wrong. Sellers need not volunteer information on the problems and wants of the business and can and do remain silent unless asked. Most sellers will disclose negative information when asked specific questions but they are under no compunction to volunteer damaging data. Regardless of the reasons, once an acquired company is discovered to be something other than what the buyer thought it was, it will have little chance in the buyer's organization unless significant offsetting assets and potential are quickly uncovered.

Buyer Deceived

Occasionally, a buyer is deceived and he finds upon possession that the business was misrepresented with a variety of fraudulent representations and his only hope is to cut his losses through prompt legal action. A seller who is disreputable enough to engage in fraud is usually clever enough to have the buyer's money and be well out of reach before the buyer realizes what happened to him. False financial statements, phantom assets, unrealistic appraisals, undisclosed liabilities, undisclosed litigation, overvalued inventory, concealed illegal practices, premature recognition of income, and product failures are examples of concealed problems or means of beguiling an unwary buyer. Fortunately, only a very small percentage of sellers would engage in such practices but buyers should never forget a few do surface from time to time. Systematic evaluations and use of experienced professionals are the buyer's primary defenses against misrepresentation.

Buyers are often quick to mumble fraud or misrepresentation when an acquisition turns sour because it is politically expedient to blame the seller rather than himself. These are serious charges often difficult to prove. Furthermore, the misrepresentation that may have occurred may be insignificant or irrelevant to the basic causes of the failure. A buyer should be very cautious with his accusations.

Paid Too Much

If a buyer's enthusiasm had the better of him and he paid a price for a business in which everything had to go just right, including a few small miracles, in order to meet his forecasts and secure the desired return on his investment, then he will almost certainly be disappointed and eventually realize he paid too much. The acquired business may be an excellent business in every respect, but if a price was paid for it on which the return is inadequate, the acquisition must be classed as a failure. Usually when overpayment has occurred, the internal relationship between the buyer and the acquired's management begins to sour. Little support is given to the business, extraordinary performance is demanded but not produced, and soon there is management turnover. A general deterioration sets in leading to an eventual divestment.

Political Pariah

If controversy existed in the buyer's organization over the decision to acquire a business, those who were opposed may do all they can in a subtle way to prove their original views were correct. The old team play spirit of "we may disagree, but once the decision is made, we are all 100% behind it" more often than not, in a business organization, is nonsense. An acquisition strongly endorsed by or under the responsibility of a controversial executive with rivals or detractors in the corporation may be unfairly criticized and not given full support and a fair chance as part of the political byplay. A newly acquired company should receive all the support, understanding and assistance from the buyer's organization possible in order to maximize the buyer's investment. Political considerations should be recognized and eliminated if a buyer wants to reduce the chance of failure.

Multidivision corporations can all too easily slip into an application of performance standards that are grossly unequal and unfair. The divisions that are out of favor are criticized for every real or imagined shortcoming no matter how trivial and miracles of performance are demanded. The divisions in favor are reviewed casually and seldom criticized no matter what their performance. This situation can develop in any corporation unless the chief executive is alert to the possibility and periodically reviews his own performance for objectivity and impartial management.

Interpersonal Relationships

The relationship between the buyer's executives and the executives of the acquired company is a critical factor. A healthy working relationship involving mutual respect is essential for the acquired business to prosper, but it will not exist if the two parties cannot communicate, do not understand, or just dislike each other. A buyer planning to retain the management of a company to be acquired, should not enter into the transaction unless there is genuine respect and a good rapport with key executives at the time of the acquisition. If it is not good at the start there is little chance it will become better during the stress and friction of the transition period. If the buyer is a large organization, the executive to whom the acquired is to be assigned should have the opportunity to become well acquainted and build a good rapport with the seller's executives. If he has a dislike for them, it will not be a healthy relationship. Racial, religious, and political factors may be illegal to consider in hiring and promotions but they cannot be entirely ignored in acquisition decisions. It is not impossible for individuals with strongly differing basic views to get along well, but it is far more difficult.

Buyer Does Not Understand Business

Each business has its own characteristics and peculiarities that must be accommodated if success is to result. Many acquisitions fail because a buyer either does not bother to learn the special characteristics and problems of the acquired or discounts their significance. Buyers who apply roughshod techniques, systems, procedures, and objectives to the acquired that were successful in their other businesses may find belatedly they are inapplicable, some modification is necessary, or the existing methods or approaches used by the acquired are superior. A business believed good enough to buy cannot be doing everything wrong.

A buyer who lacks an understanding of the acquired industry or markets and is unwilling to accept the conditions because of preconceived notions or egotistical commitments and expectations can expect trouble that will not be remedied by management changes. Managements of the acquired are accustomed to working with conditions as they know them to be and any changes in operational methods must be explained and make sense. Failure can come rapidly if the buyer does not understand the business and persists in playing an active role in its management.

Lack of Agreed Objectives

The acquired company may never have received a set of objectives that it agreed were attainable. The buyer may not have clear objectives or he kept them to himself and whatever they are remains a mystery to the acquired company's management. This condition is only slightly better than objectives forced upon the acquired that they believe to be impossible. This lack of direction or irrational objectives can produce failure. A buyer should bring the acquired into the objective setting process and secure willing agreement. If the executives of the acquired are not in full agreement, then it is the buyer's responsibility to demonstrate the objectives are attainable or revise them to a reasonable level.

Unfulfilled Buyer Promises

During the evaluation phase and courtship, a buyer will be studying how the acquired should best fit into his organization and what he will contribute to the acquired to make it grow. These proposed contributions were often critical in convincing a seller to sell. Injections of capital, combined distribution, new systems, technical assistance, new facilities, assistance in locating people, access to top professionals, and introduction to new markets are examples of often promised assistance that have the potential for synergistic benefits. Too often promises are made by those responsible only for making the acquisition who have the best of intentions but are not directly responsible for implementing the promised assistance and do not have the authority to force fulfillment of the promises. Circumstances do change on occasion and a buyer may not be in a position to keep his promises; but broken promises are demoralizing. The promised help may have been essential to the success of the acquired and unless forthcoming the acquisition will not prosper.

Improper or Unstable Position in Buyer's Organization

An acquired company should be assigned a logical position in the buyer's organization and left there. It is a high management game to reorganize and move companies from one division, group, or executive to another but this is debilitating to a newly acquired company and can result in failure. A new company management will be having enough trouble adjusting to the buyer's way of doing business without the added problems associated with being moved about and readjusting to new corporate executives and their style of operating. Every time an operating unit is assigned to report to a new executive, there is a period of discussions, trial, and error where the parties learn to work together. The difference in methods of management between executives within the same corporation can be as severe as those of executives in totally different organizations. This condition often occurs when the buyer liked the company enough to acquire it but never had a clear idea as to how it fit.

Management Changes

Some buyers believe they must promptly make key management changes after the acquisition is closed. Usually, the financial executive and the president are first on the list to be replaced. Although most buyers do not have a policy to make management changes automatically, for many it usually turns out that way. Buyers have frequently learned to their dismay that the terminated executives took with them the know-how that made the company a success and was necessary for its continued success. It is truly remarkable how buyers can rationalize their management changes and declare executives incompetent who have fine unblemished records of performance.The fired executives usually do what they know best and go with competitors or create competing companies. Few buyers will ever bring themselves to admit their personnel decisions were in error but the facts are that in many acquisitions, the road to failure starts with unnecessary management changes.

Over Dependence On One Executive

Some companies are one-man shows. These are usually small or medium-sized firms that only could afford one very good man or firms of any size dominated for years by a very strong personality who had come to erroneously suspect he was immortal and would carry on forever. Companies with only one strong executive are a real risk for any buyer. Even when the executive is to continue in his role, unexpected incapacitation or death can occur with no successor readily available. Although these solo executives may become convinced of the need to develop candidates as their successor, they have great difficulty delegating enough responsibility to develop or attract their replacement. These strong executives who cannot delegate responsibility often have equal difficulty surrendering any of their authority and independence to a new owner who wants his say in running the company now that he owns it. A company with only one key executive may have been a great performer but it can rapidly deteriorate in his absence.

Establishing Priorities by Seeking the "Ideal Company"

Buyers usually reach a stage in contemplating, researching, and planning their acquisitions program where they have a whole shopping list of company types they would like to acquire. These lists are circulated internally and to bankers, brokers, and consultants often with requests for everyone to be on the lookout for such companies. They give the impression the buyer would attempt to pursue anything on the list with equal enthusiasm. Seldom is this the actual case and never in the author's experience did he find there were more than one or two categories on a list that the issuer cared enough about to drop everything else and get on a plane immediately. Other categories are of much lower priority often because of changing conditions but also because little or no interest ever existed.

Often, categories appear that a buyer believes he would like to acquire a year or two later, but not at this time. Because few, if any, buyers have the unlimited resources to pursue every type acquisition at once, it is absolutely essential to set priorities. Furthermore, acquisitions can best be accomplished if those searching know exactly what they are looking for and doing it on a specific basis rather than merely "looking for companies to buy."

Setting of priorities can be greatly aided by the buyer periodically developing a profile of the ideal company he would most like to buy. This is not an existing company but a fictitious one. The search for the ideal company will almost certainly be unsuccessful but those searching will know precisely what they are looking for and their task is to find the existing company that comes closest to the ideal.

If the buyer is realistic in developing the ideal company profile, then it should be possible for a company close to the ideal to exist. It is a waste of time to create a profile of an ideal company possessing superior characteristics that have never been achieved or are unlikely to ever exist. The ideal may be quite different from a company superior in all respects if the buyers are seeking a turnaround situation or primarily wish to acquire a business for its facilities, distribution, or other specific characteristics. Cost and the buyer's capabilities must be taken into consideration in developing the ideal. An ideal company with the characteristics of General Motors to be acquired for $10 million is nonsense. The buyer must review his current financial condition and decide what he can afford and is readily willing to pay. The ideal will normally not have a cost that would cause the buyer a hardship or jeopardize his present position. The type of currency to be used should also be settled. Each buyer has vastly different capacities to acquire depending whether he pays with cash, stock, notes, or other forms of consideration. However, every buyer has his preference.

The buyer should determine his ideal company characteristics not only on a basis of what he really wants and would be fine to own, but also on what he really needs. A company with the ideal company's characteristics will be difficult enough to locate without including unnecessary features in its profile. For example, a buyer with a very strong cash position should carefully evaluate how important to him is the seller's cash position. The best acquisitions should be an excellent matching of the strength and weaknesses of the buyers and sellers. Every buyer's list of characteristics for his ideal company will be unique, but on almost everyone's list will be the following:

1. Product or service	11. Growth potential
2. Sales volume	12. Type facilities
3. Earnings level	13. Management
4. Net worth	14. Type distribution
5. Geographical location	15. Debt position
6. Proprietary position	16. Cash position
7. Cost to acquire	17. Percent of market
8. Acceptable acquisition	18. Number of employees
currency	19. Type ownership
9. Union/Nonunion	20. Reputation
10. Financial history	21. Cash flow

The ideal company for any buyer will change from time to time as his conditions and views change making it advisable to construct a new ideal company periodically. If a buyer is very active in an effort to acquire in several industries and has the resources to pursue more than one company simultaneously, then he should develop an ideal in each industry, but only if they have near equal priority.

Once the ideal company's characteristics are determined, the buyer should review what he would do with it if acquired and how it would fit into his present organization. Sellers ask these questions and the buyer will not help his position if he is unprepared and has no satisfactory answers. A buyer's own organization is often in the dark as to where a new company would fit. Too many buyers do not bother to plan early where they would assign an acquired business and a program of transition for the company. Using the ideal company as a theoretical acquisition, these broad planning decisions can be made.

5.
The Industry Study

The purposes of an industry study are to identify prospects, obtain information about each prospect, secure data on the prospect's industry, and provide general information that will permit the buyer's executives to become thoroughly conversant about the industry.

The scope of the industry study will be narrowed and set as the prospective acquirer establishes his objectives, which ideally will be tempered by a realistic assessment of his capabilities. The more work accomplished in identifying the industry the buyer wishes to enter and the ideal prospect within the industry, the simpler will be the task of studying the industry and determining the logical prospects. Information is so readily available and in such quantity that individuals conducting the study will find their main problem is sorting and evaluating data once they know where and how to look. Unfortunately, there is no single reliable source of information, so a study will cover data secured from a number of reference books, periodicals, and other sources.

Reasons for Industry Studies

Prospect identification is the obvious first need, but data on all companies in the industry as well as complete information on the industry is important. Information on all other companies will help establish the total size of the market, identify problems, determine the nature of the competition, and help prevent acquisition of the wrong company in the right industry. Few events are more dismaying to a management than to learn after acquiring a company that it could have acquired a superior competitor on an advantageous basis. Such blunders are seldom admitted or aired publicly, but they are amply and acrimoniously discussed in executive suites. Comprehensive data on all companies in the selected industry, regardless of size or present ownership, is an essential first step towards preventing such mistakes.

The industry study should provide detailed information on all aspects of an industry. Size, customer data, market trends, long-range forecasts, new product developments, technological advances, current problems, government influence and attitudes, labor conditions, and domestic and foreign competitive pressures are all major areas for a buyer's study to cover. As information is developed, unsuspected problems or opportunities may emerge that require greater in-depth study than anticipated. It would be most unlikely if the study did not result in some modification of the buyer's original views. An in-depth study may very well convince a buyer to terminate his aspirations to buy into that specific industry.

Another purpose of the industry study is for the buyer's executives who are to be in contact with prospects to become thoroughly conversant about the industry. The prospects will already possess far more knowledge of the industry than the buyer is likely to ever have but they will expect the buyer's executives to display sufficient information about the industry to prove they know what they are doing. With knowledge of the industry, the buyer's executives will demonstrate that they have an understanding of conditions and have made their decision to enter the industry on a planned rational basis. They will avoid the appearance of being "shoppers" looking for any company in any industry. A buyer's industry knowledge will deter a seller from making extravagant or overly enthusiastic claims about the potential of his business in hopes of improving his bargaining position. Buyer knowledge helps preserve a realistic basis for discussions. The seller has probably spent much of his life in the industry and enjoys discussing its conditions. "Talking shop" helps build the rapport necessary to eventually bring about a sale but this is only possible if the buyer is well informed.

The buyer's executives must have industry knowledge to know what questions to ask and not to ask. It will be difficult for an executive to regain the respect of a prospect once he has asked irrelevant questions or questions that even the janitor of the prospect could answer. Great insight into the management approach and capabilities of prospects can be gained if the buyer is able to question the prospect on how he is coping with specific problems and changes occurring in the industry. It is almost certain the problems any company has are also problems being experienced to varying degrees by its competitors and are well known. Most executives tend to believe their problems are unique to some degree, but this seldom is the case. Sellers, once aware of the buyer's industry knowledge, may assume the buyer has more than what is actually possessed, and will ask for information and opinions.

The buyer's representatives need to be well prepared to voice learned opinions.

The industry study is a continuous study lasting throughout the acquisition program, but it should be sufficiently complete prior to contacting prospects for the buyer's representatives to have a good grasp of the nature of the industry.

Everyone who prepares an industry study will have their own thoughts on format. However, there are several principles to keep in mind. The format should be such that new information can continually be added. Contacts with prospects often produce new information, publications appear with important data and preliminary information may prove to be misleading or erroneous. The study should be in an orderly and well organized loose-leaf book that permits revisions and additions but is durable and convenient. It will be used during the acquisition phase and also used by operating executives to whom the company is assigned once acquired. A mass of unorganized data in files or stacks will not be of much help to anyone.

Data Accuracy and Reliability

When gathering data on the industry and individual prospects, caution should continually be exercised as to its reliability and accuracy regardless of the stature of its source. An awareness of this problem coupled with an understanding of how it occurs is essential for anyone using business data.

Any published financial data on companies is out of date to some degree by the time it is published. Financial reports describe the results for a period of time that has passed. The reports summarize the results for the entire period and do not show trends within the period. They cannot be prepared until after the period is over and it may take months to complete, print, and distribute the data. (One criterion for evaluation of companies is the speed with which they can issue financial results.) Once issued, the results may be included in statistical comparisons of companies or hardbound books containing financial reports of hundreds of companies. These all require time to prepare, print, and distribute. Because companies can and do select fiscal periods ending any month in the year, there can be eleven months difference in the periods described and compared. As an example, a list of 500 companies with the largest sales volume when published in 1980 could contain companies whose fiscal years ended anytime between January 30, 1979 and December 31, 1979. Public companies' annual reports are issued yearly and supplemented by brief quarterly reports. The annual reports and forms 10-K usually are distributed two to four months after the close of the fiscal year they describe. As a consequence, for a period of one year the primary source of information on a public company describes the company's business during a period of time that ended two to fourteen months earlier.

Laws forbidding disclosure of inaccurate or misleading information by public companies have discouraged most financial reports and executive statements of this variety but some do persist. SEC enforcement actions, shareholder suits, and suits against public accounting firms, all of which are frequently reported in the business press, should remind one to be wary. Even with the best of intentions, errors do occur in publishing the vast amount of data generated by business activity. The prestigious *Wall Street Journal* has even had to go to a regular column in which it prints corrections of errors in previous editions.

Publishers of the popular business periodicals and trade magazines undoubtedly strive for accuracy but they do have certain problems and weaknesses that should be recognized. They must rely on the information given to them by others. They cannot audit financial data or readily verify forecasts or other information submitted. They depend upon the integrity of their sources and when in doubt, indicate their source. They have extreme time pressures and limited budgets to develop enough "copy" by their next deadline. This situation has enabled the public relations industry to flourish.

Public relations firms are paid well to secure publication of articles favorable to their corporate clients and suppress unfavorable news or at least present it in the least damaging manner. The PR firms activity includes arranging for interviews with executives who have been coached by the public relations firm on what to say and how to behave during an interview. If the publication does not have reporters available, the PR firm will develop the information for an article and, if permitted, write the entire article. It is usually understood that the publisher reserves the right to edit or change articles as he sees fit but the publisher's ability to do this is limited because he only has information supplied by the public relations firm. There is no better way for an executive to understand the system and develop a certain amount of skepticism about the business press than to call in public relations firms and request a proposal to represent his firm and prove their competence by describing what they have done for others. They will present an array of articles that have appeared in publications as a result of their assistance and will impress most executives. Another simple test is to make a mathematical comparison of the number of articles that favorably or blandly describe companies with the few that are negative. Regardless of the occasional doubtful accuracy of the business press, it is an essential source of information for anyone seriously interested in making acquisitions.

Gathering Information for the Industry Study

Once there is a belief that it would be desirable to enter a certain industry, the first step is to subscribe to all the trade publications that cover the industry. Many subscriptions can be made on a retroactive basis so that a few recent issues can quickly be received and studied. Some publishers may sell an entire year's back issues. To find out what are the trade publications, start by asking a person in the industry what they receive. If it is possible to secure copies, do so and review those issues for subscription information. Most contain tear-out postcards to mail in to start a subscription. This approach will identify the common domestic publications but more are required.

Everyone engaged in acquisitions will find invaluable as a basic reference book *Ulrich's International Periodicals Directory* published by R.R. Bowker Company, which lists all periodicals. This reference is a listing on an international basis of all publications arranged by subject along with information on how to subscribe. From it can be selected a broad range of trade publications from all over the world. The most important publications to select will be those with the largest circulation. They are not only more widely read and most influential but also contain more advertising and publish more industry data. Lesser circulation periodicals are also important and when one considers the cost of an acquisition, it is wise to subscribe to all appropriate periodicals for the industry. The industry study should include information on a world-wide basis regardless of how local or regional the acquisition objectives may be. Developments in other countries may greatly influence the local industry. It may also help the buyer's executives in their discussions with sellers if they can display their knowledge of international conditions.

Another source to identify trade publications is *Standard Rate and Data Service, Inc.* This publication is primarily for advertisers and appears in multiple volumes that are available at most advertising agencies or in the larger public libraries.

Using Trade Publications

There is no more important source of information than the trade magazines. The amount of information they provide on a regular basis is almost overwhelming but it is the basic data needed to understand what is going on in an industry. They contain far more than technical articles describing solutions to current problems or the state of the art. They publish lists and realistic rankings of companies, industry wide markets forecasts, reports on new products, market trends, government activities, profiles of individual companies and executives, notices and programs of up-coming trade shows, names of key executives changing jobs and news stories on companies in the industry who are acquired or acquire someone else. The advertisers will constitute a fairly lengthy list of those in the industry but it will not be all inclusive. Advertisements also provide valuable product information.

Many publishers of trade magazines have discovered another profitable use for all the information they accumulate. They publish annual surveys of the industry or suppliers directories that contain industry statistics, names of companies, and information on the companies. These are usually advertised in the trade magazines and should be ordered by anyone studying a particular industry. A visit to the editor of a trade magazine could be helpful in securing industry insight and even names of companies who would be prospects. Most will go out of their way to be helpful and if increased or continuing advertising revenues are a possibility, cooperation is assured.

Trade Associations

Most industries have trade associations or societies formed by the companies in the industry. Not all companies join their industry trade association but enough do that it is worth the effort to learn if an association exists and secure its membership roster and anything it might publish. If convenient, a meeting with the associations director would be worthwhile, because he may provide information on the industry, as well as suggest a few prospects. The simplest way to locate the trade associations would be from a friendly member. If none are known, locate the trade association through the following reference book: *Encyclopedia of Associations* published by Gale Research Company.

Trade Shows

As part of the continuing market study, all of the industry trade shows should be attended. Here, product literature on individual companies is available to anyone attending. Company representatives are on hand to discuss their products, capabilities, and companies. A skillful person visiting a company booth can learn much about a company and readily compare it with its competitors. This may prove to be the first actual contact between representatives of the buyer and seller but at this time the subject of acquisition normally would not be discussed. When setting up a first meeting with a prospect to discuss acquisition, it is advisable to include complimentary remarks about his exhibit at the trade show.

In many trade shows it is customary to introduce new products. When this is the case, it is an opportunity to indirectly evaluate a company's research and development program and marketing approach. Often at trade shows there are companies that emerge as members of the industry for the first time. These companies may be new and small or large companies attempting to enter the market for the first time or companies that limit their advertising budget to the cost of trade shows and generally maintain a low profile.

Investment Services

There are a large number of investment services that describe industries and public companies primarily from a financial standpoint. They are limited to public companies for their lists and analyses because they attempt to serve investors in public companies. If a buyer has some particular financial criteria for acquisition prospects such as low book value, debt-equity ration, or low price/earnings ratio, then these can be helpful, quick references. They also can identify industry averages for various financial ratios and these can be used to compare individual companies and also the financials of privately held companies once their data is secured. There are many services that can be very effective. The larger and more reputable usually advertise in the Sunday financial section of the *New York Times* and *Barrons* and offer trial subscriptions. They are easy to sample with little commitment. *Standard and Poors* has a service that monitors certain basic industries and is recognized as one of the best. If a buyer is only seeking to identify companies that have certain financial prerequisites, one of his executives can go through his personal stockbroker and receive the data without involving his firm. The larger investment banking firms have banks of computerized data waiting for such requests. It is free and the cost of the investment service can be avoided.

Forbes magazine publishes a ranking of corporations by various criteria each January much as the investment services publish. However, it is limited to the larger corporations. *Fortune* magazine publishes its famous *Fortune 500* and other lists of business once a year. Trade magazines publish their lists of companies in the industry and rank them by financial characteristics.

Yellow Pages

If the buyer is seeking a company in a certain geographical area, he should not forget the yellow pages of his local telephone directory or the directory in the specific location. They are very comprehensive and readily available. It is possible to order the yellow pages for any city from your own local telephone company business office.

Specialized Directories

There are also many specialized directories usually published annually. They describe banks, insurance companies, advertising agencies, investment bankers, manufacturers by product line, business by state and many other variations. These are too numerous to list but a visit to a large city library would identify the most common. There also is a book of directories called the *Encyclopedia of Business Information Sources* published by Gale Research Company.

Other Publications

When market statistics are desired, government sources should be checked, particularly the United Nations. The U.S. government continually publishes data helpful to business and a telephone call to the Department of Commerce will usually produce someone who will describe what is available. The United Nations has accumulated an incredible amount of information about the world. Here it is best to secure their catalogue of publications. In large public libraries is the *F&S Index of Corporations and Industries*, which is a business readers guide to track down desired information. Two British publications, *The Economist* and *The Financial Times*, periodically study industries and countries in exhaustive detail, but they are of excellent quality. Subscriptions to both would be a good investment for an international acquisition executive who had a secretary able to screen for articles of interest. *Predicasts, Inc.*, of Cleveland, Ohio, has a variety of fine information services worth considering by those interested in comprehensive market studies.

Field Studies and Direct Contacts

Direct discussions with industry representatives may not be practical if the program is to be kept secret. There is no point in making direct contacts with industry people until most of the published data is gathered. Then, contacts of this type will largely be helpful to confirm what already is known or to explore minor areas of interest about the industry. Executives in an industry read regularly or are exposed to much of the data the researcher already has, so most of their information and opinions will not be news. Direct contacts are time consuming and expensive and should not be conducted unless the researcher has developed incisive questions in advance and is aware of exactly what missing information is desired. In most situations the direct interview is unnecessary prior to the approach of actual prospects to discuss acquisition. The prospects themselves become another direct source of new or confirming data.

Company Names in Bulk

There are several other approaches to securing company names in an industry that may be helpful but the quantity and quality of the lists may discourage all but the most determined researcher. It is not that they are inaccurate, but they contain everything remotely fitting the category. These lists are often keyed off SIC codes and are found in both Dun and Bradstreet and Standard and Poors directories. It is also possible to secure computer printed lists of companies of specific types from Dun and Bradstreet, usually at a price per hundred. In addition, it is possible to buy mailing lists from firms specializing in this service—usually at a price per thousand. The names of companies providing such lists and their catalogues of mailing lists can be found at most advertising agencies.

Information on Individual Companies

The industry study will produce the names of the companies, but more information must be secured on those of interest or significance. Any buyer launching an acquisition effort will save time and money if he purchases certain basic reference books. An adequate acquisition reference library can be built for less than $1,000 per year and a very fine one for under $2,000. The basic books recommended for consideration are listed below. There is duplication of data in these publications and it is advisable for the prospective purchaser to contact each publisher for descriptive material. The best and quickest way to make a selection is to visit a large public library and inspect the books before purchasing any.

Name	Publisher
Million Dollar Directory	Dun and Bradstreet
Middle Market Directory	Dun and Bradstreet

Principal International Business	Dun and Bradstreet
Jones' Major Companies of	
Europe	The Greeham Press
Directory of Corporate	
Affiliations	National Register
Kompass	Kompass Publishers Ltd.
Moody's Manuals	Moody's Investor Service
Standard and Poors'	
Register and Reports	Standard and Poors' Corp.

Moody's and Standard and Poor's have a variety of excellent publications, services, and sales representatives in most areas who will contact prospective purchasers upon request.

Any acquisition library will have to be tailored to the type of program contemplated. If there are no plans to acquire foreign companies or public companies, then it can be a smaller library. The industries of interest will also be a limiting factor. A recent book, *How to Find Information About Companies* published by Washington Researchers can be helpful to a buyer attempting to locate all information possible on a company.

Once the program is started, action should be taken to locate information on specific companies of interest as soon as their names appear. The annual reports and 10-K's should be ordered on all public companies in the industry. In order not to disclose the program, an executive or secretary can write to the secretary of the company whose name was secured from one of the reference books and request copies of the annual reports to be sent to their home. A friendly investment banking broker can perform this service, but care must be taken to avoid rumors whenever dealing with brokers. If the prospect fails to send either the annual report, proxy statement, or 10-K, the SEC in Washington can be contacted for the name of a service that duplicates the SEC filings for a fee, or the buyer can visit one of the SEC offices located in Washington, New York, Chicago, or Los Angeles and make his own copies.

Dun and Bradstreet reports on private and public companies should be ordered. D&B has to rely on data given to them by the companies so they should not be faulted for the inaccuracies that occur. While financial data is sometimes misleading, the reports usually contain very accurate listing of officers, directors, and credit problems—which is their basic purpose. It is unwise to contact any private company before securing a D&B report. It is helpful to also secure D&B reports on public companies, although much of the data will be taken directly from SEC filings that the buyer should already have.

Product literature can be secured by writing a short letter addressed to the sales manager. If the buyer has a purchasing department, it can do this best and a buyer may even be surprised to learn his purchasing group already has the literature in their files. Literature can also be secured by filling in the postcards that are found in most trade magazines.

The buyer should check his own organization to see if in it are former employees of the prospect or those who have done business with the prospect. There may be vast knowledge right in the buyer's own company about the prospect and possibly employees who could provide introductions.

Files and Library

Files should be developed on individual companies that contain all information available. This would eventually include reports on any contacts with the company if such did occur. The library would be developed containing the reference books accumulated as well as trade publications and any other lists of value. An aggressive acquisition executive and department will always be accumulating reference data.

Acquisition Prices

Once a program commences, it is wise to record prices paid for companies as reported in the press. From this information it is possible to determine a general range of prices currently being paid that may indicate what is expected of the buyer in making an offer. This data is extremely helpful in price negotiations on both sides of the table. A buyer must justify to his own organization a price and one way is by comparison with recent purchases. The buyer should assume the seller is reading the same newspapers.

6.
Logical Prospects

It Doesn't Hurt to Ask

Unless an active solicitation of buyers is in progress, there is no certain means to determine if shareholders are inclined to sell other than by making direct contact and asking. Published data, rumors, and research analysis may indicate the business as a logical and available acquisition prospect, but until the controlling shareholders are contacted, perhaps repeatedly, willingness to sell cannot be ascertained. All signs may give the impression a prospect is a ready seller, but it may turn out upon contact that the owners are quite happy with their situation and have no desire whatsoever to sell. Other prospects may appear to have an ownership that would never sell, but in actuality they are hoping someone will appear and make an offer.

Price considerations are another unknown factor. There are few businesses that cannot be acquired if the price is high enough. The price may be totally uneconomic for a buyer and make no sense at all but, nevertheless, there is a price level that probably would bring about a sale. An offer so high that a seller would feel himself a fool not to accept may not look so high to a buyer who has a strong need.

Shareholder status and attitudes and pricing requirements are such important unknowns that a buyer in developing his list of prospects should not rule out any prospects that have characteristics close to those of his ideal company profile. Superficial views that the company's shareholders will not sell frequently prove to be in error. Initially, the buyer should prepare his list of prospects on the basis of how similar they are to his ideal and disregard preliminary opinions of availability. Once the complete list of prospects is compiled, priority for making contact can be influenced by likelihood of availability if other factors are essentially equal. However, a buyer would be unwise to rule out or set a very low priority on contacting any prospect whose characteristics closely matched the ideal's. Every week more acquisitions are publicly announced and most are businesses no one suspected were for sale or could be acquired. At one time they appeared on someone's confidential formal or informal list of companies that had the characteristics they sought and through some means contacts were made that led to the acquisitions.

Prospect Lists

A serious buyer who plans an ambitious program of acquisitions must maintain lists of prospects supported by all information accumulated on each prospect. Separate file folders should include the known information about a prospect and a record of all contacts and meetings. Acquisitions take a very long time to complete and because few executives are gifted with total recall, records are most essential. On occasion acquisition activity brings on litigation and accurate records of what transpired can be invaluable, if the buyer has a good case. A list of prospects that are worth further study or contact should be prepared monthly along with an indication of what happened in the prior month and what is planned for the near future. A simple report of this type is an important tool for the buyer because it is a reminder of what needs to be done and commitments made. It prevents prospects, once identified, from being ignored or lost in the system. It is a means of communicating to key executives of the buying organization progress or lack of progress. A complete list is also a means of giving an overview of the acquisition program whereby opportunities can be compared periodically with the buyer's resources and current priorities.

Reasons to Sell

A buyer should be familiar with the more common reasons business owners become sellers in order to quickly identify logical prospects and to be able to point out applicable reasons to owners for selling. A key part of any buyer's sales program is to emphasize why it would be to the owner's advantage to sell. Shareholders may not be aware that good reasons do exist for them to seriously consider selling and a perceptive buyer can greatly help his cause by tactfully weaving into his sales presentation the appropriate reasons.

Seldom do owners have only one reason for selling, although they make public statements to this effect. There may be one primary reason for a shareholder to sell, but it would be unusual if there were not supporting factors. Because businesses commonly have multiple owners, a buyer must recognize in his approach each owner may be motivated by widely different reasons to sell. As a result of these combination factors, a buyer should avoid attempting to convince shareholders to sell for one reason alone. Fortunately, there is a long list to draw upon as the following compendium illustrates, so multiple arguments should not be difficult to develop. These reasons or conditions conducive to bring about a sale can be used to identify logical prospects and conversely to screen unlikely ones. The condition opposite of a reason to sell is a reason not to sell, and its presence would indicate the owner is less inclined to sell.

Generous Price

If the offer is good enough, there need be no other reason to sell. The owners, in these situations, believe the price offered is so generous that they are better off to accept rather than hold on to their shares. Essentially, they believe the rate of return on their current investment will never equal the return they can receive from the offer invested elsewhere.

In tenders for public companies, where the buyer is offering a premium over what the market has valued the company, price may prove to be the only factor if the management does not resist. Management resistance will be tempered or nonexistent based on the amount of premium offered.

Offers for private or closely held companies on occasion are so generous that those in control believe they should sell although they had no plans to do so. They believe they have been offered more than the business is worth or will be worth in the foreseeable future. The buyer has convinced himself the company is undervalued in terms of recognition of past performance and estimated potential and justifies the offer with his view of the future. The seller accepts the buyer's offer to a large degree because he does not accept the buyer's optimistic view of the future or does not believe the buyer will receive a competitive return on his investment. Any buyer who finds himself making such a generous offer that the business owners believe they must accept should give some thought to the fact that the owners or managers who know the business and industry best may consider the buyer a fool. More often than not, it turns out the buyer who acquires businesses at a price so generous no one can understand his reasoning is a fool, but several years of ownership must elapse before this is definitely determined. It occasionally happens that the buyer had insight into the future better than all others, who eventually realize their judgment was wrong. There is growing evidence that the so-called winners of the well publicized bidding contests that occurred in the late 1970's for large public companies are turning out to be losers.

Nonparticipating Shareholders

Absentee owners or other shareholders who are not active in the business have a greater tendency to sell than those closely involved. To them it is an investment without an emotional attachment and they tend to evaluate offers objectively with price their primary interest.

Estate Planning

The owners know in some cases that to settle their estate when they die, the business must be sold. A single aging major owner with multiple heirs may have no way to divide his net worth without selling the business and he would sooner find a suitable new owner than leave this task to those handling his estate after his death. Estate taxes may also be so onerous that sale is necessary. The owner may be motivated by his belief that selling the business and creating a more liquid estate will lessen problems for his heirs.

Estate Settlements

The death of a major shareholder may open the company up for acquisition. A buyer needs considerable tact in inquiring into the availability of the company, but usually there is a banker or attorney involved willing to assist on a dispassionate basis. A buyer should very early evaluate if a sale is possible from a legal standpoint because some estates are in such a condition or filled with controversy that little can be done.

If the primary heir is the owner's widow or children who have not been active in the business, the prospect is all the more probable. Others readily notice these conditions so the acquisition of a business available to settle an estate may be fairly competitive.

A sale may be retarded by executors and professionals who have such a lucrative client that they have little interest in a speedy sale.

Shareholder Disputes

Whenever shareholders dislike each other or have differences of opinion on how the business should be run, sale of the business is a means of getting clear of each other. Unfortunately for a buyer, the animosity and disputes that made the acquisition negotiations possible will likely continue during the negotiations. In such negotiations it often seems whatever one faction agrees to, the other automatically challenges.

Often shareholder disputes are well publicized but even when the differences are not common knowledge, they can be suspected whenever there are two large relatively equal blocks of stock that control a company.

Retirement Plans

An owner over 50 years of age who has no heirs in the business who are senior executives may intend to sell and enjoy his money. For this owner it is largely a matter of timing, price, and an acceptable buyer because he has already made the decision to sell.

Owners in their 70's or 80's who have not sold are very difficult to persuade to sell because they do not wish to retire and believe if they remain active they will live to a very great age. They are convinced, possibly correctly, that if they sold out and retired, they would soon die.

Losing Control Because of Growth

Many founders of companies create very fine businesses but find it impossible to delegate decision-making responsibilities as growth occurs. As long as the business is small, they easily can make all the decisions but as it grows, delegation of responsibility and the need for complex paperwork systems becomes obvious. The transition from a one-man show to a more organized business is often difficult. During this transition period, owners are more receptive to selling, particularly to buyers who present themselves as experts on business organizations and systems.

Businesses Recently Acquired

Businesses that were acquired one to three years ago are often available. The purchasers have or may have discovered that the business is not what they thought it was or it is making too many demands in time and capital. The buyers may also have found they do not like being tied down to running a business. Another factor is that buyers often have not thought out what they would do with a business once acquired and after two or three years are ready to divest it.

Ambitious CEO

An ambitious CEO (usually young and well educated) may conclude he could and should be running a much larger business than his present one. To achieve his personal goals, he may be willing to sell his business if he has a chance for a much larger executive position in a great corporation. For the buyer in need of top talent, this can be a "killing of two birds with one stone" technique of great merit.

Cancelled Acquisition

A company that reached agreement with a buyer to sell but the buyer backed out as they approached the altar is a good prospect. These companies have made the decision to sell and know what is involved in selling.

Sometimes the insult of being turned down or the sheer fatigue and diversion of time away from their business during the unconsummated sales negotiations causes the seller to want to delay for a few months before entering negotiations again but chances are good they will consider another suitor.

New Businesses

Businesses a year or two old may be available. Often these are companies with products or services that have potential but the companies are so undercapitalized the owners are willing to sell. Companies are frequently founded by executives who terminated from larger organizations to start their own businesses and discovered there were problems never anticipated. Getting over the security of a regular paycheck is difficult for many and they would welcome a return to corporate life. After they have had their fling, they may become excellent, stable executives.

Lack of Succession

A business owned and managed by one man who has no children in the business in key positions or has all of the key executives in an age range over 50 probably has no clear cut management succession worked out. The owner is usually aware that his sudden death or incapacitation would cause a substantial drop in the value of the company and severe operational problems. To safely consider this type of prospect a buyer should have available an executive to step in and run the company if worse comes to worst.

Financial Problems

A company with a poor current ratio, large loan, in need of cash for capital expenditures may consider sale. The opportunities lost because of lack of capital, restrictions of loan terms, or press of creditors can take their toll and induce owners to consider sale as a solution to their problems.

Flat or Declining Earnings

A business that is not growing for any reason can be a prospect. A company in such a condition has fundamental problems that are discouraging to the owners and management. Perhaps the problems can be solved with outside assistance or new ownership. Obviously, a new owner must be in a position to provide solutions or he will not have a satisfactory investment.

Employee Ownership Problems

Owners who still retain control but have started a program of selling shares to employees may find they have created a monster no one likes. Whatever the motivation of the owner, the employees are seldom inspired by spending a portion of their income for stock without liquidity and a meager return. The owner may become unhappy with their ingratitude and believe he could secure more for his shares through a complete sale of the company.

Stock Buy-Back Problems

Whenever a closely held company has a scheme whereby the company must acquire the stock of shareholders when they quit or retire from the company, obligations are created that may become impossible to fulfill. The more successful the company, the more valuable is the stock, but success brings a requirement for more working capital and the company cannot afford to buy back shares without hurting the business. Buy-back price formulas seldom provide a value equal to what the shares would bring if the entire business was sold, thus creating more dissatisfaction. These companies are particularly ripe for sale when one of the major holders is ready to retire.

Partnership Disenchantment

Partnerships have such a sorry record of surviving with the working relationship of the founding partners remaining in tact for any period of time that it is a wonder any operating partnerships are created. Business organizations do not lend themselves to coownership with more than one boss. The differences of opinion and changing personal objectives of the partners create a situation where sale is a logical solution for breakup of the partnership.

Cash Heavy

Tax laws make it highly advantageous for a cash-heavy successful company to be sold. A total sale of the business is the only way the owners can get out of their business the cash and value of the business on a favorable capital gains basis. Owners of cash-heavy companies usually have an abnormal fear they will be taxed for having an excess accumulation of earnings although this rarely occurs. These cash-heavy companies are always logical prospects.

Overwhelming Luxuries

A little success can encourage an owner to become overly enthusiastic about his future and spend heavily on luxuries such as lavish offices, new facilities, excess executives, relatives on the payroll, automobiles, lodges, airplanes, and the like and soon the only way out is a sale of the business. These expenses can readily exceed the earning power of the business and soon the business is in trouble. A buyer will seldom be impressed by ostentatious luxuries in his evaluations but determine the value of the basic business after the unnecessary expense is removed.

CEO Took Over Too Late

When the owner who has run the business for several decades leaves the business for whatever reason and an heir who is middle-aged is appointed or takes over management, chances are the company will soon be for sale. It often is too late in life for one to have the drive, initiative, or interest in running the business. He may enjoy the prestige, but that is all.

Lost Orders

Loss of major orders or clients may cause such consternation that the owners will be in a frame of mind to sell. This is usually shortsighted on their part because the business will be worth less in a depressed state but they are tired and distressed. Lost clients and orders receive little publicity but awards of major contracts or taking on of new clients are given publicity, and usually for every winner, there are one or more losers who can easily be identified.

Economic Pessimism

Overall pessimism about the economy, political situations, or industry on the part of owners may cause them to believe their best move would be to sell out and become liquid. A buyer seldom knows this is the state of mind of an owner until he meets him, but it usually becomes apparent after a short conversation. Cheerful or reassuring words will not help a buyer's case.

CEO Minority Holder Fed Up With Majority

If the CEO is a minority holder and the other owners are largely inactive, the CEO is often dissatisfied with the arrangement. He feels he puts forth all the work and they reap most of the benefits and always demand more. The majority holders may believe they cannot readily or easily replace the CEO thus making a sale of the business a solution. This condition seems to be particularly true when the shareholders are related.

Desire for Liquidity

Some owners simply reach the point when they want to do things other than run a business. They may want to pursue hobbies, fishing, hunting, writing, sailing, or any one of a thousand things they consider more interesting than running a business. A sale gives them the money to do as they please. These companies often can be identified by finding an owner who already spends a large portion of his time on activities other than management of the business.

Over Focus on Problems

All managers spend most of their time on the aspects of their businesses that are wrong or need change rather than those things that are running well and in good shape. As a result, some develop a very unbalanced view of the business in which they have lost sight of its accomplishments and attributes. Discussions with such prospects reveal them to be harried, tired, old before their time, and ready to sell.

The American Way

Found a successful company, sell out, pay your capital gains tax, and remain rich ever after is the stated goal of many entrepreneurs. The concept of founding a company that will become a family company owned and operated by descendants of the founder for untold generations is seldom considered by either the founder or his progeny. Sale is only a question of timing and this is often the stated public position of the owner.

Divestiture

Any subsidiary, product line, or division that is performing at a level below that of the rest of the corporation is a candidate for divestiture. Those that are largely orphans or unrelated to the rest of the corporation, regardless of their performance, are candidates. The current fad of business is strategic planning and one of its byproducts is a greater interest in divestiture and willingness to sell off assets. "Asset management" has nearly become another way of saying "anything we have is available for a price." An aggressive buyer should never automatically strike a company from his prospect list that matches closely with his ideal profile because it already is owned by another corporation. This condition more likely should move the company to near the top of his list of logical prospects.

A buyer should have in mind all of the reasons why a prospect should sell and recognize the signs that indicate a business may be a ready acquisition candidate. Buyers with experience in acquisitions are said to develop a sixth sense that tells them very quickly if a prospect is ready or soon will be ready to sell. The sixth sense is only an automatic recognition of the factors listed in this chapter.

7.
Internal Communications and Approval

Certain key elements of an acquisition program—information gathering, evaluation of data, and approvals—tend to conflict with the need for secrecy and necessity for decisiveness. Unless these potential areas of conflict are recognized at the start and appropriate systems and procedures devised, the buyer may find himself wondering why he identifies prospects but never buys despite good intentions. The buyer who is an individual investor has little difficulty with communications and less with approvals, but most buyers are corporations where problems of these categories may become severe. Corporations are generally highly structured with a chain of command that functions on an informal and formal basis. Certain executives must approve an acquisition, others need not give approval but it is unlikely the acquisition can go ahead without their blessing, others give their opinion but can be overruled, and some have their opinions solicited but little regarded. To complicate matters further, an acquisition requires not one decision but hundreds that must be made over a period of time.

To be effective a buyer must have the ability and systems to make decisions and make them promptly, but not so quickly that they are ill thought out or based on inadequate information. Buyer's delays cause unnecessary risks that jeopardize an acquisition attempt for a number of reasons. Sellers lose interest or question the sincerity of the buyer. A lack of decisiveness reflects unfavorably on the buyer because a fundamental measure of any executive's competence is his ability to make decisions. Delays permit time to elapse in which new suitors may emerge. Procrastination is discouraging to the buyer's executives engaged in convincing the seller he should sell, because they have spent time describing the buyer as a model business organization. Delays permit information to become obsolete and misleading. However, a foolish decision is worse than none at all because no decision only risks the loss of opportunity and expenses incurred. An intelligent decision requires information upon which to decide. Information gathering takes time, but the time can be shortened if those collecting data know how to secure the information, what is really needed and not needed, and how to assemble it into a useable form.

The need for secrecy conflicts with the need for internal and external communications and the benefits that can be achieved by informing members of the buyer's organization of an acquisition prospect. Secrecy is essential because buyers demand it; word of a possible takeover would cause the stock of a public company to jump in value and in the competitive market for acquisitions, a "leak" may inform other suitors. Regardless of the need for secrecy, a buyer will find it necessary to discuss an acquisition with some of his key executives and outside advisers to secure their opinions and assistance. A well planned program of procedures and control prior to starting the acquisition program is as important for secrecy as knowing who can be trusted. Every time another person is told of the acquisition prospect, the secret becomes less of a secret.

Tailor Approval Procedure to Organization

Each buyer will have his own organization in size and structure and seldom will two be alike. Consequently, a buyer must tailor his approval and acquisition procedures to fit his own situation. Below is a composite organization chart illustrating the various individuals inside and outside the buyer's organization who may be included in the acquisition process.

Buyer's Participants

Shareholders

Board of directors

Corporate Executives
   Chairman
   President
   Executive vice-president

Operating Executives
   Group executive
   Division executive
   Subsidiary executive
   Manufacturing or sales executive

Corporate Staff
  Financial
  Legal
  Acquisition
Assigned staff

Outside Participants

Public accountants
Attorneys
Bankers or lenders
Public relations advisors
Investment bankers
Brokers

A buyer can look at his own organization and cross out those listed that are inapplicable. For the individual buyer very few will remain but the majority will remain for corporations of substantial size. With the organization identified and in mind, the buyer is ready to establish his approval procedure by matching the decisions to be made with the participants.

Acquisition Decisions

The decisions fall into broad categories for use in establishing a procedure. The fewer involved in making any category of decisions, the quicker a final decision can be made, assuming the participants are willing to make speedy decisions. However, the fewer the participants, the lower will be input of different opinions and viewpoints that can bring about the best decisions. This basic conflict must be considered and compromises evolved if a workable procedure is to be developed for assigning the following categories for decisions.

1. Establishment of acquisition objectives.
2. Establishment of acquistion policies.
3. Preliminary evaluation of identified but uncontacted prospects.
4. Whether or not to contact a prospect.
5. Whether or not to pursue further a contacted prospect including evaluation of new information secured during the contact.
6. Whether or not to make an offer.
7. What the offer will be.
8. Negotiating decisions:
     a. Changes in basic terms.

    b. Major contractual items.

    c. Items that are primarily legal or financial requiring professional guidance.

9. Transitional items or changes, if any are to be made in the acquired after closing and upon its integration into the buyer's organization.

The entire decision-making process can be greatly simplified and need not be as complicated as it first appears. A buyer with well defined policies and objectives automatically screens out most unwanted prospects without further decision. A realistic evaluation of the buyer's financial capabilities will further screen prospects and set parameters for offers. As an acquisition program progresses, a combination of confidence in those making the acquisitions and precedents established in prior acquisitions will increase the delegation of decision-making and willingness to make quick decisions.

Decision Assignments

For most buyers the assignment of decision categories to participants will be relatively simple if the roles of the executives involved in the acquisition program are clear and well established. The responsibility, if any, of the group, division, or subsidiary executives for seeking out, contacting, and negotiating with prospects and how their activity and responsibility meshes with those of the corporate office must be fully thought out. In most corporations these two levels are protagonists and without assignment of responsibilities coupled with strong leadership, a bitter and counterproductive condition may develop. A corporate office demanding acquisition activity and prospects from its operating groups that is not helpful and quick to respond to their needs but rather constantly critical cannot expect many acquisitions to result. The degree of participation other than final approval, which the board of directors may wish to provide, has to be established in a frank discussion with the CEO. Acquisition assignments at any level of an organization will be influenced by the interest and ability of the executives at the various levels as well as who is available to do the work. While individual capabilities may be inconsistent with an ideal system of organization and approval procedures, they must also be recognized and accommodated if the system is to work.

Setting up the approval and involvement system is largely a case of matching the participants to the decision categories, but there are some areas that are troublesome and need to be given special review. There is no right or wrong procedure because what is best is dependent upon the nature of the buyer's organization and the degree of delegation of authority that is practical. Answers to the following questions can greatly aid the buyer in establishing a workable procedure:

1. Will the board of directors review and approve offers prior to their presentation to sellers?
2. Will a board that approves offers also approve offer revisions?
3. Will the board approve all contacts with prospects?
4. Will the CEO approve all offers?
5. Will the CEO approve all contacts with prospects?
6. Will the CEO approve all offer revisions?
7. Who will develop offers and who will give approval?
8. What approval authority will staff executives have?

The objective of a buyer should be to have a quick approval system that all involved understand. Preferably, it is written but this is not as important as it be understood and known to the participants, and when changes occur, they are promptly communicated. The approval system should be devised at the start of an acquisition program and not after the program is underway and a likely prospect has been identified. At that time, unnecessary delays and confusion will result if the system is yet to be established.

Internal Reports

Whoever in the buyer organization is responsible for an active acquisition program should develop a monthly report for his own use that records the name of each prospect, and any recent and/or planned activity with prospects. With many prospects under consideration, such a report becomes an invaluable tool. The major question is who else should receive copies of the report. Acquisition activity is exciting fare for most executives and those with little need to know may want a copy, but the buyer should limit distribution of this report to as few as possible to maintain secrecy.

Secrecy

Secrecy is one of the more troublesome problems for any buyer. An acquisition is such a complex affair involving so many people in selling, structuring, evaluating, and negotiating that it is difficult to maintain secrecy. The financial gain possible is enormous for those willing to act upon inside information. The temptation is obviously too much for many because more often than not an increase in price of the shares of public companies occurs the week before an offer is made. Acting on inside information is illegal, but very difficult to prove, as the SEC often attests. However, there is no other logical explanation for rises in share value prior to an offer. The buying of a prospect's shares because of inside information may just as easily result from a leak from the seller as the buyer, but the buyer can only attempt to control his own people. The buyer must secure information on a prospect adequate for him to make a decision and few buyers consider data found in annual reports and other disclosure documents sufficient. Every time someone inside or outside the buyer's organization is asked a question about the prospect, there is a chance the person questioned will suspect the true reason regardless of what ruse is used. People in business who are intelligent enough to answer the informational questions are also able to suspect what may be going on and contact their broker. If they tell their broker of their suspicions, he and all his other good customers may start buying.

Time for Disclosure

The secrecy problem is compounded by the question as to what point a public disclosure of acquisition discussions and proposals must be made. Attorney opinions vary on this issue and a buyer who contacts public companies that are prospects should not do so without legal advice on disclosure. A seller's attorney may have a very different opinion from the buyer's aggravating the problem because each are likely to act on their own attorney's advice.

In a friendly acquisition of a public company attorneys do agree that disclosure must be made no later than the time of acceptance of an offer but some believe disclosure is necessary when the offer is made and a few argue disclosure is necessary when any discussion takes place with the prospect. Some sellers are suspected of making early disclosures just to increase the value of their shares either to discourage the buyer or to secure a higher price.

Secrecy in buying privately held companies is nearly as important as when buying public ones. Most owners are very concerned and insistent upon secrecy and will terminate discussions if they learn from others the buyer has not been discreet. Controlling shareholders want to be first to notify minority shareholders, employees, and others closely associated. A buyer also runs the risk of another buyer coming onto the scene creating unwanted competition if word of the seller's willingness gets out.

Every buyer must establish his own procedures for maintaining secrecy and in doing so weigh the value of secrecy against the risks associated with the information gathering and the approval process. Limiting the number of participants will help the most. Other devices are: code names for prospects, limiting typing to the CEO's secretary, hand carrying of documents, secret meetings away from regular offices, and fictitious travel to cover up meetings. All have value but in the final analysis, there is no certainty secrecy can be maintained and to some degree most buyers find to their dismay, they were unsuccessful.

Internal Politics

Political problems and pressures abound in acquisition situations. Even the individual entrepreneur is not immune because his attorneys, accountants, and his own family will all give an opinion that he may or may not like. However, the greatest problem exists in corporations where the larger number of participants creates the opportunity for political, inept and ignorant activity as well as the brilliant, decisive, and creative, which builds an outstanding enterprise.

Within the corporate buyer's organization, there must be at least one executive who is an outspoken, vigorous, and constant advocate of every acquisition if it is to be made. The champion may not be the same for every acquisition and it often varies, but someone must be convinced the acquisition should be made and stand up against all others to explain and push the acquisition through to completion. This active advocate is preferably the CEO but it may be a director, the man heading a planning or acquisition program, or a group executive or anyone else in the buyer's organization high enough up in rank to have access to nearly all of the participants. His role is one he has voluntarily chosen because of his belief that the acquisition is a good one for the corporation. He knows full well he could have held back and played it safe by not being a vigorous advocate or opposing the proposition. He may find he has far more problems convincing or motivating his own organization than he does with the seller. His role is often a lonely and discouraging one because of the following gallery of executive types that he may encounter:

1. The Ideal Executive. He is able to quickly assimilate the information given, ask intelligent questions, and make good suggestions. He acts promptly giving priority to acquisition matters and is decisive. If the disapproves of the acquisition, his

reasons are clearly stated and valid. Fortunately, there are enough executives of this type to make an acquisition program feasible.

2. The Weathervane. He delays until others make their position known before he gives his opinion. Then he selects whatever view he perceives to be politically best for him.

3. Noncommitted. He avoids in every way possible becoming involved, believing this to be his safest approach.

4. Opposed. Opposes acquisition believing this is his safest course of action. His reasons are either unstated, unclear, or unsound, but he knows his odds are best if he votes no.

5. Blind Enthusiast. He will vote for any acquisition without even learning what it's all about.

6. Too Busy. He is too busy with his other duties to look at an acquisition.

7. Disloyal Opposition. He is opposed to any venture recommended by those he dislikes or considers his rival.

8. Nitpicker. He concentrates on trivial aspects of the acquisition rather than the important features of the prospect and he does not look at the transaction in a balanced way. He will be more concerned with officer salaries than he will be with earnings levels and price.

9. Analysis Forever. He avoids decisions by demanding more data.

10. Old Timer. He has a 30-year-old frame of reference and head full of obsolete data that he tries to apply to the present situation.

11. The Expert. He suddenly discloses he is an expert on the prospect or prospect's industry and everything must be held up until he has time to expound his views and present alledgedly new data.

12. Prefers Another. There is nothing wrong with the prospect but he prefers another of unknown availability.

13. Forever Looking. He will settle for nothing less than the perfect company, which does not exist.

14. Indecisive. He simply cannot decide and make a decision.

15. Financial Technician. He is never satisfied unless he has at least a 10-year profit and loss, balance sheet, and cash flow forecast.

16. The Provincial. He evaluates acquisitions only on the basis of how they would affect him and his area of responsibility.

17. Big Picture Man. The prospect does not fit his view of the buyer's objectives, and his views of the buyer's objectives are different from everyone elses.

18. Big Deal Man. The acquisition, no matter how attractive, is not large enough.

19. Unsuitable Parent. He did not first discover the prospect so he is opposed.

20. Correct Procedures Come First. The internal procedures established for processing prospects are so important to this executive that he opposes any acquisition where procedures have not been followed to the letter. He evaluates procedure compliance rather than the prospect.

21. Devil's Advocate. He believes it is his duty to actively oppose and play the role of devil's advocate for any prospect, although he may favor the acquisition. At a later date he will claim he actually favored the acquisition all along, providing it turns out well.

It can only be hoped that a buyer will only have "ideal executives" in his organization, but chances are good he will also have an assortment of the other variety. Recognition of this condition will be a large step towards overcoming whatever obstacles occur in bringing worthwhile acquisitions to a conclusion. Internal obstacles and negative attitudes are irritating but they do force the proponents to be more careful in their evaluations. Furthermore, often those opposed to an acquisition are right.

8.
Contacting Prospects

"We would like to buy your company" is the greatest business compliment that can be paid to the owner of any company. A proposal informs the owner that the potential buyer thinks so highly of the business that he is willing to invest his money and time in the company. The owner may not wish to sell or the price eventually offered may be thought inadequate by the owner, but the fact that an offer was made is the ultimate compliment possible. Owners are not offended by responsible buyers who indicate an interest in buying their company and even when they do not wish to sell, they will tactfully decline the invitation to talk or more commonly agree to meet anyway with a warning that they are not "on the market." They are flattered by the contact and often brag about it to their close friends.

Regardless, most buyers are shy about approaching prospects and inquiring of their willingness to discuss being acquired. This irrational shyness may stem from a fear of verbal abuse or rejection and it is a reluctance many never totally overcome. Bashfulness also makes it possible for many intermediaries, such as brokers, investment bankers, and consultants, who are troubled very little by shyness, to prosper. An executive of a buyer can overcome nearly all the shyness he has about contacting prospects himself if he prepares for his contacts and realizes that a key executive of the buyer, who may be totally void of experience, can be far more effective in initiating discussions than any intermediary. A principal is more readily accepted because he has the advantages of instant credibility and sincerity, which comes from being able to speak authoritatively.

Studying all information about the prospect and having a complete understanding of why the acquisition is wanted will give the buyer confidence and help overcome shyness. This preparation for the first contact with a prospect is critically important and will encompass the entire activity that might be characterized as the contact presentation.

The Contact Presentation

The contact presentation consists of four parts: assimilation of all known data about the prospect, the reasons why the buyer would like to buy, reasons why the owner may consider sale to be to his advantage, and knowledge of the present relationship, if any, between the buyer and seller. The buyer may only find it appropriate to use a small part of the contact presentation in his first discussion with the buyer, or he may have to use most of it. He will not know what will be required and what he can insert into the conversation until his discussions actually begin, but he should be ready. The entire presentation has to be constructed to fit the prospect and his specific situation and will be far less effective if it is merely a recitation of largely bland generalizations.

Prospect Information

Knowledge of the prospect and its industry is the foundation upon which the acquisition effort is based. Enough data had to have been accumulated to bring the buyer to a point where he believes he would like to be in the industry and acquire the prospect. Additional data may cause him at a later date to reconsider, but as of the time of the first contact, he would like to proceed. This same knowledge makes it possible for the buyer to be conversant with the owner about the business and in a subtle way convey that the buyer has done his homework and has made a careful and well considered decision to enter the business. This is more impressive than appearing to only be shopping for any business.

Prior to making the first contact, the buyer's representative should review all information available. A large quantity of material may have been accumulated on a prospect and industry, but whoever is making the contact should review it again just prior to the contact in order to have it fresh in his mind.

Reasons for Buying

Why the buyer wants to buy the prospect need not be a difficult question, simply tell the truth. There is no approach as simple or effective as the buyer explaining in detail the research, logic, and internal discussions that led to the conclusion that he would like to buy the prospect. Too much time is wasted by buyers attempting to figure out appropriate reasons for buying, which they believe would be acceptable and inoffensive to a prospect. The effort that goes into concocting half-truths and rationalizations for buying could be better spent clarifying and putting into a precise statement the true reasons why the buyer wants to buy. If the buyer's true reasons for wanting to make an acquisition are believed to be so offensive to a prospect that he would reject the idea out of hand, the acquisition should never be made and almost certainly never will be.

The reason for buying can be as simple a statement as the buyer indicating he believes the acquisition would be a good investment. This sort of a catchall reason could apply to every acquisition, but it also implies to the seller that the buyer will not buy if the price is too high. An abnormally high price will cause the return on investment to be inadequate.

Most buyers have and most sellers want reasons that tell a more complete story and indicate what may happen to the prospect once acquired, "We want to have your sales organization handle our product. . . . We believe we could help you secure more international business. . . . Our facilities could be combined." Logical, sensible business reasons will be persuasive and place the buyer in the best light with the seller. Valid business reasons for buying when properly presented help to demonstrate that the buyer has ability and would be the type of buyer the prospect should sell to if he does sell. A good technique for presenting a reason to buy is one in which the buyer states an objective and informs the prospect that the best possible way for the objective to be achieved is by the acquisition of the prospect. This is flattering and a basis for continued business discussions.

A buyer usually has several reasons for buying and generally the more reasons given to a seller, the more convincing the buyer. Some reasons will be more important than others to a buyer, but degrees of importance need not be volunteered to the seller. Controversy may exist within the buyer's organization over reasons for buying, but this again is not for the seller's ears. However, any such controversy should be quickly resolved. A major advantage of presenting multiple reasons for buying is that if one proves to be invalid because of changing conditions or new information, the buyer can still continue his acquisition discussions without giving the impression his program is ill-founded. If most of the reasons for buying become invalid, the buyer had better forget the prospect.

Sellers will want to know how the buyer learned of the seller and what prompted the buyer to call on them as opposed to other companies. Regardless of the origin, a buyer can usually reveal how he first learned of the seller (unless the source is one that cannot be disclosed, such as a disgruntled shareholder or employee) and upon investigation found the seller to be very good. This is an excellent opportunity for compliments to the seller.

Reasons for Selling

The buyer should have prepared a convincing series of arguments as to why it would be advantageous for the prospect to sell. Underlying all such arguments are the economic benefits that initially are largely implied and not discussed in detail. Eventually, the owners must be convinced with a specific offer that they will be better off financially if they sell and be presented with persuasive arguments but this usually is provided at subsequent meetings. At a first meeting most buyers do not have enough data to make an offer and are still far from deciding they definitely would like to acquire the prospect.

Chapter 6, "Prospects," discusses common reasons and conditions why owners may be inclined to sell, and a buyer should know which are applicable to the prospect or any others that are pertinent and be prepared to stress them in the conversation. This can be done rather skillfully with questions, "What would happen to the business if something happened to you? . . . Do you have much time to pursue your other interests? . . . Have you been able to avoid the problem many second-generation, family-owned companies have had with differences of opinions in the families on how the business should be run?" Of course, the buyer knows in advance the answers to questions he will ask and believes the answers will help his case. Buyers should be tactful in presenting the advantages of sale and the more they can be woven into the general conversation in a subtle manner that causes serious thinking by the owners, the more effective they will be.

Just as buyers usually have multiple reasons for buying, there are normally a number of reasons why it would be advantageous for a seller to sell. The buyer is unlikely to know which are most important to the seller so he should avoid placing emphasis on any specific one. As a general rule, the more good logical reasons for selling that can be pointed out to the seller, the better.

The critical reasons for selling are those that show the advantages for the decision-makers in the selling organization, even if they just want "out," but the reasons that purport to show the acquisition having a beneficial effect on the business of the prospect as well as the buyer should not be underestimated in importance. Everyone supports synergism and believes in it although it is much more difficult to accomplish than discuss in theory. All the participants on both sides, shareholders, managers, and employees, want to believe everyone will gain if the acquisition occurs and a wise buyer will not disappoint them by failing to disseminate reasons for a sale that make good business sense. These reasons are also very helpful to the selling shareholders who will find it far easier to inform their employees they sold for meritorious reasons, such as to secure necessary capital for growth of the business or to take advantage of the buyer's purchasing power, rather than personal reasons, such as to place capital in their pockets, to place an estate in order, or terminate business quarrels among the relatives.

The buyer may complete the acquisition without doing more than briefly touching on the reasons why the seller's decision-makers should sell, although these are the reasons that will count most and will be foremost in the seller's mind. However, the socially acceptable business reasons of how the prospect's business will continue to operate and thrive under new ownership should be covered openly and frequently in great detail.

A buyer must guard against a psychological phenomenon that often occurs in the selling process. While persuading the prospect to sell, the buyer is also convincing himself to buy and he may do such a good job of convincing himself that he no longer is objective in his evaluation of the prospect. Buyers can become so impressed with the logic of their own arguments, which they believe prove the prospect would be an excellent acquisition from an operational standpoint and the seller will be much better off selling, that they lose sight of the economic realities. This phenomenon partially explains uneconomic high offers and the irrational bids that appear in contested acquisitions.

Prior or Current Relations

The buyer who is an individual investor will know of all contacts he has had with the prospect in the past, but this may not be the case for the multi-division corporate buyer. The buyer's executive who contacts the seller may be unaware of prior or current relations between his organization and the seller, but chances are excellent the smaller seller has full knowledge. It is awkward for a buyer's executive to make contact with a prospect unaware of what has transpired between the companies. To avoid this embarrassment, some checking is advisable. This internal checking will have to be restrained because of secrecy considerations, but certain areas should be reviewed if at all possible.

Has the prospect been previously contacted about acquisition by representatives of the buyer? A prospect that appears to be a logical choice for the buyer today, may have been just as logical years ago when someone else made contact to explore acquisition. A corporation with divisional or subsidiary acquisition activity, as well as a parent company department, may inadvertently have representatives of both groups make contact unless their activities are coordinated. The seller will certainly remember any such contacts and a buyer will look foolish if he is unaware.

What business is conducted today or has been conducted between the buyer and seller? A supplier-customer relationship may already exist with the buyer being in either position or both. The volume of business, products or services involved and overall relations must be known. Any disputes that have occurred must be identified and full details secured. A resolution of the dispute could be excellent preparation for acquisition overtures.

Does either the buyer or seller have key employees that once worked for the other? Employees of the buyer who worked previously for the seller can be a source of information and possibly introductions. If they were respected and left the seller on good terms, they probably can be a help in the transaction. Former employees of the buyer, now with the seller, will almost certainly be called on for their opinions of the buyer. If differences exist between former employees and the buyer, the buyer should plan a strategy to offset the problem. A candid admission of the differences and emphasis on the fact that there are two or more sides to every issue may be enough to neutralize a critic.

Do both companies use the same professionals or financial institutions? Accounting firms are the more probable of the professional groups to serve both parties because of their size and international operations. Attorneys would be much less probable, except when buyer and seller are in the same city. The parties may use the same banks, insurance carriers, actuaries, or underwriters. Whenever there exists a condition in which both use the same professionals or institutions, there will be conversation about mutual friends or quality of service. These mutual friends may be the origin of the first introductions. There also may prove to be a conflict of interest situation as the acquisition progresses that must be discussed openly very early and resolved. Care also must be exercised to avoid unnecessary fees charged by mutual friends for their assistance in introduction or negotiations.

Boasting With Facts

It would be difficult to judge the relative importance of the buyer's organization or executive representative in importance, but both should be impressive to the seller. A seller wants to be convinced that he is dealing with people he likes and their organization is one with which he can be proud to be associated. The buyer's representative cannot be one the seller dislikes because sellers of solid companies need not subject themselves to dealing with people they find unpleasant. However, the buyer's representative does not have to be a person of extraordinary charm (although it would not hurt the cause any), but he must be an enthusiastic supporter and advocate of the buyer.

The buyer's representative must be totally familiar with all aspects of the buyer's operations and objectives and present this information to sellers in an enthusiastic manner. The seller will want to learn all about the buyer and merely providing annual reports or product literature will be inadequate. The accomplishments and major assets should be stressed while problems are downplayed. If significant problems exist for the buyer, these should be mentioned by the buyer before the seller brings them up. An explanation for the problem areas should be offered and if none can be found, simply claim, "We made a mistake. Of course, there are no decisions that you have made you would like to do over, but we floundered." This candid approach of admission coupled with a slightly whimsical reminder that the seller has undoubtedly made mistakes is a very effective method of explanation.

The buyer's boasting should be well supported by facts. Most successful businesses have more than enough accomplishments to describe, so exaggerations or half-truths are improper and totally unnecessary. Presentation of favorable specific facts about whatever the buyer is doing better than others will be impressive. The buyer's representative must be totally enthusiastic in his presentation, but not a Pollyanna, as he describes financial results, sales levels, new products, outstanding fellow employees, executives, etc.

The One-on-One of Contacting Sellers

After the buyer has resolved what he intends to say to a prospect, he has the practical decisions to make of who will contact whom and by what means. At this stage, it is no longer a case of Company A contacting Company B, but now one of which executive of the buyer will contact which executive of the seller and how will this be accomplished. Here personalities do count and they become subject to much planning and conjecture.

Who To Contact

The first decision is to determine the individual in the seller's group to be contacted. The buyer's representative can best be selected after the prospect's contact is chosen. Normally, the person in the prospect's group to contact is the one in the strongest position of control; either through direct or beneficial stock ownership, as a result of his executive position in the business, or because of trustee or executor responsibilities. Only as a last resort, after other efforts have failed to produce a meeting with the person in control, should a buyer contact minority shareholders or managers who have no equity, and then primarily to enlist their aid in meeting the key owners.

Contact the founder in a privately held company where he is still active in the company. He may no longer be chief executive officer, according to his official title, but in practice it is unlikely any major decisions are made without him, and he is still likely to be the largest shareholder. If the founder is totally out of the business or physically or mentally incapacitated, then the CEO will be the best starting point, because he can explain the ownership situation and arrange appropriate meetings. The CEO is an individual the buyer must associate with before and probably after the acquisition, so the buyer should, from the start, work to build a good relationship. Absentee owners or controlling shareholders of privately held firms, such as widows, children of founders, or investor groups, can usually be contacted through the company CEO, who is easier to identify and locate.

In publicly held companies, the CEO is in nearly all cases, the logical individual to first contact. The one exception is a publicly held company that has one shareholder outside the company who owns a controlling block of stock. If stock is held by various members of a controlling family, the buyer should contact the CEO first. Contacts with directors or employees are best limited to a means of introduction to the individual in control.

If the company sought is a subsidiary or division of another corporation, then the only person to first contact is the CEO of the parent company. His attitude will determine what can be done and, in any event, any inquiries to others would be forwarded to him for decision.

The CEO will be the first contact for companies whose shares are tied up in trusts or estates. The CEO may very well welcome a responsible buyer and assist in introductions to appropriate trust officers, attorneys, executors, or others who are not basically interested in the business but have a transitional role to play.

In countries outside of North America owners are often less accessible and language differences can create further difficulties. The CEO may be used as a contact, but often the personal financial advisors to the owners, who are something of a cross between a public accountant and consultant, are ideal to start with if they can be identified. They have the attention of the owners and they will become involved in any transaction that is negotiated.

The objective of the first contact is to arrange a face-to face meeting with the person who is able to make key decisions to sell control and express interest in acquisition. Until that person has been approached and the buyer has had the opportunity to present to him his story, the buyer will not know if the company can be acquired. Minority shareholders, employees, directors, and associated professionals often have meaningless views widely divergent from the shareholders who control. Anyone who has been active in making acquisitions has quickly become impressed with the differences in attitude that more often than not exist between those in control and minority holders or employees. This situation is so common that a buyer can base decisions only on remarks of those in control, because major shareholders usually do not want others to know they would sell if a suitable offer was presented, and minority holders do not want the major holders to know they would like to see them out. Employees may believe a sale would improve their chances of promotion. Incompetent employees would fear loss of their protection. None are likely to confide such thoughts to the owners.

Who Should Make the First Contact

If the buyer is an individual investor, he will be the best one to contact the seller. He will represent himself for better or worse. The corporate buyer has more flexibility in selecting who should make the contact. If the corporate buyer has an acquisition or planning department for this purpose, the members will ordinarily make most contacts.

In the absence of an acquisition department the executives selected to make the first contacts ideally should have status approximately equal or slightly higher than the person to be contacted. The CEO of a $500 million corporation need not first contact the president of a $5 million corporation, but he should be involved from the start with a prospect of the $300-400 million sales range. Vice-presidents often are able to successfully meet prospects of all levels because they are thought of as key trusted members of the buyers organization. A vice-president of a $100 million corporation would have status in the business world easily equal to that of the president of a $10 million dollar corporation. Status evaluations are simple judgment decisions that need not be precise, but they are important along with the other factors of personality, knowledge of the business and the items previously discussed. Availability must also be considered, because whoever makes the contact should be able to follow through with subsequent meetings.

If the buyer already has an acquaintance with the prospect, then the senior buyer executive who knows the executive or shareholder who controls the prospect should first bring up the subject. Any other contact would appear to be improper and out of channels.

Contacting Strangers

The most common situation is where the buyer has studied all available data on the seller and concludes he would like to explore the possibility of acquisition, but none of his key executives know any of the controlling shareholders or the CEO. The options for introduction and expression of interest are as follows:

1. Introduction through mutual friends or lower level employees.
2. Introduction through professional intermediaries.
3. Letters or telegrams.
4. Telephone contact.

Whichever is used depends on the circumstances and to some degree on the inclination of the buyer. However, what is used should be done in such a manner that it has no elements of deceit, subterfuge, or false pretexts. It is best to handle the introduction in a straightforward manner in which the purpose is not concealed. To do otherwise is to immediately place the buyer in a bad light and get him off to a poor start. Sellers are usually perceptive and will see through most any ruse, because they are not fools and often they have seen much nonsense of this variety before. Suggestions of "We would like to become better acquainted," "We wish to explore working together," and "We believe there may be mutual opportunities that would be profitable to explore," are examples of half-truths. All of this jargon and similar statements are unnecessary, confuse the few who do not see through the approach, and give the seller the impression the buyer is at best amateurish and at worst, deceitful.

Diversionary approaches are also inadvisable. Contacts suggesting creating joint ventures, marketing cooperation, or even large purchases of products or services from the prospect as a means of initiating discussions of total acquisition can only create problems. If the buyer is not serious about the diversionary scheme, he is being dishonest. If the seller accepts the scheme, the buyer becomes locked into a program he may not want and has progressed little towards his real objective. A rejection of the scheme leaves the buyer worse off than before. The prospect may be a willing seller if asked, but he does not favor the lesser transaction. Diversionary schemes also cost valuable time that better could be spent discussing the real issue of acquisition.

Introduction Through Friends or Employees. It is remarkable how often a buyer who knows no one within a prospect discovers he does know someone well who is acquainted with key executives or shareholders of the prospect and would gladly provide introductions, if asked. Bank officers, attorneys, accountants, social or business club members, trade organization members, customers, suppliers, middle management employees, and executive's neighbors are possible categories to review if a buyer wants a third-party introduction to the seller. Even if he eventually uses other means for the introduction, he will want to know who are the mutual acquaintances because they can become topics of conversation and references.

If the buyer's reputation with the third party is unsatisfactory, this too must be known and precautionary measures taken. There also is the risk that the selected third parties reputation is poor with the prospect and his use would adversely effect the buyer.

Common problems with third-party introduction are well intentioned overenthusiasm, difficulty in their control, loss of secrecy, unexpected fees, and the usual loss of accuracy in relayed messages. Most people are delighted with the opportunity to arrange an introduction that could lead to a major business event. To bring the parties together for the first time would, for many, be participating in high drama on a grand scale. They tend to want to play an overly enthusiastic role surpassing that of introduction, which at times is difficult to contain. A sophisticated buyer normally only desires an introduction and little more, but the third party may volunteer advice to both parties, try to remain in the discussions after the introduction is made, and often just get in the way. Some third parties may want to be paid for their efforts so a buyer would do well to make his position known on fees. There also is the danger of a major breech of secrecy through a third party who was so impressed with his role that he can not keep it to himself or sees a way to profit in an insider stock transaction.

If a third-party friend or business acquaintance is used to secure an introduction, the buyer should be certain he can be fully trusted, controlled, and able to follow specific instructions. If he does not meet these requirements, he should be avoided and other means employed. The buyer must give the third party very specific instructions as to what should and should not be said to the prospect, including the purpose of the requested introduction. The purpose cannot be concealed without jeopardizing friendship with the "introducer" and the chances of productive discussions with the "introducee." So, the third party should be prepared with a brief explanation of the buyer's reasoning of why he wants to buy and why the prospect should sell but advised to use such information sparingly. The third party should also be told early that only an introduction is desired and no more, unless the buyer has great confidence in the third party and wants him to assist in the acquisition activity.

Professional Intermediaries. If a buyer has identified through his own efforts a prospect he would like to acquire, he has no need to call upon a professional intermediary to make the first contact. Investment bankers, brokers, and consultants cannot do anything to establish first contact with a prospect that the buyer cannot do as well or better himself. They have to use the telephone or mail the same as the buyer and they lack the credibility and authority of a principal in the buyer's organization. Their use for introductions also brings on fee obligations, which a buyer should equate against fifteen minutes of his own time. Professional intermediaries can play an important role in many aspects of the acquisition process, but introduction to buyer identified prospects is hardly one of them.

Mail and Telegrams. Telegrams and registered or certified letters should not be sent proposing initial discussions to explore the possibility of acquisition. They have a threatening connotation that is not conducive to friendly discussions. An unfriendly takeover attempt is implied if discussions do not succeed and this will send prospects running to their attorneys.

Letters to prospects in which a buyer introduces himself and proposed acquisition discussions are controversial as to value. In nearly all cases there are more effective approaches than a letter to introduce the buyer and a letter should be looked at as largely a last resort when other approaches fail or are impossible. In reality they take on more of the aspects of a warning than an invitation to discussions. Although letters give the seller time to consider his position and investigate the buyer before accepting or declining an invitation to meet, this decision is made with little or no input from the buyer in which he presents facts, arguments, and his best story devised to demonstrate he would be an outstanding suitor.

Letters also have an impersonal character because most companies of a type and size that makes them attractive acquisition prospects receive numerous letters suggesting acquisitions in the course of a year. Many are from intermediaries looking for companies to sell, but many others are from buyers who have broadsided obvious form letters to many companies. Unless a seller has already determined to sell to any likely buyer, letters of this type are routinely destroyed or given short negative responses. The buyer's letter may very well receive this quick treatment and be routinely processed on its way to a file cabinet and oblivion.

Letters are of no value unless they clearly state what is the next step. A request for the prospect to reply in writing is inviting disaster. How can a buyer change the prospect's mind if he responds he's "not interested"? The only practical next step is for the buyer to state in his letter that he will telephone the prospect at a designated time in the future. In the telephone call the buyer should attempt to set an appointment with the prospect.

A letter does have the advantage of firmly establishing the identity of the buyer. Annual reports, product literature, and other published material may be sent with the letter. Such material clarifies who the buyer is for the prospect. If the literature is impressive, it may help encourage interest or at least curiosity in the prospect and pave the way for a meeting. However, a buyer should realize his literature and letter can only present information which may or may not be persuasive, and are totally unable to generate a personal relationship that is so essential to an acquisition.

The Telephone Introduction. A most effective approach is self-introduction through a telephone call by an appropriate executive of the buyer to the key shareholder or CEO of the prospect. The properly conducted telephone approach will yield better results with fewer complications than any other method. The objectives of the call are introduction of the buyer, a statement of intent, and arrangements of the first meeting. The key elements of a call are as follows:

Identification: The buyer executive should place his telephone call himself and state his name, title, and company to explain who he is and eliminate any communication misunderstandings. It also gives a degree of importance to the call which will help bring prompt attention. Placing the call directly enables the buyer to develop familiarity with the prospect's system and personnel if more than one call is required to get through to the desired person. Telephone operators and secretaries can be very helpful in suggesting when is the best time to call if the executive is out of town or unavailable. Besides, it would be a foolish executive indeed who did not go out of his way to develop a friendly rapport with these people.

Some executives answer their own calls and are readily available, while others have set up barriers that make them nearly inaccessible. For some, the barriers are thought necessary because of extreme pressures on their time, but for others the barriers are symptomatic of deeper problems such as creditor harrassment, serious legal difficulties, and peculiar psychological characteristics of the executive, all of which might indicate that the prospect is not as attractive as hoped. In most cases the buyer's executive will experience little difficulty in reaching the person he wishes, but on occasion some persistance is required.

Secretaries may demand to know the purpose of the call before putting it through. For some, this is in accordance with their instructions and for others they are simply overzealous or curious. If possible, the caller should avoid giving the secretary the reason for his call. Evasive reasons may be tried such as, "It's personal," or "I want to discuss a business situation." Whatever excuse is given, the buyer should be very careful not to alienate the secretary. The prospect's executive may not want his secretary to know he would consider a sale for fear of her personal reaction or a lack of confidence in her ability to keep important secrets. In some cases, the secretary may be such a barrier that the purpose of the call must be disclosed to get through to the desired executive.

Demonstrate familiarity with the prospect: After the introduction brief comments on some aspect of the prospects business are appropriate to indicate that the buyer is familiar with the business and likes what he sees. This comment can cover any aspect of the prospect's business; his annual report, product or service, booth at a trade show, advertising, or any other aspect of the business that is impressive. If the buyer and prospect have any sort of a customer-vendor relationship, now is the time to refer to it.

The compliment: A compliment to the prospect should be worked into the conversation. This most easily can be accomplished in the reference to the prospect's business, "Your new product line is the best we have seen," or "Your booth at the trade show was outstanding." The compliment should be sincere and refer to something that the prospect is very likely to be proud of. Compliments not only are universally welcome, but they begin the process of building rapport and demonstrate the buyer is genuinely interested.

Reason for calling: The buyer's objective in the telephone call is to secure a face-to-face meeting with the prospect. He cannot expect to receive a positive expression of interest in selling the business over the telephone, although it could happen. At this stage, the buyer is still a stranger and the prospect has yet to decide his level of interest. The buyer should explain to the prospect, "My reason for calling is that everything we know of you is impressive (another compliment) and we have no idea whether your shareholders and you would consider selling your business (states the buyer's objective without placing the prospect in a position where he must comment), but if at sometime in the future you would sell (the future is anytime from one minute to X number of years and, again, does not place the prospect in the position of saying yes or no), we would like to be considered (this implies a friendly acquisition). I would like to have the opportunity to visit with you and tell you more about us so that you would be familiar with us in case there is a chance (this establishes the next step without placing the prospect in the position of having to confirm that he would consider selling) of an acquisition." In Europe, the term "make an equity investment in your firm" is commonly used to indicate an acquistion is contemplated.

From the author's experience and others' using this approach, over eight out of ten prospects will reply something to this effect, "We have no immediate plans for selling, but I would be happy to meet you." The few that decline are usually already in negotiations to sell their company or have a policy of not selling for a set number of years, or there are estate problems, or shareholder disputes that make sale at the present time impossible. Those declining to meet are usually not suitable prospects and can be dropped from immediate consideration. However, the reasons given for declining to meet should be analyzed and if they represent conditions subject to change, the buyer should so note and suggest he call again when they do change. He also might ask if he could meet the owner on a "social" basis when in the area. Agreeing to meet should not be interpreted by the buyer as agreement to sell and can mean anything from curiosity to a definite desire to sell. It also may mean the prospect may believe he has a moral and possible legal obligation to his shareholders to listen. Regardless of the prospect's present thinking, the buyer is now in a position to present his case.

Set a date: Once the prospect agrees to meet, the buyer should promptly propose a date for the meeting. This date should be within the next two weeks if at all possible. Dates further into the future often become delayed because of unexpected conflicts and the psychological momentum is lost. Most executives are sure of their schedules a couple of weeks in advance, but beyond that much uncertainty creeps in.

The buyer's best time for the first meeting is 10:00 a.m. or 10:30 a.m. This permits the prospect to handle important matters before the meeting and if all goes well, the meeting can continue through lunch. The buyer should set his travel schedule so that the meeting can last into the afternoon if the prospect so desires. It is a mistake for a buyer to break off a first meeting prematurely because he must catch a plane or attend to other business.

Immediately after the introductory telephone call, the buyer should send a letter to the prospect confirming the time and place. Literature describing the buyer can also be sent, but the buyer should not count on it arriving before his visit if the meeting is scheduled within a week.

The First Meeting

The buyer should make every effort to have the first meeting at the prospect's office, rather than at an airport, restaurant, law office, or some other neutral location. Suggestions by eager prospects for the meeting to be held at the buyer's office should be resisted. At the prospect's office the prospect will be more comfortable and at ease, but more important for the buyer is the opportunity to learn about the prospect. The typical executive's office usually provides a wealth of information about the executive's interests, background, and accomplishments and each clue is an opportunity for conversation on subjects of interest to the prospect. Photographs, trophies, books, unusual furniture, framed certificates, models, products or parts, paintings, or any other items collected by or awarded to the prospect are worth noting. During the first five minutes in the prospect's office, the buyer would do well to make a mental note of all such items. These can become a logical topic of conversation as the parties become acquainted prior to discussing the main purpose of the visits.

The overall condition and appearance of the office can also be revealing. A run-down office, overly lavish office, disorderly conditions, immaculate and orderly, a desk piled high with papers, constant interruptions or no interruptions at all are clues which, when tied to other observations, may tell much about the prospect and his business. A buyer at this stage will still be attempting to learn all he can and be a long way from a final decision to make an offer.

Another advantage of visiting the prospect is the possibility of inspecting facilities that may be located near the prospect's office. Manufacturing plants, offices, retail outlets, and warehouses or any other facilities of the prospect should be toured if the prospect will agree. A wise buyer will arrive prior to his appointment in time to drive, unescorted, around the exterior of the facilities to gain a better understanding of the assets and operations. This will also permit him to ask better questions of the prospect once the meeting commences.

The buyer should not attempt to present a canned, verbatim presentation to the prospect, because this would have an insincere ring. The buyer should be at ease, demonstrate interest in the prospect, and present his case. This requires preparation but not some sort of master salesman or executive of extraordinary charm. The buyer should totally know what he wants to say and be able to tailor it to the general tone and nature of the conversation. Here all his preparation and knowledge of the industry comes into play.

After a period of general conversation and becoming acquainted with the prospect, the buyer may lead into his subject by simply stating, "Let me explain to you how this all came about and why I am here today." He can begin by describing his company and follow-up with how he learned of the prospect. He can explain his objectives and overall program and why the prospect would fit into his program. Finally, he can explain why it would be advantageous for the prospect to sell. The buyer need not be shy about explaining all his reasoning, but it is best to maintain a soft-sell approach. Few individuals who have risen to positions of authority in a business organization are going to be bowled over by a high pressure sales approach. Most have long since learned how to say "No" and are not pleased, and often offended, with a hard sell. Even if a prospect declares he is not willing to sell at this time, it would be a rare one who agrees to meet who does not want to hear the buyer's story and would not agree to the buyer keeping in touch in case the prospect changed his mind.

A buyer should have two additional objectives for this first meeting other than stating his case and building rapport. He will want to secure new or confirming information about the prospect and will want to establish the next step which will follow the meeting.

Information On the Prospect From the Prospect

Prior to the first meeting, the buyer representative should develop a list of questions he will attempt to ask the prospect during the meeting. These questions or subject areas should be committed to memory and be worked into the overall conversation and never presented as a list of questions the buyer wants answered. The buyer may have the list in his pocket as a reminder that he peeks at when the prospect is out of the room or on the telephone, but this is done inconspicuously. The list should be prepared in general order of importance because there may not be an opportunity to ask all the desired questions. However, a moderately skillful executive can easily weave into the conversation fifteen or more questions in a two-hour meeting without becoming offensive or the prospect even being aware he is disclosing so much data. Immediately after the meeting, the buyer should write down all information learned as well as his general impressions.

While the buyer is continually presenting arguments why the prospect should sell and building his case, he is also gathering data and insight to decide whether or not he really wants to buy. These two functions run concurrently and are somewhat contradictory, but the buyer must strive to keep the basic decision his. If the prospect refuses to sell to the buyer, the buyer has wasted his time and has no decision to make. Therefore, the buyer must maintain a position of enthusiastically pursuing the prospect while he privately tries to make up his mind. If the buyer decides he does not want to buy the prospect, he should drop the matter promptly and so inform the prospect. Usually, a message of rejection in which the buyer claims he has had a change of policy or plans is more appropriate than informing the prospect that he does not meet the buyer's standards. Someday, the buyer may change his mind and the prospect will never forget or forgive comments he finds insulting.

The Next Step

Unless at the first meeting the buyer becomes convinced he does not want to buy the prospect or he concludes the prospect cannot be acquired, some next step should be decided upon. This will depend entirely upon the degree of interest and how far the meeting progressed. If the prospect shows only modest interest, then a return date for the present visitor or another buyer's executive would be in order. An invitation to the prospect to visit the buyer's facilities would be suitable if the prospect shows more interest. If the prospect professes a definite desire to sell, then the buyer should disclose his acquisition procedure for evaluation and negotiation and arrange to implement the procedure. The buyer should ask for a copy of the seller's financial statements and recognize their receipt is a milestone in the process. A seller who gives a copy of his financials to the buyer is also saying he wants an offer.

A letter to the prospect after the meeting thanking him for the meeting and confirming the next step should be sent. This should be a business letter and not a love letter that restates all the advantages of the contemplated acquisition. Some buyers tend to overdo it in their correspondence and write what can be much better said face to face.

The Romance

The first meeting has been held and the buyer's objectives are now out in the open. The key decision-maker or makers who must be convinced and kept convinced through closing have been identified. Obviously, the courtship has to be tailored to each individual to be effective, but the heart of the romance will be the building of a close personal relationship between the seller's decision-makers and the buyer's key executives. Ideally, these relationships will contain enough sincerity so that they will last long after the closing of the transaction and be invaluable throughout the transition. Personal friendships between the decision-makers are also a means of meeting and persuading their families. The majority of the shares may be in the hands of the family as a result of gifts or inheritance. Family members may play a very active role in influencing the decision-maker.

Personal friendships should be encouraged below the decision-making level. Accountants working on the evaluation or audit have an excellent opportunity to become well acquainted with their counterparts. Attorneys writing and negotiating contracts spend much time together and can develop friendships. Operational executives responsible for integrating or planning new programs must work together. These friendships can help bring about the acquisition and serve as additional avenues of communication between the parties. Even if the original contact was by someone in the buyer's organization other than the CEO and the prospect is of significant size, the buyer's CEO should build and maintain a personal relationship with the seller's CEO.

Inviting the prospect's key executives to visit the buyer's facilities is an effective technique, providing the facilities are impressive. Facility visits allow the prospect to inspect the buyer and tend to support the contention of the buyer that he has substance. Visits are also a means of exploring at the site how the companies could work together if a sale occurred. They also provide an opportunity for the buyer to have the undivided attention of the seller. When visits occur, it is most important that the prospects be provided with constant attention and first class treatment. The buyer must be prepared to answer any of his visitor's questions regarding accomplishments or problems. If accomplishments do not clearly outweigh the problems, it is advisable to avoid facility visits.

A buyer who has a collection of acquisitions still managed by happy sellers can do no better than to enlist their aid in persuading prospects to sell. Unfortunately, most buyers do not have this condition and must work to keep previously acquired sellers away from the new prospect. However, a previous seller who is still satisfied with the transaction he made and likes his relationship with the buyer can be very persuasive indeed and possibly the most convincing factor for a seller.

Some sellers suggest, "Let's work together first and get to know each other before we further consider being acquired." This request occurs commonly and, while it may appear logical on the surface, it is a no-win situation for the buyer. This comes up whenever some sort of customer-vendor relationship can exist between the buyer and seller, or when the buyer can direct substantial business to the seller. Unfortunately, the more prosperous the seller becomes, the higher will be the price if a sale does eventually occur. The seller's business will gain some of the advantages of an acquisition without being acquired; thus, eliminating part of the incentive to sell. The seller will expect special advantages from the buyer that he cannot give.

The buyer will have to establish some special system or mechanism to oversee the preacquisition business relationship or it will falter. If any errors are made by the seller, they will be magnified out of proportion. Special arrangements worked out at the top levels of a corporation for an ongoing business relationship are often resisted, and even subverted, within the respective organizations. Unless there is some clear, immediate economic advantage to the buyer to conduct business with a prospect, he should refuse to do so. The best way to counter the proposal is a candid enumeration of the problems just cited.

Purpose of Courtship

The period of romance is important in many respects to the parties. How the courtship is conducted depends upon the participants' nature and interests. There is no such thing as a standard or canned courtship because each must be tailored to the parties and conditions that exist. Whether the courtship is laden with expensive entertainment or long discussions in a business setting, it has certain objectives and functions to accomplish.

First, it is a process of mutual evaluation in which the parties decide if they want to enter into the transaction. Despite the romance, both parties continue to evaluate their situation and can back away any time prior to the final closing. If the sellers are to remain active in the company after the sale, then it is all the more important. The buyer who is about to make major commitments also must be certain he knows exactly what he is getting into. The romance is important to convince some prospects to sell, but in most cases it gives them supporting reasons to do what they wanted to do all along. It is not fully acceptable socially for a seller to simply say, "Pay me the cash and I could care less what happens to the company after you own it." The seller's decision-maker has to explain to his friends, family, employees, minority shareholders, directors, the community, and business associates why it is in the company's best interest that he sell to the buyer.

Assurances by the buyer that the management and employees will be well treated are obligatory remarks that too often are forgotten by the buyer.

Preservation of the company name is also important to some sellers and costs the buyer nothing.

Most buyers accommodate the seller by offering suggestions that portend growth forecasts, great prosperity, and independence retained by the prospect. In addition, most buyers honestly believe that upon consummation of the acquisition, synergism will abound, capital will be plentiful, marketing will be beneficial, and the acquired may even be encouraged to make a few acquisitions. Unfortunately, such a commercial utopia is the exception rather than the rule, but there are enough acquisition success stories to keep the buyers well motivated.

If all the romance is successful, the prospect will give the buyer his financial statements and state that he will seriously consider an offer. Then the buyer must develop an offer or go away. The romance now begins to serve another purpose—of keeping the parties talking when they disagree on price.

9.
Evaluation

Evaluation of a prospect commences when the buyer first learns of the prospect and continues with each contact and the collection of each bit of additional data. Buyer representatives meet with the seller, gain their impressions, and obtain answers to most of the basic questions largely in an informal context. Well organized buyers prior to each contact may use a checklist as a reminder of needed data but information gathering is initially conducted on an informal basis. All of the data and impressions should be accumulated and recorded and kept together in one place for use in the total evaluation of the prospect. The informal evaluation, which commenced when the first information was received and continued through the romance, eventually leads to a comprehensive formal study and evaluation of the prospect.

The business judgment of each buyer must be applied in deciding the extent and depth of the formal evaluation he believes is essential for a final decision. This will vary from industry to industry and somewhat with the experience, willingness to take risks, and sophistication of the buyer. However, in any event a formal evaluation is necessary and, to be worthwhile, it must be comprehensive, which will require a real effort and substantial expense. The belief that the more information one has about a prospect, and the more extensive the evaluation, the better will be the buyer's decision is not necessarily true. Much information about a company can be gathered that is interesting, but of minor or no importance to making an acquisition decision. Superfluous data will only confuse and distract those charged with the evaluation who under any circumstances will still have voluminous essential data to study. The information gathered may describe every facet of the prospect's business but it will be no better than the ability of the buyer to evaluate it. Regardless of how much data is gathered and studied, there is no way to totally eliminate all the risks in acquisitions and have a 100% certainty the acquisition will succeed.

The only way to be 100% certain not to make a bad acquisition is to make none at all.

Excess study and evaluation also brings on subtle psychological problems that tend to discourage completion of the acquisition. Because there are no perfect companies and all have some warts, the longer a buyer looks at a prospect, the larger the warts become. A buyer tends to talk himself out of going ahead and dwells on what is wrong rather than what is right. An attitude of becoming bored and tired of the deal also begins to set in. While the buyer, submerged in data, is losing his enthusiasm, the seller becomes impatient, loses respect for the buyer, and begins to consider his alternatives.

Evaluating Inaccurate or Partial Information

Buyers should be realistic in their evaluations and recognize that most positions taken by sellers are normal and explainable and not some sort of devious plot. The sellers have ample motivation to present their company in the best possible light and feel no requirement to volunteer all the negative information about the company and industry. They may be unfamiliar with some details of their business, but they know far more than the buyer and this gives them an advantage, which they may not always use because they assume the buyer knows more than he does. Sellers are in a position to control the timing of a sale and this enables them to select their most advantageous time to give the best impression.

Sellers, in providing information to buyers, may give data that later proves to be inaccurate or only partially true, but more often than not inaccurate data is attributable to reasons other than outright lying. The seller may have inaccurate information but actually believes it to be correct. He may not know and guesses rather than appear uninformed to the buyer. The seller's enthusiasm about the business may be so great that it clouds his views and he confuses his hopes with his accomplishments. Communication misunderstandings may occur because the buyer's questions are not understood. In any evaluation when facts do not ring true, the last possible cause to consider is deliberate lying. Few sellers will intentionally provide false information and equally few will volunteer unfavorable information or correct a buyer's overly enthusiastic misconceptions. Most studies of prospects will turn up some surprises and warts of which it is impossible to determine if the seller had knowledge. When they become known, a buyer should be very careful not to jump to any conclusions and evaluate the importance of the negative aspects in light of the total company's desirability.

During evaluation of prospects, a buyer should strive for a balanced view without placing excessive emphasis on either what is right or what is wrong with a prospect. A Pollyanna type of approach of looking only at the positive aspects is nearly as big a mistake as evaluating the company with the attitude of "We are going to find out what's wrong with it." Acquisition executives looking for another notch on their guns are probably the greatest offenders in over-stressing the positive, while accounting executives clearly excel in the unbalanced negative suspecting sinister plots and spooks everywhere and generally looking on the dark side.

Purpose of Formal Study

A comprehensive formal study and evaluation, if well conducted and to be of real value to the buyer, should have a variety of purposes other than just securing information about the prospect. It is more than a systematic means of asking the right questions. It is far more than a method of ferreting out "minor" items that could cause failure such as the health of a key manager, ownership of patents, tooling or patterns, or loss of a critical customer. The comprehensive study should provide a complete record of the history and condition of the prospect, insight into how it fits with the buyer's overall program, a basis for the buyer's business plan, and a record of the entire transaction. It organizes a mass of information, forces a buyer to carefully think out what he is doing, and discourages rushing into an acquisition because it is available and appears to be a "good deal."

Information on Prospects

A basic purpose of the comprehensive study is to secure historical data and complete information on the present condition of all phases of the business. This is systematically accomplished with emphasis on accuracy. The information is taken directly from the prospect's records and interviews with the prospect's management, employees, cus-tomers, suppliers, or others who would have knowledge of the busi-ness and industry. Through use of checklists and prepared questions the buyer is able to methodically gather all the information he considers essential for making decisions. The information is then assembled into a format that is useable and with which the buyer becomes accustomed as his program progresses.

A buyer should never be satisfied with his forms and continually work to improve the checklists, questionnaires, and summaries to make them more responsive to his needs. There is no one format suitable for every business and buyer or one a buyer will not be able to improve from time to time. The format should be one that can be conveniently used by executives in their evaluations and in presentations to the board of directors. The format should lend itself to becoming a permanent record, to be used in operating the acquired.

Compliance with Objectives

The comprehensive study data should provide the information necessary to determine if the prospect complied with the buyer's predetermined acquisition policies and objectives. A systematic comparison of the prospect's characteristics against each policy and objective will help a buyer determine if the prospect really fits. In practice a buyer will not have waited until the comprehensive study to decide if the prospect complies with his policies and objectives, but will have been making tentative conclusions as he went along. Noncompliance in a few areas may only identify easily correctable situations or even that some of the buyer's policies are unrealistic and should be reviewed. However, policies once established should not easily be changed and never changed to bring an acquisition prospect into compliance. Regardless, noncompliance in any area is a significant danger signal requiring attention and the buyer's best course may be to walk away.

Basis of Business Plan

Possibly most important is the business plan for the acquisition, which is an integral part of the evaluation study. It is a major blunder for a buyer to acquire a company and not have a clear plan of what he will do with it, how it will be managed, how defects will be corrected, how assets will be utilized, and how the business will be integrated into the buyer's organization. The development of a business plan can best become part of the complete formal evaluation process. Only if a buyer knows precisely what is intended to be done with an acquisition can he realistically decide if he wants to make the acquisition.

Permanent Record

Any acquisition generates an incredible quantity of information in a variety of forms. The assimilation of all this data into a useable format and permanent record should be accomplished largely during the formal evaluation process. The information not only must be available to the individual or group making the final decision, but also to those who conduct preliminary or specialized evaluations and make recommendations to senior executives. A copy of the data should go to whoever becomes responsible for operating the acquired company so that he will be able to benefit from its use. A permanent copy should be retained in a safe place as a record of the transaction for use in answering questions at a later date, for use in resolving disputes, or as evidence in litigation. A buyer will find invaluable his organized permanent record of the transaction, business plan, and study of the company and industry.

The Formal Evaluation and Study

Appendices 1 (Parts 1 and 2) and 2 at the back of this book are sample comprehensive study and evaluation forms for use in the formal evaluation. While the forms may be adequate for certain medium-sized manufacturing and service companies, they should be looked at more as examples of concepts to be tailored by a serious buyer to his own industry and requirements and also revised to evaluate large or unusual prospects. The modifications should accommodate the preferences and idiosyncracies of the buyer as well as include questions applicable to his own industry in terminology with which he is accustomed. They also would have to be modified and expanded substantially if the prospect had multiple divisions or subsidiaries. The appendices combine data gathering, policy compliance, and the detailed business plan simplifying organization and review.

Appendix 1, Part 1, contains all the basic information for evaluation, review, and approval of the acquisition. It is a combination checklist and questionnaire that constitutes a summary of the acquisition in sufficient detail for most board of directors to make a decision. Included is the business plan for integration of the acquired into the buyer's organization and verification of compliance with the buyer's policies and objectives.

Part 2 is a continuation of the basic study outlined in Part 1. For larger acquisitions, the amount of data generated by Part 2 may require several volumes to be added because it is a checklist of information and documents to be secured, with comprehensive questionnaires covering key aspects of the business that are not covered in Part 1. Some of the basic data found in Part 2, such as financial statements, are summarized in Part 1.

Appendix 2 is a final checklist for use a few days before the actual closing of the acquisition to learn if any significant changes have occurred in the prospect during the period since the original study, Appendix 1 (Parts 1 and 2), was completed. This period could be months and a final check is necessary.

It is obvious that completion of the studies will involve a great amount of time and expense. Concern over the expenditure in time and money for the study should be equated against the potential benefits from the acquisition and the possible loss if it is a failure. Usually the cost of the study is very small compared to potential losses associated with an unsuccessful acquisition. A buyer in tailoring the study for his use should strive to eliminate superfluous items but most buyers will find over a long period the studies will tend to grow rather than shrink because of the addition of what one or more executives believe to be important. Another source of additional sections of questions for the studies will be bitter experience, which comes from the acquisition of companies having major defects that were not discovered prior to the acquisition because the buyer did not ask the right questions and the seller saw no advantage in volunteering bad news. The greater the detail, the more chance of finding things wrong, as well as unsuspected assets, and this brings a greater need for wisdom on the part of the buyer to keep the defects and pleasant surprises in perspective.

When to Conduct the Study

Because of the time and expense of a comprehensive study, some controversy may exist as to when in the acquisition process to complete the study. A fundamental question is, Should the in-depth study be conducted before or after making an offer and coming to grips with the price issue? Most buyers prefer to rely upon the seller's financial statements, their own forecasts, and essential data supplied by the seller to negotiate a price before conducting a comprehensive study.

Clearly, the buyer would be better informed and prepared to negotiate a price if he had the comprehensive study complete, but the cost of the study for most buyers is considered too great until they are more confident the acquisition can be made. Sellers also resist the inconvenience and loss of secrecy associated with a buyer's team gathering information prior to agreement on price. If agreement on price proves to be impossible, negotiations are discontinued. If price agreement occurs, then the full study is conducted and assuming nothing unusual turns up and prior data submitted by the seller is verified, the acquisition will be closed.

In some situations the buyer and seller are unable to reach full agreement on price but they are close. At this stage the buyer may request a break in the negotiations and conduct his comprehensive study before making further price concessions or giving up. If discrepancies occur or other unfavorable data emerges, the buyer will have to reassess his position. He can simply accept the bad news and consider it insignificant, demand to renegotiate, or walk away. The buyer can also use the results of the study as a face-saving way to make price concessions he had vigorously argued were unjustified prior to the study.

Who Prepares the Study?

Ideally, a team of buyer executives who will continue to be associated with the prospect after it is acquired will be assembled to conduct the study, evaluate the company, and develop the business plan. Members of the team should be specialists in the areas of the study they work on. An attorney will conduct the legal review, a marketing specialist the marketing section, and an accountant the financial sections, as well as assist in preparing the forecasts. Whoever will be responsible for the company once acquired should oversee and approve development of the business plan and all projections for the future. This person will be held responsible so the plan should be his.

Someone must be charged with the responsibility of coordinating all study activities and seeing that the work is completed on a timely basis and assembled into the volumes. This person may also complete some of the sections himself. The job will never get done unless someone sets schedules, assigns work, and ramrods the program to completion. Much of the information regarding the prospect's history and current condition could be secured by a competent accountant. If one is not available in the buyer's organization, outside auditors can be employed for the job. When full financial audits are required, then the outside auditors will be involved automatically. If outside auditors are used, the buyer should be very precise in defining the scope of their work.

Buyer representatives who gather data at the prospect's office must be tactful and perceptive. They must be able to get along well with people and be very courteous with the seller's employees. They will be looked at as typical members of the buyer organization for better or worse, although the buyer has no "typical" employees. They must be perceptive in what they see and hear and be able to develop a rapport that encourages the prospect's employees to speak freely.

Seller Preparation

Most sellers have a vague understanding that if they agree to sell their company, the buyer has a right to inspect what he is about to buy. Few realize the depth of the study contemplated by the buyer and expect little more than for him to "kick the tires," so, a buyer should explain why it is needed. The buyer should assure the seller that the study is highly confidential and will not be disclosed to anyone outside the buyer's organization and particularly to any government agencies.

Owner's Tax Concerns

Owners of privately held companies normally operate on a basis to minimize taxes and are more interested in cash retention than bottom-line income. As a result, they tend to expense everything possible, including items that should have been capitalized, write off receivables if questionable at all, write down inventory, establish excessive reserves, and do whatever else they can think of to delay taxes. They also may make a practice of the company paying some personal and family expenses, which more properly should have been treated as personal income. It should be emphasized that most privately held companies pay few personal expenses and are only delaying and not avoiding taxes with their other schemes. European companies have a reputation for tax avoidance but most are no different from those in North America and contrary to popular belief, the Americans are often more aggressive in delaying taxes. The buyer should explain that he understands the seller's tax approach and will take it into consideration in his study. More often than not the study will reveal the taxes delayed have not been significant.

In recent years there has been much more interest by U.S. government agencies in perquisites, political contributions, commission payments, which may more accurately be described as bribes, boycott violations, and other activity whose illegality has not been universally accepted. If such practices are thought to exist in the seller's business, the buyer can not promise to refuse to disclose their presence if asked, but he can assure the seller that he is not interested in seeing such matters exposed. This is a very delicate matter that a buyer should review with his attorney.

Evaluating the Study

The most comprehensive and well organized collection of information about a prospect is only of value if it is properly evaluated. The old political maxim of "it does not matter so much who votes as who counts the votes" also has a certain application. The comprehensive study and business plan for an acquisition prospect constitutes a voluminous amount of data and it is a real task for anyone to read it all and come to a conclusion, but it must be done. Because acquisitions are business decisions of major importance, the final decision whether or not to acquire will fall upon the investor or top decision-makers of a corporation, and intelligent decisions require adequate information. Structuring the study into two or more volumes simplifies the task for busy directors or CEO's in that a sound decision can be made relying largely on volume one, but even that is not a ten-minute project.

Evaluation can be partially delegated to those with expertise in areas such as accounting, law, personnel, or marketing who can be called upon to give an opinion for items that fall into their areas, as well as an overall opinion of the entire acquisition. Their participation and opinions will not detract from the responsibility of those who must make the final decision to fully study and evaluate the acquisition prospect.

Whoever is responsible for seeing that the entire study is completed also should be the person who reads every bit of data accumulated and is able to answer any questions that arise or know where to go to secure the answers. Despite the detailed nature of a comprehensive study there probably will be more questions whose answers must be sought. This person must also be responsible for highlighting any problem areas in the contemplated acquisition that are not readily apparent, but could have great significance. Threatened litigation, problem jobs in progress, dubious inventory values, and unfunded pension liabilities are only a few examples of problems that may not be discernable from financial statements but could cause any acquisition to be uneconomical. Unless someone has called these to the attention of the buyer's decision-makers, they may be overlooked. A seller may even have informed the buyer of their presence, but unless the information goes to the proper people in the buyer's organization, it will not help the buyer. A buyer can lose his right of recourse against a seller if negative information was provided to buyer personnel conducting the study, but was ignored. A buyer has no reason to complain if adverse information is provided by the seller but it is ignored, not acted upon, or never reaches the decision-makers. Someone in the buyer's organization with enough stature to make himself heard must become totally knowledgeable about all aspects of the prospect's business.

Beware of Overenthusiasm

In larger organizations the responsibility for securing the comprehensive study usually falls to the executive in charge of the acquisition program. Anyone in this position has some conflict of interest in that he is graded short-term on the number of acquisitions made, and stressing the shortcomings of prospects is not conducive to securing agreement for their purchase. It is possible to rationalize almost any wart as insignificant or offset it by other positive attributes. Acquisition executives' views are also affected by an awareness of the difficulty of buying any company and the work that goes into bringing a prospect to a point where it can be bought, and they do not want to see all that effort lost. They have been selling the prospect so hard on the transaction that they have completely sold themselves on the wisdom of the acquisition. Their conclusions may be valid but they should not be the final word.

Evaluation Standards

To evaluate any company some standards must exist on either a formal or informal basis. Criteria must be used that determine whether or not characteristics of a prospect are acceptable, superior, or cause for rejection. Predetermined buyer policies will be important as criteria and should cover the basic characteristics. As a buyer's acquisition program continues, his views on what is acceptable will develop and expand. Some of these views will evolve into formal policies and others will remain unwritten, but they will be known and complied with as though they were written. An advantage of a continuous acquisition program is that as experience is gained, learning results from errors, certain characteristics take on added importance, a buyer becomes more certain of what sort of company he wants to buy, and he more easily recognizes a desirable company when he sees it.

Established policies of acceptability help guard against the halo effect whereby several very good attributes of a prospect may tend to distort a buyer's perspective and he overlooks the deficiencies and problem areas. A favorable general impression of a company coupled with a strong need or desire to acquire the type of business can cause a buyer to look at the prospect through rose-colored glasses. Buyers caught up in bidding contests also seem to experience this phenomenon. Because no companies are free of defects, it is all too easy to use this as a basis of rationalizing the purchase of a prospect that makes a favorable impression but has many serious defects. Unemotional and mature business judgment is needed in evaluation, but there also must be a favorable general impression of "good chemistry" for a buyer to go ahead. The reverse situation is also true. Even if a prospect fully met every test and policy of the buyer, but the buyer had an uneasy and unenthusiastic feeling about the prospect, which may not be rationally explained, it would be best to drop the prospect from consideration. Though a general impression may be part intuition and can not be fully explained, it can not be ignored.

Policies can cover specific characteristics of a prospect, but they cannot provide standards for overall opinions and decisions. Some characteristics will be more important than others, and while any trait can be bad enough to make a company fail, no one trait can be so good it guarantees success. It will be the task of the buyer's decision-maker to evaluate the problems and positive aspects and arrive at a balanced decision.

Buyers should not have qualms about applying double standards, one for their existing businesses and one for acquisitions. Most buyers do just this and while they may be accused of a degree of hypocricy, their self-interest requires that they try to improve their level of operations and apply high standards to new acquisitions. However, the acquisition standards for new acquisitions should be attainable goals for existing operations. Alert sellers will point out differences in performance quality in price discussions to justify their position, but buyers can counter by claiming the current lower performance of existing operations will be tolerated only a short time and improvement programs are underway. This should be the case in any aggressive, well managed company.

Procedural Paralysis

A comprehensive study is lengthy and its completion should be accomplished if at all possible but, in some cases, because of time pressures, lack of personnel, inferior work, or difficulty in securing data, there may be minor errors, omissions, or inadequate data. While defective work is not to be encouraged or tolerated, a buyer's final decision-makers should not become unduly concerned and involved with the mechanics of completing studies. Their first question when confronted with a deficient study should be "Is there enough valid information to make a decision?" and not just send it back until they get it right. Sending it back may also terminate the chance of making an exceptionally fine acquisition. Excessive concern over format, insignificant details, minor omissions, typographical errors, and not following precise approval procedures usually indicate an indecisive management more than a policy of excellence.

Legal Audit

Studies of acquisition prospects tend to concentrate primarily on financial and operational aspects of the business, but in recent years there has been increased emphasis on and need for a comprehensive legal audit. In the legal audit the basic information about the legal structure of the prospect, shareholders, types of securities, locations and names of officers and directors are secured to draft the definitive agreements, the first drafts of which are normally the responsibility of the buyer. Equally important is the legal study of the prospect to learn of obligations that exist or are possible, a review of compliance with governmental regulations, interaction with governmental bodies, and a determination of what government approvals both state, federal, or foreign are required to complete an acquisition. The legal audit section in Appendix 1, Part 2, gives detailed questions of the type that should be included in the review. An attorney will be required to answer most and conduct the evaluation. Most attorneys active in acquisition work have developed their own checklists that can be used to supplement the buyers. The proliferation of attorneys in business and government as well as the expansion of government has created an inescapable requirement for legal review and competent legal services to protect a buyer attempting an acquisition.

Surprises

Few prospects will survive the comprehensive study and evaluation with the buyer finding the company in exactly the condition he thought it to be without any surprises. A buyer starts with a generally favorable impression of a prospect based on published data and early observations. Because his information is limited and superficial, his early impressions tend to be simplistic but ample to spark his interest. As more information emerges through direct contacts and the comprehensive study, the prospect and its industry appear to become more complex and the buyer's overall opinion can either become more positive or turn very negative. This is usually caused by new information and surprises rather than finding original information to be erroneous.

Unfavorable surprises that emerge in the evaluation do create serious problems for the buyer. A buyer can ignore them, renegotiate, or walk away, but to decide his course of action, he first must measure their importance. Some sellers use as a strategy a program of first disclosing all the good features of their company in the hope of developing some sort of blind enthusiasm in the buyer so that he will still conclude the acquisition after the withheld unfavorable information is discovered. This strategy seldom works. Evaluation of the unfavorable surprise must take place before any conclusion is reached and this can only be accomplished when all the facts are gathered. Hasty conclusions should be avoided.

Special Problems and General Advice

The decision to acquire a company requires the best of mature judgment. Possibly one of the ultimate tests of a business executive is his ability to make successful acquisitions. Clearly, it requires skill and luck, but the fact that some buyers can acquire with high percentage of success indicates skill plays the major role.

Successful buyers have their own favorite approaches and evaluation techniques but many of the basic concepts are the same. Some are presented here for use in evaluations.

1. A buyer should not make his decision solely on the financial statements of a prospect. The financial statements may or may not be accurate even when backed with a full audit and "clean" opinion of a CPA. Scandals and litigation against CPA firms appear from time to time and reveal their clients have been less than candid and often very clever, but this situation fortunately is relatively uncommon. More common is imaginative but proper accounting that is misleading and audits by small obscure CPA firms not adequately staffed or possessing the procedures and disciplines of the major accounting firms. There are many excellent small CPA firms but as a general rule, the smaller they are, the more wary should be the buyer.

2. Information that does not appear on a prospect's financial statements is every bit as important as what does appear. Management quality, market share, competitive position, undisclosed liabilities, such as litigation and conflicts with government agencies, are all examples of critical items for a buyer's evaluations.

3. Companies with strong past earnings records will tend to continue to do well while those with erratic or poor records will probably repeat their performance. Past financial performance is an unreliable prophet for the future, but it is the best available.

4. The buyer can not expect to work miracles and change overnight a company acquired. Whatever changes and improvements are contemplated will probably take much longer than anticipated.

5. Beware of any sudden increases in earnings levels. Large increases may be the advent of prosperity or only preparation to sell.

6. Prospect's management quality and its willingness to continue can not be underestimated in importance. The compatibility of the management with the buyers is also a critical factor.

7. The buyer should include in his evaluation answers to the questions: What happens if he does not buy the company? What

will be the impact upon the buyer's organization if the acquisition is made? What if the acquisition is completed and it fails?

8. A buyer should not assume that anything done differently by a seller is done wrong or is inferior to the buyer's methods. Avoid the "we are the buyer, so we are the best" attitude. An acquired company can be a gold mine of ideas for a buyer, but unfortunately most buyers do not look at an acquired in this light and lose much of the benefit possible from an acquisition.

9. A buyer never should become so involved with a prospect either because of personal relationships or business transactions in progress that he can not say "No" and back away from the acquisition.

Flow of Information

Information in the acquisition study and evaluation must continually be made available to those involved in the final negotiations and preparation of the definitive agreements. These activities usually occur concurrently. A system must be provided for the immediate flow of any significant information to company negotiators. Buyers who are large structured corporations with a team conducting the study, another group negotiating the definitive agreement, and the decision-makers awaiting the results can find coordination a serious problem. Of course, the buyer who is an individual investor handling all phases of the acquisition process or closely involved has little or no coordination problems.

10.
Common-Sense Pricing

Pricing a business need not be an unduly complicated procedure limited only to self-acclaimed experts in the field. Any businessman capable of good judgment and simple mathematics who follows certain basic principles is able to adequately evaluate a business and develop a rational price for what the business would be worth to him. Pricing always has been and will remain an imprecise, subjective exercise, a poker game on a massive scale—and the first step to sensible pricing is to recognize it as such.

Whether a price proves to be too high or low for the buyer depends upon the future results of the business, which are never predictable with total certainty. Possibly one of the rarest events in business would be a five-year forecast for a business that proved to be accurate for all five years. Regardless of the techniques used in valuation studies and pricing of acquisition prospects, the validity of any price conclusions rests upon forecasts and assumptions of what may or may not occur in the future, and this produces a most unsteady foundation. People have trouble enough believing everything that has happened in the past ten years to feel confident about forecasts for the next decade. With all the risks and uncertainty associated with pricing, it clearly is not an activity for the fainthearted.

Valuation studies by outside professionals do play an important and necessary role in estate settlements, divorce cases, tax litigation, condemnation suits, and other legal actions, but their role in acquisition pricing is controversial. There is little that an investment banker or other professional can do in valuing an acquisition prospect that a buyer could not do himself if he elects to do so in terms of developing the price a prospect would be worth to him. The buyer probably would not have a splendid voluminous appraisal he could use to justify his actions to his critics, nor would the buyer have an appraiser who would claim to be a model of professionalism support the buyer's position in arguments with other credentialed professionals who reached substantially different conclusions because they were employed by disgruntled shareholders or other detractors to challenge the buyer. But, the buyer would have a valuation prepared totally on the basis of what the prospect is worth to him, knowing that he must live with his conclusions rather than collecting a fee and walking away. In some instances a buyer may need an outside professional to produce a valuation conclusion similar to what the buyer expects as a defense measure, but this can usually be done once the buyer finds he is under attack.

What the buyer can afford and justify and what the seller will accept eventually combine to set a price for any transaction. The process they go through to reach their conclusions is one influenced by economic and psychological factors. Any buyer will want to pay as little as possible and will base his initial offer, to some degree, on how strongly he believes the seller wants to sell, his alternatives, and any other "straws in the wind" that indicate the lowest acceptable price level. The buyer's appraisal and price calculations may justify a much higher price than need be offered, but there is natural extreme reluctance to offer a price greater than necessary to bring about a sale. However, very low bargaining offers substantially below the price a buyer has calculated he could justify and pay usually are promptly rejected because they can not be adequately explained and, of course, sellers can do their own calculations. A buyer should guard against being offended when his low offer is rejected after having become convinced of his own sales arguments developed in an attempt to justify the offer.

Sellers and buyers have totally different points of view in evaluating offers. A seller will look at a stock offer primarily in terms of what is the market price of the stock and total value of the offer. The market price of the stock is secondary to the buyer because his concerns center around preventing earnings dilution, dividend obligations, and any loss of control he may experience upon issuance of the shares. In cash transactions the sellers are again primarily interested in price and have little concern about whether the buyer can afford the price, what return he will receive on his investment, or any adverse effects the buyer would be living with once the seller is long gone with the money.

Pricing Fallacies

Myths, dubious practices, and terms without agreed definitions surround pricing activity and these deserve comment to eliminate misconceptions and permit sensible pricing policies. A buyer's best approach to pricing is one in which he does not deceive himself or the seller, but if the seller persists in approaches and arguments that are nonsense, the buyer should be able to play the seller's game to his advantage. The following topics are not in any order of importance because importance varies with each transaction and the times.

Fair Price

There is no such thing as a fair price in the sense that established rules and guidelines exist that are useable in setting a price. The term can be used to righteously describe one's own position, but the user should know that no definition exists. Society does not set rules for calculating a price that could be judged fair. It can be argued that any price is fair if the parties agree, but this is unrealistic if one party must agree to a price he does not like but has to accept. Even if this definition is moved a step further to where both parties are pleased and enthusiastic about the price, we find the concept lacking because their satisfaction may be based on false or incomplete information or an ineffective search for better alternatives.

The final step comes when both parties are convinced they each received the best of the deal, but this now is interpreted to mean the opposite of "fair." Fairness in pricing is a state of mind rather than a mathematical calculation. If one party to a transaction believes a certain price is fair, whatever the amount, then to him it is regardless of how it was determined, the existence of uninvestigated alternatives, or any other factors. The buyer's task in convincing a seller that an offer is fair is comparable to persuading a traveler he has reached his destination while he is really still lost.

Competitive Prices Paid

Meaningful statistics do not exist that accurately show what is currently being paid for companies. With a little effort a buyer can select his own statistics and use them to support almost any position, but he should never be trapped into accepting statistics supporting a conclusion he does not want. An active buyer should accumulate published data on acquisition prices to use to his best advantage, but he should not fully accept either their accuracy or completeness and not base his offers upon such data.

The reports on individual prices paid and surveys on prices that do appear from time to time are misleading for the following reasons. The actual prices paid for privately held companies are seldom disclosed and could never be fully determined in any transaction without a complete analysis of the agreements. Prices announced as paid for the shares of public companies often involve different types of consideration such as stock, cash, debentures, and/or combinations thereof eliminating ready comparison. Even in public company sales, there can be significant components of the price found in the terms that are not published. Prices are influenced by industry type, the condition of individual companies, and the capability of buyers, thus rendering statistical tabulations of prices to be of little value. The actual number of comparable acquisitions for statistical comparisons is small, and it is unlikely that more than one or two in the same industry that have sold within the past year are similar in size and type to the prospect under consideration. The economy also changes rapidly, which, in turn, affects acquisition thinking to an extreme degree, thus causing price data and past practices to rapidly become obsolete. The volume of similar acquisitions would not be large enough to establish a "going price." Surveys of acquisition prices are not like wage surveys where data is available on hundreds of employees all performing the same job.

Price Earnings Ratios

PE ratios are continually used in price discussions but seldom are the participants talking about the same thing or thinking about the meaning and implications of this nebulous term. There is a PE number before the market quotations in the financial pages for public companies listed on the American and New York Stock Exchanges. These are the defined price earnings ratios for a relatively small quantity of shares in a public company. Any substantial purchases of shares would likely run up the share value and increase the PE, but not change the fundamental earnings or potential earnings of the company. Heavy sales of shares could force down the price and PE ratio, but this may be totally unrelated to the earnings of the company. This is a vastly different situation from a buyer acquiring majority control or all of the shares of a company. Because financial page PE's are calculated on current earnings and are revised quarterly, a high PE can either mean that the market believes the company has great earnings potential and a real record of growth, or the reverse, where the company's earnings have rapidly declined and prospects are not bright but its assets are so valuable the stock remains at a relatively high level.

While financial page PE's are calculated upon current earnings, in acquisition situations a variety of earnings bases are used to suit the prejudices and positions of the participants. Five-year earnings averages, three-year earnings averages, last fiscal year's earnings, current year projections, and in some instances, projections of future earnings are used. The sensible way to choose an earnings base is select the one(s) that helps your position.

PE's as guidelines also have limitations in that they do not reflect book or market values of the company's assets nor do they weigh the relative values of currencies that may be used in an acquisition. For example, no consideration is given for cash as opposed to a high multiple, unregistered common stock or promissory notes of little promise. PE's of public companies are not even of much value in comparing companies for pricing, because few companies are similar and the forces that determine a stock price in the market are often unrelated to the performance of a company.

Acquisition prices based on PE's are nonsense, but if a buyer can use PE arguments to support a price developed by more rational means, he may as well do so. Chances are the seller will have a bag full of fallacious PE arguments to plead his case.

Return on Investment

A buyer who uses this term in his acquisition program should define it for his own purposes and apply the definition in his own organization to reduce confusion. He has considerable freedom in creating his definition because a satisfactory, fully acceptable one does not exist. Return on investment is a common business term but if ten business people were asked to define it, ten different definitions could result. Just what is "return"? Is it pretax or after-tax income? Are reinvested earnings return or are only dividends the buyer can use elsewhere? How are foreign earnings treated prior to repatriation? How are foreign earnings in a blocked currency that cannot be repatriated treated?

Investment also has its share of problems. What is the value of stock used as currency in an acquisition—market value, book value, or some other amount? Is the price of the stock fixed at closing time or will it go up and down with the current market price or book value? Is cash in an acquired company deducted from the investment? Is money borrowed by the acquired company or the buyer using the acquired company's assets as collateral investment? Do earnings retained within the acquired after acquisition become investment? How will depreciation and amortization of goodwill affect the buyer's investment? Are surplus assets of an acquired upon their sale to be treated as a reduction in investment or as income (return)?

This obviously can become a jungle of confusion unless a buyer who wants to use the concept also defines it. The companion terms "return on capital deployed" and "return on equity" are just as vague and subject to most of the above questions and a buyer should be equally cautious about their use. The buyer's awareness of these terms' uncertain definitions may work to his advantage in price negotiations, because if a seller uses them, the buyer may be free to construct as advantageous a definition as possible.

Book Value

Book values are important but there is a tendency to distort their importance in valuation of a business, pricing, and price negotiations. Book value is not related to earnings history, capacity, or potential, which are far more important in setting a price. Largely because of inflation, book value seldom reflects liquidation value or market value of the assets. Book value does not reflect the condition of assets or their salability, and it may include amounts for assets of little or no value such as goodwill, patents, capitalized expenses, and slow moving inventory. It will not be fully discounted for undisclosed or unrecorded liabilities or the cost of liquidation if the business was shut down. Arbitrary depreciation rates always affect book value.

Book values become a false standard in pricing upon which a buyer should place only secondary importance unless he can use book value arguments to his advantage. A buyer who by any other means calculates a company's worth close to book value will usually consider an amount equal to book value a convenient offer to make.

Prices above book value are often justified by earnings, but they create goodwill, which must be amortized. Because this can be done over a 40-year period, the impact in any year is usually small in relation to total earnings. Prices below book are quite justified if earnings are low and the business is being acquired to operate rather than liquidate. A wise buyer will avoid pricing decisions based on a book value and will largely limit its role to that of a point from which a price arrived at by other means can vary up or down as the condition of the company changes during the period between the date of a prospect's latest financials and closing. Offers of book value are fine if book value is below the price calculated by other means a buyer is prepared to pay.

Tax Free Exchange

This refers to transactions where the buyer pays the selling shareholders for their shares by issuing to them shares of his stock. If properly structured, there will not be income tax payments due by the seller at the time of the transaction. However, when the sellers sell the stock they received, tax payments will be required if they sell for more than their original investment. As a result the term "tax free" should more accurately be replaced with "tax deferred."

Price Varies With Buyers

Businesses are worth far more to some buyers than others and some buyers can justify paying more than others. The concept that a business can be appraised and its worth determined to be X dollars for any and all buyers is not sound. The earnings that can be realized from a prospect under the ownership of one buyer can be vastly different from those earned under another. The following basic categories of buyers illustrate this fact from an operational viewpoint:

1. The passive investor who buys a company and contributes nothing towards the success of the business has the lowest earnings potential. Earnings from the prospect would only be what the prospect can generate alone.
2. The corporate buyer who is able to effect savings in the acquired by combining facilities, distribution, or the addition of technology, systems, or other benefits should enjoy greater earnings than a passive investor.
3. The corporate buyer who is able to effect cost savings or other benefits to his existing business as a result of the acquisition also has an advantage over the passive investor.
4. The corporate buyer who is able to enjoy 2 and 3 above should receive the maximum total earnings from the acquisition and can justify the greatest price.

Operational advantages clearly can affect price but the type of currency available to a buyer for use in acquisitions plays an equally important price role. These categories are in approximate order of low to high price capability:

1. Common stock, low PE: A common stock with a PE under 6 is seldom used in acquisitions because too many shares would have to be issued to create an attractive price. A high dividend also makes a common stock difficult for a buyer to use in acquisitions because of the higher minimum level of cash earnings that must be generated by the acquisition to survive the dividend obligations.
2. Preferred stock and debentures: These securities are only practical for acquisitions where the price is low.

3. Borrowed cash: If the buyer has to borrow funds to pay the seller, retirement of the principal as well as interest obligations will prevent a buyer from paying a premium for a prospect.
4. Available cash: A buyer with cash reserves available for acquisitions is in a position to equate the pretax income of the seller against the income he presently receives and justify a price higher than any other currency, except a high multiple stock.
5. Common stock, high PE: Highest prices can be paid with a high PE multiple common stock. The higher the PE, the higher the price possible without a dilution of earnings.
6. Seller financing: If the seller provides financing on a very generous basis, price can become a secondary factor with only the terms being important. The only limit on terms is at some point the sale may not be treated as bonafide by the public accountants or government. An example was a sale several years ago of a very unprofitable subsidiary of a Dallas, Texas company to its janitor on terms that amounted to a giveaway.

A buyer must look at each prospect strictly in terms of what it is worth to him. An owner desiring to sell will be wise to seek out a buyer of the type who can pay well and has operational advantages. Generally, the optimum for both sides will probably be the buyer who can help most of the prospect's business.

What Is To Be Acquired and Retained

The first step in pricing is to decide what is to be acquired. If the prospect is a public company and shares are to be acquired, as normally would be the case, there will be little opportunity for decision. The buyer will be buying it all. However, if the prospect is privately held, more careful decisions must be made to decide what precisely is being acquired and what will remain with the seller. For example, the following illustrate just a few of the myriad possibilities:

1. Largely for tax purposes, owners of private businesses often create multiple corporations and carry certain assets in their own or family members' names.
2. Operations in geographical locations other than where the headquarters is located may be in different corporations and the ownership may not always be identical.
3. Certain corporations may have been set up to contain management benefit plans and charge management fees.

4. Leasing companies may have been created to own and lease assets to the business.
5. Real estate is frequently owned by key shareholders and leased to the business.
6. Patents may be assigned to a separate corporation or retained by the inventor.

There is an endless number of variations to these conditions and they all must be evaluated and the buyer decide which can be included or excluded. The evaluation must include all of the fees and intercompany charges to determine if they represent normal fees comparable to those charged in a competitive or "arm's length" situation or if they are artifically high or low to distribute income in a manner the shareholders believe to be to their advantage. Equally important is the level of charges that will prevail if the buyer does not acquire certain corporations or assets but continues their use. These charge levels must be settled before any meaningful forecasting of profits can be attempted.

Some assets will best be retained by the seller. The most common is key man life insurance, which insured the lives of one or more key shareholders with benefits payable to the company. Usually, this can be transferred to the shareholders, but they will have a tax liability. Favorite perquisites such as yachts, hunting and fishing lodges, and aircraft are also candidates for exclusion from the acquisition. A problem still exists if the seller has a subsidiary located in Canada because it can not be acquired by a non-Canadian company without the approval of the Canadian government, and this approval is not easy to secure. It is a time consuming and costly procedure that must be followed under the Canadian Foreign Investment Review Act and a buyer must prove the acquisition will be of "significant benefit to Canada." The buyer will need the assistance of an experienced Canadian attorney.

If the acquisition is a divestiture, the buyer should be very careful to study the business and ascertain what parts will be missing. Subsidiaries or divisions of large corporations often lease or share facilities and receive financial services, research, staff assistance, and marketing assistance from the parent that will not continue after the acquisition and must be replaced. These missing segments must be accounted for in the financial evaluation of the divestiture and in the buyer's forecasts.

Assets the buyer expects to acquire but liquidate must be identified, valued, and a time schedule for their disposition established. The after-tax proceeds from these liquidations will reduce the buyer's investment. Unless a buyer has experience and possesses a capability for asset disposition, he should be cautious in establishing the time to complete the dispositions, the cost of such activity, and the amounts anticipated to be realized. All of these factors will have to be incorporated into a buyer's forecasts.

Forecasting

The next step in setting a price is to develop an earnings, cash flow, and balance sheet forecast for the business of the prospect to be acquired. This forecast should be for five years, although the buyer must realize that the latter years will become increasingly unreliable despite his best efforts. The emphasis must be on the first two years because that is the critical period for a new acquisition. If then it does not make its forecast, it probably never will and is unlikely to survive.

A prospect's financial history is an unreliable prophet, but it is the point of departure from which a buyer can forecast future earnings. Over reliance on past financial history as a guide to the future is a basic mistake for a buyer. Simple annual financial projections showing even proportioned growth each year starting with the latest financial statement is not realistic and also a mistake. The forecast should be carefully constructed with realistic sales and costs of sales estimates and include all costs and cost savings, capital requirements, and recoveries from liquidations that the buyer projects. The buyer should not deceive himself that the effects of his new management will be instantaneous regardless of how incompetent he perceives the present management. The forecast should also be done conservatively and not be distorted by a buyer's enthusiasm to acquire the prospect.

A buyer must construct his own forecasts as he cannot rely upon those of the seller, but he must recognize his forecasts are only his best educated guess and they will become distorted by all the uncertainties of the future. A buyer's price arguments to a seller will normally center around the prospect's past performance rather than anticipated future earnings, but the buyer must base his price calculations on the earnings and cash flow projected for the future. Earnings prior to the acquisition will do him no good at all. The seller will argue the potential of the company and future earnings and attempt to downplay past failures.

Forecast Effect on Buyer

A separate forecast showing additional expenses, savings, or profits to existing segments of the buyer's business as a result of the acquisition should also be constructed to give a complete picture. Profits arising in other parts of the buyer's business because of the acquisition are usually very difficult to accurately measure. This is because they are often buried in operations where overhead allocations could have a major effect and sometimes, despite the logic that benefits should exist, they just are not there. A buyer who believes he will enjoy incremental benefits to his operations but finds them impossible to measure should question his basic assumption. The logic of the probable existence of such benefits is usually persuasive to the point where it can become rationalization to support an acquisition. However, this may prove to be only an illusion and trap for the buyer if the benefits cannot clearly be measured.

Format of Forecast

When constructing forecasts, a buyer should develop them in the format to which he is accustomed in order to avoid confusion. If he follows a practice of assessing each subsidiary or division a management or parent company fee, this fee should either be omitted or forecasted earnings clearly depicted on a pre-fee and after-fee basis. The objective of the forecast is to show what additional income will accrue to the buyer as a result of the acquisition and such cannot be done if arbitrary charges are assessed out of proportion to services provided.

Forecasters should recognize that few businesses grow in even increments each year and even fewer businesses, other than high technology, new product companies, have much hope of enjoying a continuous five-year period of uninterrupted growth in which not one year will show a sales or profit decline from the prior year. It is politically difficult to include a bad year in a five-year forecast with only the rationale that it will probably happen. The valid argument of any board of directors will be that if a bad year is forecast, what steps will be taken to prevent the bad year. Regardless, a buyer would do well to include at least one poor performance year in his forecast to be realistic.

Another factor is that businesses seldom go on forever as they existed when acquired, making it necessary for the buyer to consider how long the business must survive to recover the investment. If a business will begin to decline within the first five years of ownership, the buyer had better reconsider his position unless his objective is to liquidate the company. Of course, businesses can continue indefinitely if they change, but change usually requires investment that must be included in the forecasts.

Cash Flow Forecast

The cash flow forecast is more important than the profit and loss forecasts and the result can lead a buyer to a very different conclusion. Cash flow projections will show how much and where the cash will come from to pay for the acquisition. Acquisitions by private companies are usually structured to maximize cash flow, delay taxes, and retard income recognition. Acquisitions by public companies tend to be structured to stress income rather than cash flow. If the acquisition has an international aspect to it and earnings occur in a country other than where the acquisition costs occur, careful study of currency regulations and taxes must be made and reflected in the cash flow forecast. Intense effort should go into developing as realistic a cash flow forecast as possible because it is so critical to the buyer.

A buyer faces a dilemma when deciding on whether or not to reveal his forecasts to the seller. The forecasts will be better and more accurate if from the seller's executives the buyer receives constructive comments and suggestions and agreement that the forecasts are attainable. No one knows a company better than the existing management. Because the forecasts also tend to become performance standards a retained management will be expected to achieve, it is only fair that they be informed of their contents. It is unreasonable to expect anyone to jump a hurdle they cannot see. However, the problem arises because a sophisticated seller can gain great insight into the buyer's position on price and use it against the buyer if he has access to his forecasts. Forecasts will also reveal contemplated changes in personnel, capital expenditure plans, facility closings, and other items that the buyer may prefer not to disclose. There is no ready answer to this question and each buyer will have to weigh the advantages against the disadvantages and recognize that whatever course he does take may cause regrets.

Structuring the Transaction

Structuring the specific transaction requires the assistance of financial and legal experts. For pricing purposes, a buyer must know if he will be buying the stock or selected assets and liabilities of the prospect and whether he intends to pay with stock, notes, cash, or whatever else. The characteristics of what is acquired plus the type of currency are critical factors in income projections and determination of the buyer's costs. A buyer should have a general understanding of how transactions can be structured, when each structure is applicable, the advantages and disadvantages of each, and their current status in light of any recent accounting, tax, regulatory, or legislative changes. An attorney active in corporate acquisitions can provide this information and it is a good test for a buyer to determine if his attorney is on top of his subject. A buyer can ask for an explanation of the basic types of acquisition structures which are:

1. "B" reorganization
2. Statutory merger
3. Triangular merger
4. Reverse triangular merger
5. "351" consolidation or nonstatutory consolidation
6. "C" reorganization
7. Statutory consolidation

He also should request a discussion on acquisitions of selected assets and liabilities. The buyer can easily read up on types of structures prior to meeting with his attorney to enable him to ask better questions, but only an attorney active in corporate mergers is qualified to discuss the complete ramifications of each structure and when they are applicable. A buyer will readily learn that few will ever be appropriate for his circumstances and he only needs to retain a familiarity with those that do apply.

Tax Implications

The tax implications of each structure must also be evaluated from the standpoint of the buyer and the seller. Each structure has its own peculiar tax characteristics that are extremely important to the parties and often the primary reason why a certain structure is selected. The buyer cannot take the position that a seller's tax problems are only the seller's. Although a buyer should structure the transaction if he can to reduce a seller's tax liability, he should not enter into transactions guaranteeing specific tax treatment. The seller must be encouraged to rely on his own tax advisors for opinions rather than the buyer.

The Internal Revenue Service of the United States will, upon request, issue letters of determination advising the parties in advance of closing of the government's position on tax questions, but most buyers find this route inadvisable. The IRS has such a deserved reputation for slow, narrow, and unpredictable rulings that relatively few wish to apply for such letters. Most prefer to rely upon their tax advisors and if the advice is challenged by the IRS, fight it out in court. It is years before a tax case is settled in court and if the parties acted in accordance with the advice of competent tax experts, there is little chance it will be challenged, and even less taken to court where the taxpayer is ruled against. In the meantime, the acquisition has long since been completed.

A buyer should take an aggressive stance in structuring a transaction by deciding what type of structure he wants and then advising his professionals to figure out how to do it. The professionals are then placed in the position of having to try and comply with their client's wishes or coming up with a superior solution. They are not able to simply pursue some easy course that may not be in their client's best interests. In most cases the direction received from their clients will be welcome.

The Basic Principles of Pricing

There are two basic principles upon which common sense pricing rests and a number of secondary principles, which are of varying degrees of importance but seldom applicable in every case. The principles will give the parties much more to work with than the common speculation of a buyer, "What do you think they will sell for?," or a seller, "About how much do you think they will pay?" Both types of speculation will always exist but more definite guidelines are needed. A buyer who refuses to violate the basic principles of "no dilution" and the "alternate investments rule" should find pricing relatively simple. With these principles he can determine the maximum prices he can afford to pay and still have a profit for his effort. A buyer who can establish his maximum price should have no difficulty in working out an offering price.

No Dilution of Earnings

The first basic principle is that every acquisition must contribute to a corporate buyer's earnings per share and under no conditions reduce earnings per share. The fundamental question about any acquisition is, "What will the acquisition do to a buyer's earnings per share next year?" The minimum amount of contribution to per share earnings acceptable should be established as a matter of policy. If the buyer acquires the company for stock, then the buyer must anticipate earnings per share of issued stock to equal earnings per share of the buyer's existing company plus an additional amount that we will call "earnings risk premium."

For example, a buyer with a 25% earnings risk premium policy, whose currently outstanding shares are forecast to earn $4.00 per share next year could issue to a seller only, the number of shares that would earn $5.00 per new issued share based on his forecast (divide forecasted earnings from the acquisition by the desired earnings per share to determine the maximum number of shares that can be issued). The number of shares offered multipled by the current market price per share would determine the value of the offer to the sellers. In this example, the buyer had decided he must have 25% as "earnings risk premium" ($4.00 + 25% of $4.00) for the transaction to be attractive to him from an earnings standpoint.

The percentage required for earnings risk premium is a basic decision each buyer must make for himself. A buyer should not go below 20%, and 50% would not be unreasonable. A buyer is actually basing his price on a forecast for the prospect and a forecast of his existing business. With two forecasts, the opportunity for error increases and arguments for a high earnings risk premium percentage take on considerable validity. Because the earnings risk premium percentage determines only the maximum price permissable, a buyer will find it practical to set a fixed percentage for all transactions and then reduce down further individual prices to reflect negative factors such as low net worth, earnings history, and management deficiency. Attempts to vary the percentage based on an overall judgment of the prospect and its desirability will unduly complicate the pricing process.

Obviously, the lower the earnings risk premium percentage, the higher the price a buyer can pay, but he also will be taking a greater risk if his forecasts prove inaccurate and he will receive less benefit for his effort. A high percentage will reduce the maximum price, lower the buyer's risk, and increase his return, but it will also reduce the chances of the buyer making acquisitions because his price becomes less attractive to the seller. A buyer must weigh all these factors in setting his percentage. The earnings risk premium does more than provide a cushion to cover errors in forecasting and constitute an incentive to buy. It also creates the funds that can be used to retire stock issued or debt created, or replace cash used to acquire the prospect, because every acquisition is expected to eventually pay for itself out of its own earnings. Creating a number of examples for his own industry will help a buyer decide what is a reasonable earnings risk premium for him.

A corporate buyer who uses cash or notes to acquire should follow the same principle. If he borrows cash or issues notes or debentures, then he must equate his forecasted earnings for the prospect against the cost of the borrowed or loaned money plus the earnings risk premium. As an example, a buyer who forecasts annual pre-tax earnings of $1,000,000 and used an earnings risk premium percentage of 25% would have $750,000 available to service debt. If interest rates were 10% on his borrowed cash or notes, the buyer's maximum price would be $7,500,000 ($750,000 = 10% × $7,500,000).

If the buyer need not borrow the cash or issue debt instruments and can pay from his available cash, then his base is the amount presently being earned on the money. As an example, assume forecast earnings of the prospect to be $1,000,000, and the buyer decides to apply a 30% earnings risk premium, which would mean $700,000 of present earnings from his money could be replaced by earnings from the acquisition and the buyer still gains $300,000 of additional earnings. Assuming 10% is the interest the buyer was earning on his money, his maximum price for the company would be $7,000,000.

The Alternate Investments Principle

The second basic principle for a buyer to follow is that an investment in an acquisition must have an anticipated return greater than the return readily attainable from relatively risk-free alternative investments. All acquisition investments have a high degree of risk and regardless of how convinced a buyer may be of the wisdom of an acquisition, he should receive a return on his investment better than what he could receive buying treasury bills, certificates of deposit, government obligations, or high-grade corporate bonds. How much premium return over safe alternative investments a buyer should have is an individual decision, but it should be at least 25%.

The forecasted return should also exceed the level of the buyer's present return on investment or whatever other return criteria is used. The buyer's definition of return on investment may produce a return higher or lower than that of safe alternative investments, but whichever is higher sets an absolute minimum acceptable return. A buyer presently receiving a 10% return on investment would have as a minimum level acceptable 12½% if his acquisition policy required 25% over the alternative safe investment level, which was at the time 10% (10% + 25% of 10% = 12½%). However, if the alternative safe investment level available was 16%, then the buyer's minimum acceptable return from an acquisition must be 20% (16% + 25% of 16%). If during the pricing process and subsequent negotiations, a buyer continually reviews the return possible from alternate investments, there is less chance he will become carried away and over pay. He also will have a persuasive argument to use with the seller by pointing out the reasonableness of his offer when compared to safe alternatives.

Calculate Total Investment

The buyer must include in his calculations all aspects of his investment and not just his initial price commitment. He must look at his
total investment. Acquisition costs in professional fees, travel,
studies, executive time, broker fees, and the like are not insignificant
items in any transaction but they become proportionally more important in smaller transactions. The cost of capital expenditures, research
and development, new facilities, personnel, benefit programs, etc.
must also be considered as investment or factored into the forecasts to
reflect, at least temporarily, a reduction in earnings. Most buyers will
prefer treating post-acquisition operational expenditures such as those
listed above as items that are expenses to be financed by the acquired
business without drawing on the funds of the buyer. Regardless, these
items must be accounted for in the buyer's investment calculations or
forecasts.

Return Calculations

Emphasis on the earnings level and rate of return for price calculation purposes will center around the first two years of ownership but
the long-term picture cannot be ignored. Ideally, the acquired company will grow at a faster rate than the rest of the buyer's business and
it must grow at a rate at least equal to the buyer's or eventually
dilution of earnings can occur. The long-term rate of growth for the
acquired and buyer must be estimated, and if the acquired's will slow
to less than that of the buyer, before the buyer recovers his investment, then the entire acquisition should be reconsidered. Of course,
any long-range growth projections possess the usual uncertainty, but
they are helpful in preventing obviously unfavorable acquisitions.

If the earnings of the acquired are all needed for expansion and the
buyer must use other funds to pay dividends on stock issued or to
service debt, the buyer's cash return may be inadequate. This may fit
very well with some buyer's program of increasing investment and
building equity, but for others the reinvestment requirements may be
incompatible and such an acquisition impossible. Every buyer must
carefully study the projections for an acquisition to determine the
excess cash that will be generated *by* the business and not required *in*
the business. Short-term cash forecasts can prove to be very different
from earnings forecasts and only cash will pay the interest, dividends,
or other obligations of a buyer.

Secondary Pricing Principles

The cost of consideration to be given sellers in relation to anticipated earnings does set a maximum price that a buyer can afford. However, other factors, which determine how much below the maximum a buyer should make his offer, enter into the pricing process. This is a very subjective decision that brings into play all the buyer's judgment and intuition about human behavior. A buyer can calculate mathematically how high he can go in price but not how low. The maximum price is of the greatest importance while the difference between it and any lower acceptable price constitutes a further benefit for the buyer, which makes the transaction all the more attractive. These secondary considerations should be explored in every acquisition.

What the Seller Wants

Most sellers have some idea as to what they want for their business although they may be reluctant to disclose the number, often on the theory that by some chance the buyer may offer a higher price. Both parties also know whoever presents their price first is at a disadvantage in the negotiations because that proposal will represent the maximum position for the party who proffered it and any bargaining concessions will result in a deterioration of the position. However, some sellers do decide they want a certain amount for their business and will sell at that price and not one cent less. This phenomenon of a seller's price being "set in concrete" is relatively common and can present a nearly impossible problem for a buyer if the price asked is higher than his maximum. If the price is lower, the buyer should have an easy negotiation. Exactly how a seller arrives at his price is often mysterious and not disclosed to the buyer. If the reasoning is disclosed, the buyer has the opportunity to challenge the logic, but that still may not change the seller's price.

Regardless of any calculations or rationale of a buyer in determining his price, the seller's views and logic or illogic as to what is wanted must be accommodated in some fashion or there will be no acquisition.

Going-price Illusions

Earlier in this chapter, it was argued that there are no such things as "fair" prices or "competitive" prices that set a going rate for certain types of businesses. This does not imply an absence of conversation in which people claim a certain price level is now standard, i.e., the "going price." Either party may seize upon these reports if it helps their case. In time they become self-fulfilling if transactions start to be made on a basis of what one or both parties believe to be the going price. A seller who has been led to believe by anyone that a certain price earnings ratio or multiple of book value is the present price for companies of his type will be difficult to dissuade, particularly so if he likes the result the so-called going price produced. This can be serious and present an obstacle for the buyer if the resultant price is too high, because few sellers are psychologically prepared to sell for a price lower than they believe others have received and they can receive if they look for other buyers.

Close questioning of a seller who claims going-price knowledge will invariably break down the concept revealing the going price was based on rumor or knowledge of one or possibly two acquisitions and the price *thought* paid. Unfortunately, the questions and logic may only further convince the buyer that a going price is nonsense and he may even convince the seller, but it may not change the seller's views on the price he will accept.

One exception when a going price of sorts does exist, is the case where the buyer has been very active in acquiring businesses of a certain type. If the buyer is the most active in making acquisitions in a certain area or an industry, then he will have established a price level. Here the price level is acceptable to the buyer so seller demands for the buyer to pay what he has paid others should be reasonable and most buyers will be willing to do so.

A well publicized acquisition of a company in the same industry as the prospect by someone other than the buyer will be an unavoidable point of discussion. Chances are good the prospects' decision-makers were personally familiar with the sellers. If the price paid is not a problem for the buyer, then he can use it to his advantage. However, if the price paid was high, the buyer had better be prepared to offer arguments as to why the companies are not comparable or the price was unreasonable.

Time Pressures

Either or both parties may be subject to any variety of pressures that would cause them to want to rapidly complete the acquisition. The party in the greatest hurry will usually be willing to make the largest price concessions. Being anxious to retire, seeing the business declining, needing capital, needing money for personal use, and/or having minority shareholders pressing for a sale are some of the conditions creating urgency for sellers. Buyers may want to complete a transaction within a fiscal year, need to show some results of an acquisition program, want to buy before their stock declines in value and/or want the seller's cash among other things.

The reverse condition may also prevail where either the buyer or seller act only if conditions are entirely to their liking and under no pressure at all. A seller may decide he will never sell unless he gets his price and if no one offers his price today, he will retain ownership and wait until someone comes along who will and, in the meantime, he will keep improving the business. Some buyers will only buy if they can make an extremely attractive deal at a very low price. They will keep shopping until what they believe is the right situation comes along oblivious of the cost of their shopping and the loss of earnings from companies they could have acquired while shopping.

Regardless of reasoning and motivation, time pressures and how urgently either the buyer or seller wants to act can be a major factor in setting price.

Perquisites and Salaries

The seller's decision-makers may enjoy benefits from their position that are very dear to them. High salary levels, hunting and fishing camps, free travel, club memberships, and the like may be of such importance that a buyer can secure the business at a lower price if he provides for their continuance. Any benefit to a selling shareholder or decision-making executive can be evaluated and the cost quantified. This cost simply becomes part of the price and is recognized as such. A wise buyer will not become too troubled with how any personal benefits retained by a seller or his decision-makers fit with his overall policies if the entire price of the acquisition is attractive. Generous salaries and benefits retained by executives of acquired companies that exceed those granted executives in the balance of the buyer's organization can become a source of controversy and even jealousy as time passes and the pricing rationale fades from the participant's memory. Perquisites are under increasing attack by the IRS as taxable income, but this will largely be a problem for the sellers.

Premium Over Market

If the prospect's stock is publicly traded, the buyer must be prepared to offer a premium over the present market price. The amount of premium necessary will be determined by a number of factors that the buyer must judge as to their importance, which will vary greatly with each prospect and the times.

A key factor at any time will be the amount of premium others are currently paying. A buyer can easily make his own calculations to determine true averages and select acquisitions as examples to give a seller when the premium was not exorbitant. Buyers with an active acquisition program who expect to acquire public companies should, on a continuous basis, record the prices per share being offered with the prices of the stocks a month before the offers were made and at the time the offers are made. Acquisitions of public companies and the prices paid are routinely announced in the *Wall Street Journal*, which can be saved for enough weeks to provide the month-old market data. Because of the problem of insider leaks and resultant heavy purchases of stock in the few weeks before an offer is made, the premium over the prior month's market price is more realistic. Sophisticated prospect shareholders realize that any increase in their share values caused by insider trading can vanish as quickly as it appeared if an offer is not forthcoming from a buyer.

In a study of premiums paid, a buyer will find that premiums vary greatly with each acquisition reflecting the condition of the companies and the desire or lack of desire of key decision-makers to sell. The amount of premium being paid by others is of such importance in negotiations that the buyer must be prepared with facts to support the reasonableness of the premium he offers.

Public company prospects whose shares are heavily concentrated in the hands of one individual or a small group will require a premium that reflects the present desire of the controlling shareholders to sell. Controlling shareholders cannot easily sell all or part of their holdings without following strict procedures established by government regulations. If they are uncertain about the company's future or they simply wish to diversify their holdings, they may be content with a relatively small premium. However, if they have little desire to sell, the premium will be large as they present all sorts of arguments to support their contention that the market has undervalued their shares. The market price is partially an expression of opinion regarding the prospect's management and controlling shareholders, which creates further problems for sellers attempting to prove their shares are undervalued.

The buyer has an obligation to present a convincing case that his offer is generous in light of current performance and the company's prospects. It is not the buyer but the prospect's officers and directors who are sued by disgruntled shareholders if they accept and recommend a price to the shareholders that they cannot justify. The buyer must help them by providing a convincing and documented case. These same directors and officers may be sued by shareholders if they reject an offer as too low if the buyer's offer was generous by current standards.

Financing Difficulties and Cash Buyers

When economic conditions cause financing to become difficult to secure or virtually unobtainable as occurred in 1980, the buyer with cash is in a strong position to drive a hard bargain with those who want to sell. Unsettled financial conditions also cause a decline in the market price of listed companies' stock, making stock unattractive for use by a buyer. Under these conditions, a seller has to accept cash or notes from a buyer or wait and hope for improved times. No matter how bad a shape the economy may be in, some can imagine it worse and will choose to sell now for a low price rather than wait for better times. The buyer with cash need not be reluctant to take advantage of the situation. Some buyers accumulate cash with the expectation of making advantageous acquisitions when other buyers are out of the market during the low point of an economic cycle. There is a problem with this approach in that only with hindsight can one determine the bottom of an economic cycle and it can be a long wait trying to decide when is the right time to buy.

Stock Market Performance

If the buyer expects to acquire with his stock as currency, then its past performance in the market as well as its market value at the time of making the acquisition will be important to the seller. Past performance in the market is far from being a reliable guide to its performance in the future. However, a stock that has shown steady increases in value will be looked on more favorably than one that has been erratic or has shown consistent decline.

A buyer should attempt to use favorable stock performance as an argument for holding down the price, but he must be cautious in his presentation. Under no conditions should a buyer indicate his publicly traded stock will attain a specific price. He can point to the past record and say he knows of no probable cause why it will not continue to increase in value and he can claim great optimism, but conclusions on future price levels should strictly be left up to the seller. A buyer does not want to express such confidence in his future success and the stock's performance that the seller will demand a guarantee of the stock's performance or bring suit after the acquisition that he was misled into believing the stock would increase to a certain value.

Some foolish buyers attempt to use in price discussions the value of their stock as they speculate it will be at some time in the future. This is not only a dangerous approach for a buyer, it is one that will convince only the most desperate and naive sellers.

Regardless of the uncertainty and problems, a strongly performing buyer's stock should be a factor in setting the price. Sellers tend to look favorably on a company whose stock has out-performed the market.

Comparison with Public Companies

How a prospect stacks up financially against public companies in similar businesses can easily be determined and used as a factor in pricing. For many industries surveys already exist and are found in trade publications or in studies of the industry performed by investment bankers. If surveys cannot be located, annual reports of the leading companies can be secured and the buyer may conduct his own comparisons.

The main areas of comparison will be financial ratios such as percent of pretax profit to sales, percent of gross profit to sales, current ratio, inventory turnover, receivable turnover, debt-equity ratio, compounded annual sales and earnings growth, and any other data the buyer considers important. This information will give the buyer an indication of how well the prospect compares in its industry and what level of price may be justified. If one of the companies studied was recently sold and the price paid is known, it is all the more essential the buyer have full information on the industry.

Currency Exchange Rates

If the transaction is international and the buyer is located in a country other than the seller, currency exchange rates can be a major factor. All one has to do is review the ups and downs of the dollar within the past five or ten years against other major currencies to see how significant a factor this can be. Few buyers would classify themselves as currency speculators, but in an indirect sense, this is what they are doing when they make an international acquisition. They have all the usual business risks associated with an acquisition plus those associated with currency exchange. This should be taken into consideration in setting a price.

Prospect and Price—The Moving Targets

An offer should be structured to recognize the fact that the business condition of the prospect has been and will continually change. A period of time will elapse between the date of the financial statement upon which the buyer bases his offer and the date of the offer, and between the date of the offer and the closing. Both periods can be relatively short or quite prolonged, but in any period significant changes can occur that could change the value of the business.

If the acquisition is made on the basis of acquiring the stock of the prospect for cash or notes, then it is simplest to peg the price to the net worth on the last financial statement and let the price vary with the net worth. If the acquisition is structured on a purchase of selected assets and liabilities basis, then the price can vary with their value at time of closing. However, in both cases great care and precision must be used to define the accounting rules and principles that will be used in valuing net worth and assets. This must be negotiated by the buyer and seller and it cannot be left up to the accountants to select the rules they will use. Reputable ones will not conduct the valuation unless their clients approve the rules and methods.

If the buyer uses stock to acquire, the added problem of placing a value on his stock occurs because its market value can change each day the exchanges are open. This problem can be attacked in a number of ways. A price range for the buyer's stock can be set and if the price goes above or below the range, the transaction is subject to renegotiation. The average price of the shares for an agreed number of days prior to closing may be used in calculating the number of shares to be issued with the total price having been negotiated. A total price may be negotiated and the market price on the day before closing used to calculate the number of shares to be issued. In cases where stock is being exchanged for stock, a ratio can be negotiated whereby the seller receives for each of his shares an agreed number and/or fraction of the buyer's shares and this ratio remains fixed unless either party's shares exceed a certain range. The number of methods of accommodating changes is only limited by the imaginations of the parties.

No approach for accommodation of changes in the prospect's business or stock values is without its faults, but a negotiated concept is far better than none. It is much easier to negotiate a procedure at the time an offer is made when future changes are only speculative than it is after the changes have occurred. Establishing early in the negotiations and/or at the time of making an offer the concept that the price can change with the value of the prospect's business and the value of the buyer's shares will prevent at a later date possible charges of bad faith bargaining or reneging on an agreement if significant changes do occur and no mechanism exists for price adjustment. A buyer is not placed in the position of either accepting the changes or walking away. Regardless of any negotiated formula, if extreme changes in value do occur, either one or both parties will insist upon a renegotiation or abandon the transaction. Because, prior to closing, either party can always find a way to get out of a deal they no longer wish to make, this is the ultimate protection.

Price Calculations

A buyer should calculate his highest possible price using the no dilution and alternate investment principles after he has completed his forecasts of earnings anticipated from the acquired and new earnings in his present operations if such will occur. From this maximum price he can scale down his price by evaluating the importance of applicable secondary factors. Care must be exercised to include all of the investments in the calculation and not just the amounts to be paid to the selling shareholders. The establishment of a maximum price a buyer can pay with the transaction remaining financially attractive clarifies the entire pricing process and gives the buyer a sensible basis from which to develop an offer and negotiate. In common sense pricing the buyer works from the top price down rather than starting at the bottom without a maximum amount that will be offered under any condition. A buyer using this approach to pricing must have the self-discipline to refuse to exceed his precalculated maximum price level and pursue other alternatives regardless of how much he may covet the prospect.

The offer finally developed should be reviewed to see how it will personally affect the key decision-makers of the seller. The offer must be attractive to them and this is the primary objective for the buyer in structuring his offer. If it is not attractive for the decision-makers, the offer must be modified so that it will be. This can be accomplished by increasing the price or by techniques such as proposing generous employment, pensions, incentive compensation, or consulting agreements on top of continuation of existing benefits. The cost of these must be factored into the forecasts and earnings projections modified accordingly. Fringe benefits and perquisites should be granted if necessary and accounted for the same way.

Legal review of any special consideration for seller decision-makers is always essential to avoid later charges of impropriety or even commercial bribery. Often in the negotiations the key decision-makers are primarily concerned about how an offer benefits them and have minimal concern about meeting legal obligations to other shareholders, the employees, and/or the public. When large sums are to be paid out as occurs in acquisitions, avaricious self-interest will not be far away.

The status factors for the seller decision-makers are also of great importance and usually cost the buyer little or nothing. Position titles are of such concern to some decision-makers that they will not accept unless they retain their title or have an even better one. The buyer should be perceptive enough to see the status needs without the seller having to bring it up. Automobiles, club memberships, participation in community affairs can all be status symbols that must be retained if a deal is to be made.

Tax Implications

Any offer developed by a buyer should be reviewed by a tax expert to determine the tax implications and if the transaction and offer could be structured in another way that would be more advantageous to the buyer, seller, or both. Much of this activity will center around depreciation, how it is treated, and values placed on assets that can be depreciated. A buyer will normally want to write up assets in value to permit greater depreciation and cash flow. Sellers may have added tax liability if the assets are booked by the buyer at a higher value than the seller has them prior to the sale.

Tax ramifications are broad and varied and a buyer will be wise to have a top tax advisor at his side throughout the acquisition process. Tax advantages or disadvantages can be the key factor in whether or not a transaction should be made using a particular structure or possibly made at all.

Liquidation Values

The value at which a prospect could be liquidated is a factor to consider in price calculations, but its importance is not great if the buyer expects to operate the acquired. Liquidation values usually provide more psychological comfort to a buyer than anything else, because prices for used assets vary greatly from year-to-year and liquidation costs are seldom known in advance. The condition of assets is almost certain to decline if the time of the new buyer's ownership was largely a time of losses. However, the buyers are not usually acquiring the business to lose money and liquidate assets but expect to generate operational profits with the assets.

Acquisitions with high assets values are easier to finance because of the collateral they provide. Lenders feel more secure if they believe they have hard assets they can liquidate if default occurs.

Final Price

After a buyer calculates his maximum price and then considers all the other factors described, he will evolve a price which is a synthesis of his best judgment as to what would be appropriate. The price should be in round numbers; otherwise, the buyer will have to justify how he arrived at the precise numbers and open himself up for unnecessary criticism of his approach and concepts. Imprecision has its merits in pricing. The last digit in every price should be "0," and the number of zeros at the end increases with the price.

The final price should not reflect a buyer's desire to nearly steal a prospect. Buyers must be willing to pay top prices for quality companies that have strong management and earnings records. They can pay lesser prices for companies of lower quality. Trying to buy at a lower price is a natural desire but a low price does not necessarily mean a favorable deal. Some companies are so bad, they can not, and should not, be given away.

Two Tough Pricing Problems

In pricing there are two types of companies which are particularly difficult to price. The most difficult is the growth company with very high earnings and earnings projections in relation to net worth, and the next is the company with a high net worth or high market value of assets and little or no earnings. The discrepancies between earnings and net worth create problems for the parties that can only be resolved with compromises supported by strong desires to conclude the acquisition.

High Earnings, Low Net Worth Company

In this type of growth company a buyer is confronted with a potential extreme goodwill assumption. Paying a price based only on an earnings record and expectations would leave the buyer exposed with his investment largely lost if the earnings did not materialize. He would have few assets to fall back upon to liquidate and recover at least part of his investment.

From a buyer's point of view there are no fully satisfactory solutions. He can negotiate the lowest price possible and accept the exposure. He can propose to purchase a minority of the shares with rights to acquire the balance over a period of time if the earnings materialize.

The other alternative is a contingent payment plan where a portion of the price is held back and not paid unless certain earnings targets are met. Contingent or earnout payment plans are frought with pitfalls and inequities, largely for the buyer. All too often the buyer and seller end up in court if the buyer does not eventually pay the full price, because a seller can allege he was prevented from earning the forecasted amount because of the buyer's acts. Plans for contingency payment should be looked upon as a plans of last resort after all else failed. For some sophisticated buyers offers of contingency payment plans are presented as bargaining positions, while knowing full well that upon close study by the seller they will prove unacceptable, but will set the stage for another proposal that is firm.

High Net Worth, Low Earnings Company

Prospects with high asset values and low earnings present the problem for a buyer primarily interested in a going business of being asked to pay a value for the assets and business that the earnings do not justify. The seller's lowest price is what they believe the business will bring in a liquidation. The buyer who is reluctant, as well as ill prepared to enter into a liquidation, can not afford to pay a price that is not based on earnings potential. Valuable assets that produce no income is like cash deposited in non-interest bearing accounts. Again, compromises have to be evolved if a transaction is to occur. In some cases a partial liquidation is the solution, but seldom does a solution exist satisfactory to both parties. Regardless of any asset values, the buyer must make his earnings forecasts, base his price on the forecasts, and not place a high value on the assets unless he is prepared to liquidate the company.

Making the Offer

The offer should be made by the buyer executive who has the best rapport with the seller's key decision-makers. The better they have come to know each other, the better advantage it will be for the buyer. Not that the buyer should expect price concessions as a result of the friendship, but rather he will have a full opportunity to explain his offer and when disagreement occurs, discussions will more likely continue. The buyer should not be disappointed if he does not receive immediate agreement and should be prepared for a long campaign. If the relationship is excellent and both sides can openly present their views and opinions, the chances are good agreement will eventually result. Even if the first positions of the parties are too far apart and appear beyond immediate compromise, the views or circumstances of one or both can change in time with an agreement the result. An early objective in presenting the offer is simply to keep talking.

The most effective means of presenting an offer is an oral presentation consisting of a detailed explanation of a formal written offer, which is given to the seller simultaneously, with an account of how the offer was developed and its rationale. A common problem is that sellers often do not understand the offers made partly because they are poorly presented and partly because the sellers are not familiar with the terms and procedures occurring in acquisition situations. Offers should not be mailed or telexed because this method of communication precludes the effective face-to-face explanation and sales arguments.

The buyer's first step is to prepare a written offer that he himself fully understands and is approved within his own organization. Placing the offer in writing will also force the buyer to make decisions on all phases of the offer and bring all issues out into the open for resolution. Another factor is a seller can only agree if he knows the complete offer. Any written offer should also have legal and accounting review, although the buyer should guard against an offer that is full of legal jargon. Ideally, the offer will be placed into the format of a letter of intent that contains all significant provisions of the offer and closes with space for both parties to sign. The buyer should give a copy signed by him to the seller. If he has not signed it prior to presentation, the impression is given that it is only a bargaining offer.

The letter of intent is not legally binding on the parties but it does constitute something of a gentleman's agreement to proceed. Misunderstandings are avoided through its use and it can constitute clear instructions to the attorneys as to the basic terms to be incorporated into the definitive contracts. Basic provisions commonly found in a letter of intent are: names of parties; what exactly is being acquired; price; description of consideration to be used if other than cash; terms of payment; reference to warranties and representations; special provisions covering items such as employment agreements, competition covenants, stock sales, perquisites; and any other items important to the agreement. The letter of intent should also include time limits for completion of the definitive contracts and state what additional approvals are required.

The presentation to the seller of the offer should be a paragraph by paragraph explanation of the written offer. The buyer should explain in detail the meaning and purposes of each paragraph and will be wise to over-explain rather than skim over parts he considers to be clear enough. The buyer should remember that most sellers are not accustomed to looking at formal offers.

The offer should include all key aspects of the transaction, such as employment agreement, directorships, and continuation of perquisites, although these personal benefits for the decision-makers may be in general or near cryptic terminology. However, the most important part of the offer will be the price and this will command the first attention of the seller. It is not enough for the buyer to simply give the price without explanation of how it was developed. An explanation of how it was determined and all of the factors that went into the buyer's thinking will be the best approach. The buyer's emphasis will be on past earnings and present net worth, rather than on future projections. The buyer's explanation should convince the seller that while he may be disappointed in the offer, the buyer did not just pull the offer out of the air, but has carefully studied the prospect and concluded this is what it is worth to him.

An intelligent, logical explanation of how the price was developed will largely preclude making of undesirable, extremely low offers for which there is no logic. Very low bargaining offers that the buyer can not defend and has little expectations of being accepted repel the seller and discredit the buyer. A wise buyer should leave some room in his position to make a few concessions from his initial offer for bargaining purposes, but the initial offer should be fairly close to the buyer's final position. The buyer should not be making offers for which he need apologize, which will be the case if he attempts to explain very low bargaining offers. He will lose his credibility if at a later time he attempts to justify the higher price he should have made initially. The buyer must make a case that his offer is reasonable based on his understanding of the prospect and he is proud to present it. This puts the seller in the position where he can argue price by presenting new facts or challenging the buyer's assumptions, which will keep the price negotiations on a rational, rather than emotional, plane.

11.
Negotiation

Negotiation is any activity between two or more parties in which an exchange of philosophies, concepts, information, and respective positions occurs for the purpose of bringing about an agreement. In acquisitions this is a continuous and complex process often involving many levels of authority and different people, most of whom do not look at themselves as negotiators or as participants in negotiations.

Contrary to popular belief, acquisition negotiations seldom consist of executives seated on two sides of a table utilizing all sorts of clever and devious strategies to induce their opponents to accept distasteful positions. A wise buyer realizes negotiations for a friendly takeover commence with the first informal meeting of the parties and continues until either discussions fail and are discontinued or an agreement is reached and closing occurs. This interchange of information, ideas, and positions occurs during many meetings, telephone calls, or other modes of communications in settings ranging from small private meetings to brief conversations during entertainment activities, but rarely in formal meetings with negotiators going at each other hammer and tongs. In fact, the basic objective of every buyer should be to avoid bitter confrontations and the stereotypical picture of negotiations. The buyer should strive for a series of cordial information exchanges with both parties attempting to jointly develop a mutually beneficial agreement. Conflict, strategies, defeats, and victories do occur but these are concepts to be avoided as much as possible and the optimum negotiation would be the one where the participants did not realize it had occurred as they signed the contracts.

All meetings between buyer and seller are in a sense negotiating meetings. A buyer describes himself to establish his capabilities for the seller to evaluate as acceptable. The seller explains the needs of his business and the shareholder's requirements, which the buyer may or may not be able to fulfill. The buyer presents his philosophies and policies that a seller finds reasonable or impossible to accept. The seller gives the financial condition of his company and its outlook, which tends to establish a broad price range for a buyer. Each bit of information and communication helps establish a framework for the parties, which becomes tacitly acceptable by a willingness to continue discussions after the information is communicated to the other. The more information presented and the more views communicated and accepted, the broader becomes the framework of agreement and the area for differences continues to narrow. Eventually the parties reach the point where both want to go ahead with the transaction and they reach agreement on price either orally or in a letter of intent.

Preliminary Agreements Often Fail

Agreement may or may not be publicly announced at the price agreement stage, but there is still a long time and much work to complete before a closing occurs and often a closing never occurs. Every buyer should study why so many preliminary agreements are reached but a final agreement is never achieved. At times, it appears the financial press has as many announcements of preliminary acquisition agreements terminated as consummated. The reasons and combinations of reasons vary greatly with each case but some do prevail more often and are described below.

1. Circumstances for one or both parties may change, such as major shifts in the market price of their stock, unexpected improvement or decline in business, changes in the economy, changes in government policy, or simply loss of nerve.
2. There may never have been full agreement and when the items not agreed to had to be settled, the parties found agreement to be impossible. Often, parties to negotiations erroneously assume an issue has been settled to their satisfaction because the other party no longer brings it up, but actually, the other party is assuming the same thing. Bargainers may assume settlement of what they perceive to be the major issues will assure settlement of the minor ones. However, what may be minor to one is very major to the other and pride will increase its importance once the dispute is in the open.
3. Those who entered into the agreement could not deliver on their promises. Trust officers, minority shareholders, or employees refused to go along with the negotiated deal. Either board of directors may refuse to approve the acquisition and repudiate its negotiators.

4. The buyer or seller turned out to be different than represented. Usually, it is the seller who has defects exposed during the comprehensive evaluation that scare off the buyer, but the seller can also learn enough of the buyer to decide he does not want to proceed.
5. The buyer's key executives cease the romance too soon and leave negotiating the definitive agreement and transitional program up to weak subordinates. The subordinates are not capable or interested in concluding the deal.
6. The acquisition may prove to be contrary to government policy and be disallowed.
7. Acquisition negotiations and transactions are highly specialized and complex activities requiring the attention of able experienced executives and professionals. Inexperienced participants who assume they know far more than they do can foul up a negotiation. They differ from all other business negotiations and must be recognized as such to succeed.

The Uniqueness of Acquisition Negotiations

An awareness of the unusual characteristics and unique requirements of acquisition negotiations and negotiators will help a buyer to succeed in bringing negotiations to a favorable conclusion. Every acquisition is different and at least the circumstances for the sellers vary greatly, creating a real need and opportunity for imagination. However, there are similarities in a broad sense that should be recognized.

Negotiation is a continuous process commencing with the first contact and not ending until the definitive agreement is signed. All the discussions, comments, revised positions, and agreements on sections of the contracts are of no value until the final agreement is signed. It is on an all or nothing basis with nothing final until all is final. This is best for both parties because many parts of an agreement are interrelated and a final decision can not be made until the entire picture is clear. If bargaining has occurred with tradeoffs and compromises, a participant has to weigh the points he achieved against those he did not and decide if in balance the transaction is good for him. Actually, all parties must believe the acquisition is beneficial to them or they will find a way to back away.

Nearly every decision and every move of both parties comes under review by members of the buyer's or seller's organization as well as by accountants, attorneys and other specialists. The transactions are so complex and the ramifications of seemingly minor points so great that extensive advice and review of decisions is inescapable. As a result of the reviews and participation by professionals, the chances of one party or the other succeeding with bargaining strategies designed to mislead, beguile, or deceive another into unknowingly agreeing to unsound provisions is remote.

The personal positions of the negotiators are very different. The sellers attempt to secure the best price and protect themselves because they are giving up control of what has been a major source of livelihood or, in distress sales, they are giving up hope of the business improving and bringing prosperity. They personally have more at stake than the buyer's negotiators, who tend to look at the negotiations more as a challenge and game, the outcome of which can advance their careers or further their personal ambitions. Buyers can simply look for other prospects if negotiations fail and they will find it easier to explore alternatives than the sellers who are stuck with their limited situation. Buyer negotiators find it easy to blame failure on the intransigence of the sellers while sellers must partially blame themselves for failing to convince a buyer of their worth.

Buyers who seek out sellers are the aggressors and they are generally far more committed to their positions and policies and obligated to make themselves understood than are the sellers. Whatever information a buyer presents to a seller commits him from the first meeting on, and he can not easily change his position without loss of credibility, even if he has an opportunity to change. As an example, a buyer who initially announces to a prospect that in the past he has only made acquisitions with unregistered stock may find that the seller will not see him again if such stock is unacceptable; while the buyer's real position may be that he has used only unregistered stock for acquisitions, and prefers to do so in the future, although cash is available for fine acquisitions if required by the seller. A seller is free to frequently change his position on selling and terms with the justification that he is now thinking more seriously about selling and his views are changing because of the buyer's persuasive arguments. The seller is more free to claim he misunderstood the buyer, as was the case in the example where the buyer's position, essentially a bargaining one, cost him the opportunity.

Most executives in senior management positions have substantial experience in negotiations and fancy themselves to be competent negotiators. Some are and some are not, but generally there is a minimum level of competence. However, the individual differences in background, motivation, and experience of the sellers is so diverse that a buyer can not always rely on any one negotiator, negotiating approach, or a standard style, but must adjust to each situation and the observed competence of the sellers. The buyer negotiators may have a superior knowledge of the technical and legal aspects of an acquisition, but they are not necessarily better in understanding human nature, recognizing values, and negotiating price. The seller who is selling his life work and income source has plenty of incentive to represent his own interests as well as possible. The seller also has the advantage of knowing and understanding the business being sold better than the buyer. More often than not it is an even contest with strengths and weaknesses offsetting each other with neither party doing more than a fair job of negotiating and looking after self interests. When one side finds the other's actions and positions incomprehensible, it will more probably be correct to suspect bungling and ineptness, rather than some subtle ingenious bargaining strategy.

In acquisitions the stakes are high. No other nongovernmental activity can involve such large sums as a major acquisition. The individual participants' careers and net worths can be affected by the outcome to a degree greater than that of almost any other business activity. The opportunity for large gains as well as huge losses is present and the participants' perception of the future, skill in negotiating, and to some degree good or bad fortune will determine their success. An ability to make one hundred thousand or million dollar demands or concessions while keeping sight of the penny items is essential. The participants must be able to look at the total picture and be prepared to make large moves while not losing track of the lesser components of the transaction.

Preparations for Negotiations

The importance of thorough preparation for any meetings with prospects and continuing throughout the negotiations can not be over estimated. In-depth preparation will do more to bring about a successful negotiation and conclusion of an acquisition than all the bargaining strategy and techniques ever promoted to business executives. Ample preparation to provide the buyer with a complete understanding of the situation including his own objectives coupled with common sense gives the buyer almost everything he needs to conduct the negotiations.

A traveler who knows precisely where he is and where he wants to go can usually find his way if he has the determination to do so. The buyer must assimilate all the information accumulated about the prospect's business, industry, and owners, and develop his own positions on the issues anticipated. The quantity of information is large and can not possibly be 100% committed to paper, making it advisable for a buyer to have a continuity of personnel throughout any acquisition. Preparation involves a continuous analysis of the situation based on all information available and determination of the buyer's position on every issue that might conceivably arise both with bargaining positions and objectives. A buyer must first know his own position on an issue before a seller can be persuaded to accept it. Buyer representatives who have not done their homework and must continually tell the seller they will "check back" for an answer soon lose their credibility. This is unexcusable because most issues are foreseeable and a buyer can develop his position and justification of the position before the sellers bring up the subject.

An analysis of the positions, motivation and aspirations of the seller's decision-makers also should be conducted continually throughout the acquisition process and every effort should be made to understand the acts and reasoning of the sellers. In the typical acquisition endless amounts of time will be spent speculating on what the other party's decision-makers will or will not do and reading into their comments and acts, which would be better taken at face value, all sorts of hints, nuances, and implications that do not exist. Their positions should be respected and not immediately depreciated as unimportant or clever bargaining strategies. Understanding can lead a buyer to finding ways of accommodation or develop means to bring about a change. Opinions and positions do change and a buyer's negotiator should be perceptive enough to recognize changes have occurred rather than hang on to first impressions. On occasion, the seller may appear to change, but only because the buyer has new information and insight that has transformed the buyer's view.

Seller evaluation also includes determining whether or not the seller representatives can follow through and do what they claim. Can they clean up problem areas in the company, control the board of directors and "deliver" other shareholders? The buyer has every right to direct these and similar questions to the seller representatives. His questions should not be limited to "Can you do it?" but also "How?" and "When?" The ability to perform as claimed is so basic to the negotiating process that these questions can not be deferred on the belief that they are too sensitive to ask.

Preparations involve an understanding of the type of sale and its effect upon the outlook of the participants. As owner, founder, or manager of a profitable business will have very different views and command a totally different negotiation than a CEO conducting the divestiture of a marginal subsidiary. The negotiations to acquire a seller's equity in a profitable business with which he is not involved will be totally unlike those where the seller desperately wants to dispose of a sick company. The type of sale is a basic determinant for the motivation to sell and is one factor that is normally readily apparent.

Preparation that builds a conviction of the desirability of the acquisition helps instill the buyer with the patience and enthusiasm necessary for negotiations. Patience is needed to permit the sellers to assimilate the information and offers presented and understand the reasoning behind them. Patience is also needed to persuade key members of the buyer organization that the acquisition should be made. Enthusiasm keeps the entire process moving and builds as the buyer becomes more and more convinced the acquisition would be desirable both for him and the seller. Buyer executives who are also enthusiastic and proud of their present company make a strong favorable impression on sellers. Preparation brings confidence and understanding that helps remove many of the doubts and emotion that can creep into a negotiation.

Negotiating Decisions and Approvals

When the relationship between the buyer and seller progresses to a point where an offer can be made and seriously considered, the negotiations enter a new phase. Prior to this time philosophies, general information, and descriptions of policies and precedents have been exchanged to establish a general framework. Now, very specific and precise positions must be presented in an offer, counterproposals, if necessary, and the completion of the definitive contracts to be signed at closing. The nature of the decisions to be made, their approval, and how they will be presented to a seller is of critical importance to any buyer. The individual investor, who is something of a one-man band, only has himself to look to for decision approval, but all the decisions are still there to be made.

Negotiating decisions or bargaining latitude and the various approvals of those decisions are interrelated and must be analyzed together. Each buyer must evolve his own system, that will surely be influenced by the amount of authority delegated by a board of directors, the competence of the negotiators, the confidence the board has in the negotiator, and the prior experience the buyer has in making acquisitions.

Types of Decisions

Negotiations with prospects involves numerous and frequent decisions, many of which can not be anticipated in advance. In any acquisition easily over one hundred identifiable decisions will have to be made during the course of the negotiations with a substantial number of these after agreement is reached on basic terms. It is best for decisions to be reached promptly because it is psychologically detrimental to have long delays before decisions are made as a result of cumbersome approval procedures or inability to decide. The buyer's negotiator should have established in advance his position on most subjects or have bargaining latitude in which to negotiate. There always will be some items that a negotiator may want to study or seek advice or approval on, but frequent "checking back" will reduce his credibility. The negotiators will be confronted with four general categories of decisions.

1. *Foreseeable Basic Decisions.* Basic decisions are those which establish the general terms of the acquisition and upon which the buyer can establish his position in advance. In this category would be items such as price and, whether or not to use cash, notes, stock, or other debt instruments. Registration and sale rights of stock and basic terms for any debt instruments are other questions for advance decisions.

2. *Unforeseen Basic Decisions.* Critical, unforeseen problems or basic questions can and do arise during negotiations and require decisions. These are of major importance to the buyer and usually are items of the type listed in 1. above, where the buyer's first position proved unacceptable to the seller or modifications in the buyer's position become justified by new developments. It would be a rare negotiation if the seller fully accepted whatever the buyer first offered.

3. *Decisions Decided on a Basis of Policy or Practice.* Decisions in which an adequate body of past practice or predetermined policy existed for the negotiator to have a general frame of reference should be the largest group of decisions and also the one where the decisions can most easily be made. The better the buyer has done his job of constructing acquisition policies and the more comprehensive are his policies, the easier will be these decisions. The length of time a buyer has been actively seeking acquisitions and gaining experience will also enter into this category of decisions, because the experience will have involved decisions that can now serve as precedents. Positions on warranties and representations, employment agreements, minor asset valuations, amounts to be escrowed, and scheduling of closing are examples of decisions in this category.

4. *Professional Decisions.* These decisions usually are made or greatly influenced by professionals such as attorneys, accountants, or actuaries. While the importance of these decisions can

not be downplayed, they are ones that normally can be resolved between professionals and will not hold up an acquisition. Often, these decisions are more "how to do it" rather than "what to do."

Communication and Guidelines

If the buyer negotiator has the authority to make all major decisions as a result of his ownership position, control of the board, or powers delegated by the board, there is no approval problem. However, most buyers are more structured with the negotiators having their work reviewed and approved by some higher authority. A buyer's negotiator can recommend for approval or be given bargaining guidelines that are approved in advance by key executives or the board of directors for major decisions in category 1 above. However, no guidelines will be adequate to cover all the unforeseen problems and questions that come up in a complex acquisition negotiation.

The practical solution for prompt decision-making is for the buyer's principal negotiator to routinely make the decision of category 3 above and have available an executive or very small committee with whom he can consult to arrive at decisions for the major questions in category 2. Decisions made in these consultations would be considered to have a very high probability of acceptance by the board of directors, and those who participated in the consultation would be expected to vigorously support the decisions before the full board. The executive involved would normally be the CEO, but it could be a small committee of board members. Often in these category 2 items, it is less a problem of making a decision as one of exchanging ideas and trying to develop the best approach to solve a problem. The system is predicated upon the buyer's negotiator having ready access to the executive or group responsible for making acquisition decisions. If these people are inaccessible because of travel, lack of interest, or heavy time requirements by other facets of their positions and can not give a high priority to acquisition decisions, they become a real hindrance to the acquisition program.

It is not an ideal arrangement of a buyer's negotiator to negotiate a complete agreement covering the entire range of issues without the benefit of guidelines or consultation, reach total agreement on all points, and then submit the package to a CEO or board of directors for approval. Regardless of how the agreement is presented to them for review and approval, they are actually placed in the position of being on a "take-it-or-leave-it" basis. In practice, if they pick out one or two items they find offensive and instruct their negotiator to renegotiate their content or existence, they not only reduce the credibility of their negotiator but they run a high risk of losing the acquisition, because they have essentially rejected the entire agreement. Owners will find rejection at the last minute of points previously agreed upon highly offensive and they will have every right to claim bad faith bargaining. Those who do not have to sell probably will walk away from the sale.

Most boards of directors have set schedules for their meetings that are planned well in advance. Items such as acquisitions usually must be placed well in advance on the agenda for a meeting and material distributed to board members in time for them to study it prior to the meeting. Because few boards meet more often than once a month, a substantial period of time can elapse before another opportunity occurs if approval is not given for any reason at a board meeting. Delays in approval will always increase the chances something will happen and the acquisition will be lost. However, an aggressive buyer can call special board meetings to secure the timely approval of an acquisition.

Those evaluating the provisions of a negotiated agreement must look at the net result of the entire agreement and all the terms rather than dwell on one or two that are distasteful. Of course, negotiation involves some give and take and a buyer can hardly expect quality companies to be acquired totally on the buyer's terms. It takes experienced executives knowledgeable in acquisition transactions to evaluate the net result and not become overly concerned with a few points. The negative points must be weighed for risk and cost to keep them in perspective. In some cases it may very well be that the risk or cost is too high for the buyer to accept.

If the negotiator because of his position or confidence in his judgment is able to make final decisions, he still should have a confidant who possesses good business judgment talk over problems and contemplate decisions with him. Several points of view will help bring about the best decisions.

The last category of decisions, those largely made or influenced by professionals, can vary in scope with each buyer. The more transactions made by a buyer using the same professionals, the more the working relationship will develop. With each acquisition the professionals will have a better understanding of their client and the client will be more knowledgeable as to what is possible. The result will be the professional feeling more free to make decisions he believes are in his client's best interest and his client will fully approve. Regardless of the relationship and a client's respect for his professionals, he should never assume they have all the answers and can not be challenged or provide an explanation when requested. There always is a tendency for professionals to base their opinions on what is "customary" rather than what is absolutely best for the client. Of course, the standard of "customary" is a hard one to oppose. Skillful lawyers can be very helpful in bringing the parties together in the final negotiations because their special relationship permits exploration of possible solutions without committing their clients. They can send up trial balloons and they can tactfully explore the sellers reasoning to gain insight into a position the buyer finds difficult to accept.

Lawyers will be needed more as the negotiations progress into the final stages, when offers are made and contracts drafted. A buyer should seek their advice prior to the final stages and have them familiar with the companies and transaction contemplated. While there is some difference of opinion, most buyers believe it is best to keep attorneys out of direct contact with prospects until after a general offer is made and accepted. If an attorney accompanies a buyer to a meeting prior to an offer being made, it frequently will be disturbing to a seller and may damage the overall relationship.

Strategies

As mentioned earlier, the majority of any buyer's strategy should be intense preparation coupled with patience and enthusiasm. Much has been written and is being presented in seminars on negotiating strategies and techniques, which allegedly will enable a negotiator to beat his opponent. How many, if any, of these programs on negotiating skills help those involved in acquisitions remains very controversial. Acquisition negotiations are very different and not comparable to any product sales where the transactions can occur quickly and the parties separate. The entire concept that the other party is the opponent is all wrong for acquisition negotiations, where instead of becoming combatants the buyer and seller should strive to become partners in an endeavor to find reasonable solutions to each other's problems that will make possible a mutually satisfactory definitive agreement.

All parties will want to maximize their position in the negotiations, and for the buyer this will mean the lowest price and most favorable terms possible, while for the seller this will be the highest price possible with terms advantageous to him. If the parties explain to each other their positions and the reasoning that brought them to a particular conclusion in a cooperative atmosphere, there is a much better chance the other party will be sympathetic. The parties begin through the interchange of ideas to understand what is possible and what is not possible for the other to do. Total agreement may not immediately be achieved, but if the relationship remains good, the differences usually can be worked out. Wanting to achieve the best deal possible is perfectly normal and expected of all participants, and no one should have qualms about admitting and stressing his position.

The buyer's negotiator must maintain a very positive attitude that eventually he will acquire the prospect. He should be so convinced of the value of the prospect to the buyer and of the benefits to the seller that he will persist in the negotiations, and when obstacles occur, take a position of, "if we can't agree today lets stay friends and keep talking, maybe we can tomorrow." A positive attitude is infectious and will influence the sellers. Along with the positive attitude of buyer negotiators should come a sense of humor. The stakes are high and people's livelihoods are involved, but that does not preclude some humor in the discussions. Nothing can keep matters in perspective, soothe frustrated negotiators, and encourage agreement like a well-timed humorous observation. An example would be the comment to a seller of a consulting company reluctant because of alleged conflicts with professional ethics, "Belonging to a professional society is like virginity, it is a great honor, but has very limited commercial value."

Importance of Listening and Honesty

A positive attitude also builds the overall rapport necessary between buyer and seller executives. Good relationships can be promoted by all the usual means of social contact and creating of friendships, but two traits for a buyer representative are of particular importance, an ability to listen and complete honesty. Listening can of course be a means of flattery, but equally important the buyer can not fully understand the seller's position and motivation if he does not listen to what is said. Chances are neither party will disclose all of their thoughts to the other, but it is a mistake to be deprived of the use of what freely is disclosed simply by failing to listen. Buyer representatives can easily be so caught up in their enthusiasm and extolling the virtues of their company and the proposed acquisition, that they talk too much and listen too little. The chance of damaging the negotiations by listening is remote, but the chance of damage by excessive talking is great by bringing up irrelevant or controversial matters all sides should ignore. Negotiators should remember the salesman's adage of "Leave your briefcase closed, once you have the order."

Integrity is of critical importance for the buyer negotiator. He must continually be on guard to protect his reputation for honesty because in an acquisition there is so much opportunity to be misunderstood as well as temptations to "color" facts. Hundreds of subjects are covered often employing terminology with which one party is unfamiliar or may have a different definition. The complexity and multitude of details also increases the probability of making a mistake. When mistakes do occur, the negotiator should be the first to admit their existence in order to retain his integrity. If a negotiator makes errors to the point where his credibility is destroyed, then he will have to be replaced or the acquisition will not likely be consummated.

Switching negotiators in the middle of a negotiation should be avoided if at all possible and only for extreme conditions, such as loss of credibility and effectiveness. The loss of continuity and knowledge of the overall situation is a very heavy loss for a buyer and a change should never be lightly made. If the seller has no concern for honesty as evidenced by dishonest behavior, the buyer will be better off to walk away. The idea that if one recognizes a dishonest person for what he is he can be outsmarted is far too risky a game to play when the stakes are so high.

Price Negotiations

In Chapter 10, "Common Sense Pricing," development of an offer and presenting it to sellers was discussed. The price will more readily be acceptable if in meetings prior to the one in which an offer is made some preparatory observations have been made to the sellers to discourage unrealistic price expectations. Comments to the effect that the buyer is willing to pay reasonable prices but will only pay a price on which a satisfactory return can be achieved will be helpful. The buyer must stress that no matter how much he likes the prospect, its industry, and the people he has met, he refuses to be a business fool and overpay. "Reasonable price" and "overpay" are nebulous terms, but they will convey the buyer's thinking to the seller.

A seller who gives a price counterproposal that is outrageously high or simply states an amount far greater than the buyer can justify should be confronted with the very reasons why the buyer considers the price too high. A calculation showing the income the buyer would have to receive from the prospect's business to receive a reasonable return if the price was paid can be an effective argument. Of course, any other legitimate arguments such as PE's, return on investment, what others have paid, and the like are fair ammunition to bring down a price.

An important part of the buyer's bargaining strategy must be accommodation of the psychological and financial needs of the seller's decision-makers. The buyer should tactfully present as much as possible the terms of the acquisition agreement that favor the decision-makers as provisions the buyer wants and believes he must have, or conditions that the buyer strongly believes are ones to which the decision-makers are fairly entitled. Employment or consulting agreements with generous terms, exchange or sale of assets, such as hunting or fishing camps on a favorable basis, retention of perquisites, and transfer of key man insurance plans are examples of items that can be very important to the decision-makers. There is a certain amount of gamemanship in a perceptive buyer proposing personal benefits to sellers that are costly, but their proposal may be not only prudent but result in reducing the total price. Don't ever discount greed.

Procedures and Process

The entire acquisition process of efforts that succeed is one that starts slow, rapidly gains momentum, and becomes difficult to stop. The further into the process and progression of events necessary to conclude an acquisition, the greater becomes the time required and the expenses of the parties as the number of participants increases. It is important for any buyer to keep in mind what stage of the process he is in and plan for what lies ahead. A buyer who is intent upon acquiring a prospect should attempt to maintain an accelerating pace for completion of necessary activity and work to prevent periods of restraint or no activity. Gaps in activity usually have the effect of moving the parties apart by providing time for reconsideration.

The major milestone after initial contact and receipt of financial data is agreement on price. The buyer should go on the assumption that if agreement on price can be reached or even closely approached, then all other problems can be resolved if both parties really want to conclude the acquisition. It may turn out full agreement can not be reached but the odds are so good that with imagination, the help of experienced professionals, and the determination of the parties all issues can be resolved and the final phases of the process be set in motion.

Once price agreement is reached and the basic terms are settled, a number of activities begin to run concurrently. Attorneys draft the definitive contracts and the formal evaluation, study of the prospect is completed, the buyer's approval procedure becomes active, planning for operational takeover of the prospect commences, the seller begins accumulating data for the exhibits to the definitive contract and the seller cleans up liens and litigation whenever possible, audits are conducted, and, if securities laws require, the preparation of registration statements and prospectuses commences. All of this activity must be coordinated and little occurs without frequent decisions being required of the buyer and seller. Negotiations in some form becomes a daily affair for the six or more weeks it takes to reach the day for closing. Six weeks would be very fast for most transactions and over three months would be involved if prospectuses are required. At the time of reaching agreement on the basic terms or shortly thereafter the parties should select a day for closing the transaction so that all activities can be scheduled for completion on or before that day.

Finally, the day for closing occurs. If all the work is complete closing can take only an hour or two for signing of documents, transfer of ownership, and payment. More commonly there are still documents to complete and even items still to be settled, so the closing activity may go on for a full day, or even longer. Frequently, the principals are exhausted and bored with the proceedings they have mentally closed but the documents have not caught up. Often, the activity is further delayed while the opposing attorneys quarrel over the contents of their legal opinions that generally interest no one but the attorneys. Closings can be routine and dull or an activity full of uncertainty with the outcome in doubt until the last signature is signed.

Hazards and Special Problems

Any type of business negotiation can have problems and pitfalls and all are common to acquisitions, but acquisitions have some that create more than normal complications. A buyer should be aware of the possibility of their presence and take steps for their control.

Exhaustion and Boredom

Tiring of the deal is one of the most insidious psychological conditions to inflict the participants. As the work goes on to bring about a closing, the participants tend to begin to lose interest in the transaction and become bored with it all. Reaching agreement on price and other basic terms was the highpoint for the participants and whatever occurs thereafter is not only anticlimatic but drudgery. The challenge of identifying and contacting a prospect and the intellectually stimulating activity of persuading the owners to sell on acceptable terms are all very exciting fare that culminates with the agreement on the basic terms, but from then on it is all routine work coupled with endless minor decisions necessary to bring about a closing that wears down the participants to a point where the entire transaction can be jeopardized. The longer it takes to close after price agreement is reached, the more tired of it all the participants become. Small issues become major ones and minor defects in the prospect begin to grow to a point where the buyer begins to question his original judgment. This loss of perspective and interest can be guarded against in several ways. First and foremost is to recognize it is going to happen so that when it begins to set in, the participants realize what is occurring. Next, most importantly, is to keep sight of the objective of closing and the fact that all the time and effort that has gone into the acquisition is lost if closing does not occur. Finally, the participants must have the patience and discipline to drive themselves to exert the effort to conclude the acquisition.

Keeping the Romance Alive

During the period of romance and bringing about agreement on price, the buyer's executives had to be very attentive to the sellers. They tried to treat the sellers as though they were the most important and interesting people in the world. There is a tendency once price agreement is reached to slack off on the attention given and treat the acquisition as though it were complete. This is a mistake, because the acquisition is not finished until closing occurs, and there will invariably be many problems to resolve prior to closing. Executives experienced in acquisitions know they must not reduce in their contact and relationship with the sellers once price agreement is reached. A basic rule to follow is, "Once you reach agreement, that's when you really start selling."

A good practice for a buyer to follow is to establish a schedule of making contact with the seller's key decision-maker at least once a week. If, by the end of the week he has not been in contact with him, he should find an excuse for at least a telephone call. Contact is of greatest importance in cases where it is an owner-founder selling his life's work and has doubts as to whether or not he should give up his "baby."

Deal Killers

Watch out for the deal killers. Any acquisition affects the interests of many people and not all will perceive it to be in their best interest for the acquisition to be consummated. It would be a rare acquisition if there were no dissenters. Some will openly be opposed, while others will be more subtle in their efforts to subvert the transaction. A buyer would be wise to make a list of those whose interests they believe would be adversely affected and those who are just opposed for any reasons whatsoever. Identification of these people and how they will be contained, controlled or won over should be of paramount importance to the buyer.

The prime dissenters are to be found in the following groups. Executives who believe their careers will be adversely affected or they will be fired will be very concerned. Professionals presently representing the sellers know they will almost certainly lose the account. Shareholders who do not like the agreement and price negotiated can cause endless problems. Particularly in family controlled corporations, some shareholders have such a dislike for each other that whatever one agrees to, the other will oppose. Shareholders may not like the buyer or prefer to see a sale to a different company. There may be some executives or shareholders who had wanted to buy the company themselves but are unable to raise the money. There will be some who have nothing against the buyer and they believe the offer is fair, but they prefer to see the company remain as is with its present ownership. These are the major categories of potential dissenters, but a buyer should not limit his search to them.

Deadlines

Time limits and deadlines do affect acquisitions and a buyer should be alert to their presence. The fiscal year for both buyer and seller often causes very important deadlines. A buyer may want to be able to include an acquisition in his list of accomplishments for the year and will go to great lengths to conclude a transaction in time. A seller also may want to conclude a transaction before his fiscal year ends when all new financial statements will be available that may not show the best news. Labor agreement expiration and dates for major contract awards can easily affect timing. Most buyers would do well to avoid acting on the basis of deadlines or timing to coincide with anticipated operational events. In acquisition negotiations, one of the great problems is the subject never stands still. The companies change, industry changes, economic conditions change, and while these are occurring, the time periods upon which decisions were made pass.

Securities Laws

The securities laws are designed to protect investors and even attempt to make certain that investors know what they are doing. Compliance can require legal documents that are nearly terrifying to non-attorney investors. It is most important that the buyer have an attorney who is sensitive to the problem non-attorneys have in comprehending the documents, and in needing patient explanations of what each document is and why it is needed. After a buyer acquires a few companies, he will become accustomed to the language and documents, but most sellers will in all probability be engaging in their first and last sale of a business.

Warranty and Representation Provisions

In the definitive agreements there are two areas for unlimited arguments and debate because every solution tends to be a compromise. The warranty and representation sections of the agreement contain provisions describing the conditions of the company. The basic dispute arises because a buyer will want the agreement to state precisely what is the company's condition, while the seller will only want to warrant that which he knows for certain to be the conditions on the date of closing to the best of his knowledge. Only compromises or capitulation can resolve these issues and a buyer would do well to discuss at length the importance of the issues with his attorney and his key executives. A buyer should look at the warranty and representation section of his agreement, primarily as a device for forcing full disclosure of all facts about the prospect so he can decide if he wants to make the acquisition on the agreed basis, rather than creating language that will help in future litigation if the acquisition fails.

The other area where only compromise is possible is in employment agreements if they are given as part of the package. A buyer can not grant an employee the unrestricted right to perform a job as he sees fit without any direction but if the employee concedes the right to receive direction, the employee can be given all sorts of distasteful duties. A buyer must have the right to fire an employee for "just cause," although "just cause" will prove to be very difficult to define. A buyer wants protection to prevent the employee from quitting and going into business in competition, but an employee wants to exercise his trade if he is run off or unfairly treated by his employer. Compromises must be made.

Many compromises will be made by the parties to most acquisitions. Often, the concessions made simply represent the abandonment of unreasonable positions that should not have existed in the first place. The issues that were contested most and were most difficult to resolve are usually forgotten or considered insignificant a year or two after an acquisition has occurred. A buyer would be wise to review each negotiation a year or more after it has transpired to find out what really was important. Chances are that there was little dispute over items of greatest importance.

12.
Transition

All the time, all the effort, and the expense that went into bringing about an acquisition is lost if the acquisition proves to be a failure and whatever educational benefits may have accrued from the experience are very small indeed when compared to their cost. The damage to the careers, livelihood, net worth, and even mental health of the victims of a failure can prove to be an even worse consequence and one no responsible buyer should want on his conscience. The period of transition following closing, which may last several years, is one that a buyer can not expect to go smoothly and he will have to exercise exceptional judgment and understanding to succeed in bringing the acquired into his organization on a basis where the management and employees are enthusiastic and productive.

Different managements do not automatically mesh together, and buyers tend to become disillusioned as they discover how little they know about what they acquired and find the solutions, practices, and instincts that worked well for their other businesses do not necessarily work for the new one. Management changes that follow disenchantment often create more problems and inhibit success.

Buyer Is Responsible for Success

It is the buyer's responsiblity to make the acquired succeed. The buyer evaluated the company, usually was the aggressor in pursuing the prospect, persuaded the owners to sell, bought the company, and now is the owner with no one to blame if the acquired does not perform as forecast. An expanded definition of a successful acquisition is one the buyer does not regret making and is consistent with or better than the preacquistion forecasts. This definition of success provides a reasonable standard for any buyer but one that will not easily be met without a great deal of continuous effort on the part of the buyer. Most buyers' tasks are even more difficult because their plan for the acquired is for it to grow each year and become an increasingly more profitable and stronger company. The buyer bought the company on the basis of his own expectations, which he must now fulfill. If the acquisition fails he has no one but himself to look to and no amount of rationalization will change that fact. Therefore, a buyer must recognize his responsibility and all members of a buyer's organization must know it is the objective and policy of the buyer to help in every way possible the newly acquired succeed and any activity detracting from that objective will not be tolerated.

Of course, neither buyers nor the acquired company's management intentionally cause acquisitions to fail. Both groups normally want the acquisition to be a great success and have more to gain if it does succeed, so it is surprising such a high percentage fail because of problems and misunderstanding that could not be overcome. Actually, most could if both sides tried more to understand the other as evidenced by the common cycle of a successful company being acquired, failing, being divested, and returning to success under new ownership. At times some decisions are so inept, clumsy, ill-mannered, and downright foolish that it may appear someone is deliberately attempting to foul up an acquired company but such motivation would be irrational and very rare. In the worst managed companies plagued with bizarre management styles and executives convinced they alone have been annointed with the insight to manage a business in today's world, the business decisions are thought excellent by their makers regardless of the results. Failure of the parent and speedy divestiture is about the only hope for a company acquired by a very poorly managed buyer.

Executives make decisions upon the basis of the facts as they understand them with their background of experience and at the time of making the decisions, they believed them to be proper and wise. In no time at all the decisions may prove to be terrible and have disastrous effects, but at the time they were made, they were thought to be excellent. Bad decisions commonly result from inaccurate information, a lack of understanding of true conditions, and from attempts to achieve unrealistic goals. All these conditions abound in the transition period for an acquisition. Bad decisions breed more bad decisions and unless prudent moves are made an irreversible decline in relationships will set in causing certain failure.

Most buyers are concerned about the loss of managers and other key employees but little seems to be done about the problem. Buyers proclaim it is their intent and policy to retain the management of acquired companies (they would buy very few companies if it was their announced policy to replace all the managers immediately after the acquisition) and often include pronouncements of this policy in their press releases, but as time goes on very high turnover frequently occurs. Of course, some owners active in a business sell because they do want to retire, pursue other interests, or are experiencing ill health, but the majority of an acquired's management usually have a very productive portion of their business careers remaining and could, if properly motivated, continue to contribute to the success of the business. These are the same managers who helped build the company to a point of success where it was so attractive the buyer bought it.

Buyers believe the quality of the management team to be acquired in any acquisition is one of the more important factors in their evaluation and even pay a premium price for outstanding management. However, once the acquisition occurs, adequate attention is seldom given to preserving these important human assets, which in many acquisitions are far more important than the physical assets. Loss of the human assets more often is caused by neglect and misunderstandings rather than overt acts.

A successful transition is largely a matter of persuading the management and employees of the acquired to stay on their jobs and perform diligently and enthusiastically while they cooperate fully with the buyer. Such noble objectives are not easy to achieve even for the most sagacious of managements because there are basic conflicts that work against the buyer's good intentions.

Transitional Conflicts

A buyer will want to preserve the acquired management team unless he has acquired a company to liquidate or a sick company with either gaps in management or managers clearly over their heads and responsible for the unsatisfactory performance. The management team that has run a successful company should not readily be replaced on the logic of upgrading personnel or the convenience of having managers do things "our way." Buyers without inhouse replacements must resort to external recruiting to fill executive positions, and this is an expensive activity for which results are never 100% certain. Furthermore, it is a rare buyer who has the luxury, (and can afford the expense) of a stable full of available high powered managers who can step in as replacements and are actually superior to the acquired incumbents. Even in companies where the management team has failed and changes must be made, it is likely that the team contains some members who are quite competent and should be retained. The wise buyer will do all he can with the team he buys before replacing any managers and to do this he must be aware of the inherent conflicts and plan to mitigate their effects. There is a minority of buyers whose ability to learn is as low as their ability to retain management that automatically plan to replace the management of the acquired regardless of their performance. This practice in time becomes self-defeating because of frequent failures and difficulty they experience in finding sellers willing to be acquired under such conditions. Those successful in building companies through acquisition make a real effort to preserve talented management and recognize the basic conflicts.

Change vs. Stability

Unless a buyer is truly only a passive investor, he acquires a company with the idea of making changes that he believes will increase profitability. Change invariably means change in people's jobs with some being favorably affected, but probably more being adversely affected. An even greater number will not be adversely affected but will be worried that they will be. The results a buyer expects normally can not be achieved without traumatic changes in job content or even job loss for some. Conversion of a corporation to a division will automatically eliminate the board of directors and corporate staff personnel who are no longer needed.

If the acquisition was predicated upon the consolidation of facilities or marketing organizations, then by definition employees will be terminated, perhaps in the buyer's existing organization as well as the acquired. Even if the changes are additions of capital, products, and technology, which will help the acquired grow, there will be new stresses and instability.

Profitability vs. Compliance

Most buyers expect an acquired company to comply with their policies and procedures regardless of the effect compliance may have upon the business's profitability. Even in highly decentralized corporations some degree of uniformity is essential because of legal responsibilities of the parent, government pressures, union threats, or public pressures. The tendency by these outside groups to look at a parent company as not only being responsible but also knowledgeable about every act of every subsidiary management employee causes a trend towards a more centralized operational approach with its by-product being a need for policy compliance.

Corporations tend to concentrate their more able executives in their corporate offices. These people generally wish to make their impact upon the corporation and this normally involves intrusion into the autonomy of the subsidiaries or divisions. The larger the parent company corporate staff regardless of their abilities, the more active they will be in the affairs of each subsidiary or division. A buyer can not be considered serious about a policy of decentralization and encouragement of initiative at subsidiary levels if a large corporate office staff is maintained. Even when corporate ideas or policies are excellent and practical, there is no assurance they will be readily accepted, particularly if they modify long established relationships or practices. Unwilling acceptance brings a subtle challenge to render the parents ideas unworkable. Uniformity of corporate policies also has its hazards. They simply may not fit every unit of the corporation or for some be totally inapplicable and the result is a lack of respect for the parent and a deterioration in relations.

Judgment Conflicts

A buyer who acquires a company normally expects to exercise some influence and control. This involves the right to give directions and also review and approve decisions made by the acquired company's management. These rights also tend to imply superior judgment, which is not always the case. The parent management claims to have a broader view of the total enterprise's needs while local management should best understand their own situation and its needs better. The local managers will believe they know best how to run their business and will not readily accept approval procedures from others who do not understand the business as well.

Conflicts in Management Style

Great differences in management methods, approaches, and style exist and, its impossible to say one is superior to another if the results are good. There are successful, highly centralized organizations with subsidiaries having virtually no autonomy and others equally successful and decentralized to the point where they border on commercial anarchy. Some businesses rely on very sophisticated business systems while others often do quite well on "gut feel." Cash flow and management may be all important with certain businesses while reportable income is paramount with others. In the area of employee relations a paternalistic approach may be very successful for some, while others believe their success is due to a tough "perform or out you go" policy.

Most styles fall in between these extremes and few are all one way or the other. There are also great differences in style because of objectives and backgrounds. The professional manager's views can be very different from that of the owner-operator entrepreneur, and the passive investors' attitude different from both. Change is difficult for any business executive who has existed in one business environment for years.

The problem in acquisitions is the more different the styles of the parent and acquired, the more difficult will be the transition. The exponents of any style have found what works for them and usually can see no reason why it should not work well for others. An acquired company's resistance to changing their style to that of the new parent will be considered insubordination rather than an heroic effort to save the company from ruin. Style provides an organizational framework for a business in which employees know what is expected and what are the overall rules. Attempts to impose a new style without adequate explanation and a tailoring of the style to the acquired business will bring on confusion and adverse reactions.

Expectations vs. Reality

Usually, the buyer and the acquired management find the acquisition and the new relationship different from what they had expected. The buyer acquired the company on the basis of his business plan and forecasts. Forecasts were used to justify the price paid and the buyer must see the forecasts become reality or he has entered into a bad deal. The forecasts may have been cast very optimistically because of information and remarks provided by the sellers who wanted to enhance their bargaining position. When the forecasts are not met, an acrimonious atmosphere sets in that makes it all the more difficult to achieve the plan.

The acquired company's management may be in for its share of disappointments. There is a naive attitude that often develops particularly when a small company sells to a much larger one. The acquired management believes the larger firm will provide unlimited capital for expansion, new business systems, new technology and the like, at no cost and with no strings. This, of course, does not readily occur as the acquired management had anticipated. There also is a tendency for the acquired management to believe once the acquisition occurs all their problems will be over, but they find not only are all their old ones still there, but a host of new ones are emerging. The period of selling each other is over and all the expectations fanned by the selling process now must either become reality or bitter disappointment.

Continuity with Preacquisiton Activity

During the preacquisition discussions and negotiations, the parties may have shaded their remarks on how the companies would fit together and the compatibility of managements in an effort to promote the sale. With both parties favoring a transaction there is a tendency to look at how the companies could function well together rather than the operational difficulties that might arise in the proposed relationship. It is quite possible to rationalize and plan how any two companies might function harmoniously together if one ignores basic human traits and needs and assumes all managers and employers will enthusiastically subvert their status and personal interests to what others see as being the best interests of the buyer. Such a miracle of human nature can not be counted on. If the owners are not active in the company or intend to retire, there will be less concern on their part as to how well the company can function under a new owner, and they will not have to live with their remarks on compatibility.

The buyer's acquisition executives are usually in highly structured companies and are primarily concerned with seeing the transaction completed, and do not have to live with their sales comments. Seeking out and acquiring companies is a very specialized activity and those in this role most of their time are seldom involved with a company once it is acquired. They are responsible for making acquisitions and in their zeal to succeed tend to describe their company more as they would like it to be rather than how it is. They also tend to minimize the transitional problems because that is not their responsibility and they may not be fully aware of their nature or magnitude. Once a company is acquired, the acquisition executives have succeeded although it will be a year or more before the acquisition can be judged a success.

Individual investors who negotiate their own acquisitions also have to exercise care in their comments on how the company will be operated so that they do not confuse how they want things to work with how they probably will. Everyone's intentions are usually very good but the realities of execution are not easy.

Buyer executives would do well to evaluate very carefully with sellers the present management styles and discuss in depth their compatibility and the kind of relationship that is contemplated. There is a tendency to gloss over this area for fear of issues arising that will prevent the acquisition but if issues of this magnitude exist, it probably will be best the acquisition not occur because of the low probability of it's being a success. A candid discussion between all parties involved prior to the acquisition on how the reporting relationship will function, the authority exercised by the parent and discretionary latitude retained by a subsidiary, reports required, and financial backing to be provided by the parent will bring the key issues out in the open. These are the basic areas to be covered, and a buyer should promise only what he is certain to do. A buyer who makes outlandish promises of nearly unlimited autonomy and financial backing to managers he considers expendable in an effort to bring about the acquisition is not only deceiving the sellers but also engaging in a self-defeating exercise.

As part of these candid discussions, a buyer should consider showing the seller copies of his policy manual if he has one, the financial reporting package, which must be prepared by a subsidiary or divisions, and whatever budgets or profit plans are required. For some buyers, to do so may mean the end of acquisition discussions but for the majority it will be a solid foundation for the future relationship. Most sellers will not be surprised and will expect corporate policies and more paperwork as part of their new way of life in a larger corporation and some may even see the advantages as well as the need. The systems and policies of any buyer exist because he believes they make sense and fill a need and he should be prepared to willingly explain their purpose. This all has to come out some day, and it is much better presented by a responsible executive who can explain it. The chances of an acquisition being successful is very low if there is not an open and candid relationship.

Continuity of personal relationships is important in the transitional period. If the owners or decision-makers are expected to continue managing the acquired, the buyer executives active in the negotiations should continue in contact with the sellers during the transitional period. These personal relationships can be a source of communication and understanding of great value in smoothing the transition. The practice of some buyers to march in a whole new team to direct the acquired's management the day after closing and those involved in making the acquisition totally disappearing to pursue other acquisitions is a mistake. During the transitional period, the manager of an acquired company can use a friend who is outside the normal organizational structure, and can advise and mediate when necessary, and no one can fill the role better than an executive who developed a strong friendship during the negotiations.

Continuity is also enhanced by early introduction of the acquired company's manager to the buyer executive to whom he will report after closing. In some situations this executive will play a key role in the negotiations, and in others, not be involved at all. However long before closing, whoever he is, he should be identified and active in building a solid working relationship with the management of the company to be acquired. This not only provides continuity but also provides him the opportunity to develop the business plan and detailed forecasts for which he will be responsible. Preparing the plan requires contact with the management and this itself is an opportunity to develop a good relationship. The complete comprehensive study and evaluation of the company should be turned over to this executive for his reference during the transition. This probably contains more information in one place about the acquired than ever will be accumulated again, and it should be put to use.

Taking Over

In a friendly takeover, the transitional activities usually start in an informal way shortly after price agreement is reached, but prior to closing. Major decisions, such as capital expenditures, selection of executives to fill key vacancies, opening or closing of facilities, new borrowings, and selection of new professionals are often made only after consultation with the buyer, or the decisions are delayed until after closing. Participation in these decisions is an ideal way for the buyer executive assigned responsibility for the acquisition to become involved. He can not totally make the decisions at this stage, but under the circumstances his opinions will be given considerable weight. The more consultation on operational matters prior to closing, the smoother should be the transition, and the working relationship between the managements.

Board of Directors

Immediate decisions are needed on what to do with the directors of the acquired company, who will be the new directors, and what will be their role. In a typical acquisition they resign at closing, but this is not always the case. What happens depends upon the degree of ownership of the buyer, his plans for the acquired, and the laws of the country in which the acquired is located. If the acquired is to be converted into a division, a board of directors will no longer be required. If it is to become a wholly owned subsidiary, then usually most of the directors will be replaced with buyer employees. The activities of the board become largely that of fulfilling legal requirements and rubber stamping the decisions of others. A member of a subsidiary board has nearly the same responsibilities and opportunity for personal liability as the member of any other board, which is a fact not all consider. Retaining key members of the acquired company's management on their board can be an important status factor for these executives, although they will normally be outnumbered by new buyer members, seldom meet, and have little, if any, actual responsibility for decisions.

It is most important for the status of the CEO of the acquired that he select the members of his management team who will be permitted to remain on the board. The management can argue that they still report to a board of directors but now they only have one shareholder, which sounds fine, but in practice it's meaningless. The relationship that counts is the one between the CEO of the acquired and the executive in the buyer's organization to whom he reports.

If a buyer has acquired only a majority of the seller's stock and a sizable minority of shares remains outstanding, then the board will have to continue to exercise its normal role in overseeing the company, although a majority of the directors will be selected by the buyer and control the board's actions. Proper board action will have to be taken on all matters that legally should come before it to lessen the risk of litigation by dissident shareholders.

Election of the key decision-maker of the seller to the board of directors of the buyer can be a great psychological move to promote the acquisition but eventually the new board member must take his seat. He can become an excellent contributor to the deliberations of the board or a serious problem. The success or failure of the relationship with the executive will be more likely determined in the daily management decisions of operating his company than in the periodical lofty deliberations of the parent board. Just as election to the parent board was important in bringing the parties together, removal or resignation from the board is the end of the relationship with the seller executive.

Installing the Plan

Implementation of the buyer's business plan should commence immediately after closing. At this time the newly acquired company's management and employees are expecting changes and are best prepared to accept them. The more the initial changes clearly benefit the business, such as captive orders or working capital additions, as opposed to changes to bring the new subsidiary into compliance with the parent, the more readily they will be accepted. The activities to immediately benefit the business will also benefit the company's profits, which will further encourage a good relationship with the parent. Introduction to new customers, providing assistance in locating personnel to fill job openings, and the addition of needed equipment are all examples of items that can have immediate impact. Early emphasis on taking care of the most conspicuous deficiencies or shortcomings is also a way of improving profits and morale. The management and employees usually know what is not right, and welcome steps that make sense to improve the company.

A backlog of operational decisions may have built up during the acquisition period because of management delaying to see if the acquisition would actually close, delaying until the views of the new owner could be ascertained, and because the seller executives were all tied up in working out the acquisition, and did not have time to evaluate facts and make operational decisions. The last few weeks prior to closing are particularly hectic for the seller's executives, and they now need a little time to catch up. They also may be exhausted and need a period of rest before launching any ambitious new programs. An astute buyer will recognize that until the management has caught up and rested, it will not be wise to introduce heavy new demands or controversial changes. It takes only a few weeks for the management to recover, and that time should matter very little. However, if the management is in good shape and needs no breather because it was involved very little in the acquisition process, the program should start immediately.

Most of the task of implementing the business plan will fall on the chief executive of the acquired company. He is responsible for the company and must give the orders to put into action the plan regardless of his degree of agreement with the plan or where the plan originated. This executive and the executives reporting to him will have the task of convincing themselves and employees in the company to cooperate in making the desired changes and also convince their new parent of their ability and willingness to execute the plan. The CEO of the acquired company, and those reporting to him, who can accomplish the business plan or let it fail, are the ones most important to retain. They are the executives with whom a buyer must develop a working relationship to accomplish the business plan and effect a successful transition. The buyer, in developing his business plan for scheduling the implementation of changes through the company management has to use exceptional judgment to effect a balance between his desire to rapidly receive the benefits anticipated and the recognition that moving too fast may bring unnecessary adverse reactions that will reduce or prevent any benefits. There also is the practical problem of there being a physical limit as to what can be accomplished in a period of time by even the most enthusiastic and able management team.

Changes in management personnel can have a greater impact for good or evil on the transition than any other event. Being acquired is one of the most traumatic events that can happen to a company, but the acquisition plus replacement of key executives can be a doubly severe blow. In some acquisitions, there will automatically be a change in the CEO if the sale was because of the present CEO's desire to retire, ill health, or death. Perhaps it was a poorly performing company whose CEO is clearly not up to the job. In these situations a change is expected and usually wanted by the acquired organization. The key questions become the competence of the replacement selected and whether or not there are passed-over candidates who felt they should have been selected and what will be the consequence of their disappointment. The buyer should have had the replacement selected before closing the acquisition and be ready to install him in office to take charge immediately after closing.

Replacement of managers reporting to the new subsidiary's CEO can be troublesome, particularly if instigated by the buyer, and the CEO does not agree with the buyer's assessment. These key executives were usually selected by the CEO, or have been close associates, and demands that any be replaced can cause serious disputes with the CEO. Any efforts to make such moves by the buyer will usually be so controversial that the buyer should be prepared to find a replacement for the CEO. Many buyers lose sight of the importance a CEO attaches to his prerogative of selecting or terminating his own staff. It is a responsibility that lies at the heart of his authority. Final selection of executives to fill vacancies in key positions in the subsidiary also must be retained by the CEO. A buyer can locate and propose candidates to fill a vacancy and this assistance is usually welcome as long as the final decision remains with the CEO, and it is understood his decisions will not be challenged. Promotions from within the organization are always popular when the chosen is the obvious selection. If there is no one qualified within the acquired organization, the buyer should make every effort to find a suitable candidate from other parts of his organization. From a management morale standpoint, the ultimate situation is filling from within the acquired, the vacancy created by a promotion to another unit of the buyer or to the buyer's executive office.

In many companies there are executive changes that should have been made long ago and the CEO knows it and so does every employee of the acquired. Nepotism, longevity, extreme compassion, or promotions beyond an executive's competence may have brought about the situation, and the excuse finally arrives for the CEO to do what he should have done before. He conveniently blames the decision on the buyer. Most executives are naturally reluctant, and find it extremely difficult to move against associates with whom they have known for years, who no longer perform their job, and they delay as long as possible the demotion or termination. Moves of this kind attributed to the buyer will probably bring no adverse reaction, and enhance respect for the buyer if the replacement is an improvement, and the removed executive is treated generously.

Relations with Outside Companies

Employee relations are not the only ones that are sensitive. Over the years a successful business will have built up a productive relationship with suppliers, an accounting firm, law firm, insurance broker, and advertising agency to name the major ones. These are usually functioning well with the acquired receiving service it finds to be satisfactory. Often strong personal friendships have built up between executives of the acquired and those of the organizations providing service. Frequently, a substantial portion of the individual's income who has the close friendship with the acquired is dependent upon a continuation of the business relationship and this fact will not make breaking the relationship any easier. The first question a buyer contemplating changes must ask himself is just how important is it to change? Will the buyer's choice be superior with service better and the expense less? Must the changes be made immediately? Are compromises a possibility involving splitting some of the service? Obviously, the attitude of the acquired management must be considered and for some they may not care or will welcome a change. However, if opposed, it is not the type of issue that causes resignations, but it is one the buyer can grow to regret because the acquired management can take a passive position that they have no responsibility for the quality of service forced upon them by the buyer.

Organizing During Transition

There are a number of organizational structures that are used once a company is acquired. The type of buyer, overall circumstances, present structure, past experience, and ability of the buyer's executives, as well as their availability, will influence to varying degrees the structure selected and only in hindsight could a buyer say one should have been used over another.

A "do nothing" or "leave everything as is" approach may be used by an investor who does not wish to be active in the operation of the business. The acquisition is looked at as a business to which he can contribute little or nothing, and he believes its best chance for continued success is for him or his representatives to limit their role to that of directors. Such an approach is dependent upon a strong existing management with internal management development programs capable of providing new executives as time passes.

Immediate assignment to a permanent place in the buyer's organizational structure is surely the most common. Here the CEO reports to the executive responsible for the new addition. This can be anyone from the buyer's CEO to a divisional or group executive. A large acquisition will usually retain its identity and become a new division or group reporting to the buyer's CEO. It could also be the CEO of a subsidiary if the acquired's business was to become closely allied or integrated with the subsidiary. This assignment has some aspects of a "sink or swim" approach, and its success will be dependent upon the skill and understanding of the buyer executive responsibility for the acquired company.

An incubator approach is used by some where the senior executive responsible for making the acquisition has it report to him for the transition period until it is permanently assigned to its place in the buyer's organization structure. This is particularly effective where the senior executive is a CEO who played a major role in persuading the sellers and negotiating the transition during which time he developed a good relationship with the management. The acquisition executive for some buyers fills this role but time spent managing a new acquisition will not be time spent looking for the next one.

A combination approach is possible, involving one of the above, coupled with the temporary assignment of an executive who is preferably older and has been with the buyer a long time. This executive is assigned to the new company to assist in implementing the business plan, resolving differences, acting as close friend to the CEO, and explaining the buyer's reasoning behind any requests. This person would work outside the normal organizational channels to smooth the transition. The executive would clearly have a temporary role in the new company as a friend, helper and expediter and not be a threat to replace anyone. His activity would include some of the load for installing the business plan under the general direction of the executive with line responsibility for the subsidiary. The system can work very well, but executives able to fill the role are scarce.

Whatever the organizational structure and transition approach used, it should be clearly explained to and understood by the management of the acquired company. Even those with the best intentions can not play the game if they do not know the rules. Once they understand the reporting relationship and what is expected, revisions in the system should be avoided if at all possible. A reassignment of the acquired to another group or even another executive can set back the program of transition.

Management Attitudes

Even under the best of circumstances, it will be a very difficult adjustment for an executive who has been CEO of his own company for years to accept the role of heading up a subsidiary or division where his word is no longer the last word, and broad objectives and policies of the parent intrude on what he believes is best for the unit he manages. He no longer is as concerned how his company functions in the entire business world as how it functions in the buyer's organization and this loss of the "big picture" will be missed. For many the adjustment from leader to follower will be impossible despite the best efforts of the executive and the parent company that want very much for it to work. Loss of the CEO of the acquired brings the risk of the additional loss of the able key executives reporting to him. Most strong executives have built up a team of subordinates who are ready to follow the executive to a new company if he chooses to change positions. Because of this fact a buyer could lose his entire management team overnight.

Coddling and capitulation in every dispute are not only impossible for most buyers but in time they are self-defeating. However, the buyer should present an attitude of "what can we do to help you succeed" to the acquired management with the understanding that "just leave us alone" is not an acceptable response.

The buyer management must maintain open communication with the acquired management and promote an attitude of everyone thinking in terms of what is best for the entire corporation. Usually, open discussions will reveal there is no conflict and what is best for one is best for both. It is utopian to assume all differences can be resolved through calm reasoning and in matters important to the buyer, he will simply have to take a stand. No acquired management can expect to have everything its own way and operate as though the parent did not exist.

An objective of the buyer should be to cause the acquired management to feel they are part of the entire organization and not just the unit to which they are assigned. When executives say "we," they should be referring to the entire buyer enterprise. Frequent contact with other executives throughout the buyer's organization will help encourage "we" thinking on the broad basis. Visits to other operations of the buyer by key executives also help to encourage pride in the organization. Everyone wants to be proud of the organization with which they are associated.

If relations should begin to deteriorate with an acquired. management, the problem should be recognized early and remedial steps taken to reverse the trend before it is too late. The first step is to find out what are the causes and commence discussions for their resolution. When relations begin to go sour, communications have usually stopped and nothing will be resolved until candid discussions resume in a constructive context.

Improving the Odds for Success

Companies that were performing well when acquired have subsequently managed to fail for many reasons and combinations of reasons. Others upon being acquired have flourished, retained and inspired the management, and steadily increased their profits. For the successes, the period of transition passed with relative ease but never totally free of problems. The conditions favorable to a successful transition, as well as their importance, obviously vary from one company to another. A list of fifteen actions or conditions conducive to success appears below. Not all are practical for every buyer or even applicable but most are. The opposite of each of these represents a proven way of demoralizing the acquired management and increasing the probability of failure.

1. *Preserve autonomy.* As much autonomy as possible for the acquired company should be preserved. The CEO who is accustomed to independent action should be permitted wide freedom to run the company consistent with the business plan and general objectives of the buyer. Keeping the company as a subsidiary rather than a division helps preserve autonomy.

2. *Preserve management prestige.* Allow managers to retain their titles and status. Have them continue active in public affairs and business associations just as though the acquisition had not occurred. Continue or increase contributions to local charities. Follow organization channels and route all contact between buyer executives and the acquired's executives through the acquired's CEO. The acquired company's CEO must be aware of the content of discussions and approve all discussions with subordinates.

3. *Meeting goals to preserve autonomy.* The management by objectives approach of agreeing with the acquired management on the profit goals and then staying out of their way for them to meet the goals is effective. It is also understood that failure to meet goals will bring on heavy parent company involvement.

4. *Staff assistance.* Parent company staff employees should be used sparingly and then to accomplish specific tasks that the CEO of the acquired agrees he needs and wants done. Their role must be one of staff employees working to help the company improve in their specialized areas of competence and they should not begin assuming a line function. For some acquired managements anyone with a title from the corporate office is assumed to have some authority and this creates confusion. The best way for a buyer to minimize staff conflicts is to keep his staff small.

5. *Reporting relationships.* The CEO of the acquired should be assigned to report directly to a person he respects. Preferably the parent executive is intellectually stronger and has greater experience than the subsidiary CEO. To ask a mature executive to report to a young ambitious favorite of the buyer is asking for trouble.

6. *False superiority.* An "I'm the boss" mentality and belief that the buyer executives are automatically better and wiser business

executives because they are part of the buyer organization are attitudes to be discouraged. The acquired management will accept this view only until proven otherwise. An attitude of building a team is a much sounder basis for the relationship with the acquired.

7. *Realistic goals and plans.* The goals for the acquired company in the form of budgets or profit objectives should be realistic and the management responsible for their attainment should believe it can do it. Grandiose forecasts developed by a buyer to rationalize a price or for any other purposes should not be forced upon a skeptical management.

8. *Compliments accepted.* Buyer executives should be quick to compliment executives of the acquired for their accomplishments and ideas. Sincere appreciation can do much to develop a good relationship.

9. *Speedy decisions.* Prompt action on requests to the parent company for decisions are essential. A buyer would be wise to somehow short circuit or otherwise speed up his decisions-making process for requests from newly acquired companies. A CEO accustomed to making his own decisions for years can usually adjust to submitting major decisions for review if the decisions are quick and rejections are fully explained. Procrastination, incessant demands for more data, and negative decisions without explanation or opportunity for appeal will be debilitating.

10. *Executive compensation.* If the salary levels of the CEO or other executives of the acquired are excessive compared to the buyer's, the excess is looked at as part of the price or an unavoidable cost of doing business. When the differential is considered necessary to eliminate, it should be done over a long period of time. Salary cuts or freezes will never be popular.

11. *Perquisites.* These should be recognized by buyers as part of an executive's compensation that may even be more important than salary. A greatly enjoyed tax-free benefit can not be omitted without adverse reaction and most buyers elect not to make immediate changes. Changes believed necessary can not be accomplished in a short time without severe reactions.

12. *Meeting mistakes.* Meetings with the parent company at their offices should be scheduled well in advance, the agenda known in advance, start and end on time, and their frequency limited so as not to interfere with the participants' regular activities. A CEO of a new subsidiary is not accustomed or inclined to sit in meetings which he does not chair, are poorly run, and are tedious in nature.

13. *Task force disasters.* Changes in the acquired are accomplished through the acquired's CEO and in accordance with the business plan. The practice employed by some of sending in a task force of young MBA's or others to make massive immediate changes is best avoided.

14. *False loyalty.* An atmosphere in which executives can speak up and present their views, regardless of how controversial, should be encouraged. Executives whose definition of company loyalty is decisions of superiors, and particularly their own, are not to be questioned will cause resentment to build against them and the company. The CEO of an acquired company faced with reporting to an individual of this type will have a difficult time because blind following is not in his background.

15. *Accountants and reports.* No function causes more friction, irritation, and conflict in more acquisitions than does that of accounting and reporting. A buyer who acquires a company must have financial statements that can be consolidated with his existing statements and reports he can understand. Prior to being acquired, the acquired company may have had a financial reporting system that served its purposes well but almost certainly is different from that of the buyer. Accountants seem to take great pride in authorship and the system and formats for financial statements vary widely. A buyer who has been using one style of statement for a period of time becomes familiar with the format and readily understands it. The buyer also has his system installed throughout the enterprise and if conformity is required, the acquired can most easily be changed. The executives in the acquired company will then have to adjust to the new system, which will take some time. A wise buyer who finds the acquired has well functioning financial systems should explore changing as little as possible of the system.

Buyers owning multiple units usually have tight time deadlines for preparation of reports, both financial and otherwise. In some organizations the preparers become convinced precise formats and meeting deadlines are more important than content. Any company finding this attitude prevailing should take a hard look at itself.

Transfer of Ideas

During the transition period the buyer should not just be concerned with installing his business plan but he should be looking for the best ideas, systems processes, suppliers, and customer contacts that the acquired has and attempt to use them in other parts of his operations. It should not be just a one-way street with the buyer concentrating on installing what he considers his best ideas into the acquired. The management of an acquired company will normally be delighted to share their proven ideas and contacts throughout the buyer organization. To have been good enough to acquire they must have a great deal to offer that could profitably be shared. Unfortunately, this rarely happens on a systematic or organized basis of any sort and if any transfers of ideas occur, it is by an aggressive executive who inadvertently stumbles upon its existence. Psychologically, the transfer of benefits is a fine means for any buyer to use in introducing the acquired to the rest of his organization. A buyer who fails to aggressively make use of all the acquisition can offer is simply not receiving everything he paid for.

The task for any buyer is to "enjoy the meal and avoid the indigestion." This requires an aggressive acquisition program as well as planning and executing a program for what is to happen to a company once acquired. The activities are interrelated with true success only possible if a buyer is successful in both activities.

Appendix 1
Part 1–
Transaction Summary
and Management
Reports

This appendix, which consists of two parts, illustrates the concept and sample questions to be used in the comprehensive evaluation of prospects. Part 1 of this appendix contains the questions relative to the business plan and policy compliance, as well as a total summary of the acquisition, including questions concerning the operational aspects of the business. This first part of Appendix 1 covers the following:

1. Description of transaction
2. Summary of financial history
3. Forecasts
4. Management report
5. Comparison of acquisition prospect with buyer's policies and objectives
6. Literature of selling company

Description of Transaction

1. Summary of transaction, price, terms, etc. . . .
2. Special factors affecting negotiations, the position of the sellers or buyers.
3. Short history of company and description of present business.
4. Who are the major shareholders, and what is their motivation to sell?

5. Summarize any additional financial requirements the company will have after acquisition during the next five years for working capital, capital expenditures, or research and development, and what will be the source of these funds?
6. What effect will this acquisition have on the buyer's earnings per share? What will be the return on the investment? Define terms.

Summary of Financial History

1. Past four years plus most current interim income summary.
2. Past four years plus most current interim balance sheet summary.
NOTE: If company to be acquired is composed of major operating units or diverse products, separate summaries of their financial history should be prepared, as well as the composite totals.
The summaries should include calculation of significant ratios to indicate trends.

(Summaries should be restated into format by buyer.)

Forecasts

1. Eighteen-month income forecast by month, plus quarterly three more years.
2. Eighteen-month balance sheet forecast by month, plus quarterly three more years.
3. Eighteen-month cash flow forecast by month, plus quarterly three more years.
NOTE: 1. Notes to financial history summary are applicable.
2. The first month of each forecast should be the actual for the most recent month available.

Management Reports

Basic Investment Justification and Business Plan for the Future

1. Describe the long-range objectives of the buyer, and how the acquisition will meet these objectives and fit into his overall program.
2. What changes will be made in this company under new ownership, and what is the schedule for such changes?
3. What will the new owner add to this company in terms of

additional business, financial backing, business know-how, or other positive contributions?

4. Describe how other entities of the buyer will benefit as a result of this acquisition.
5. What systems, techniques, technology, contacts, or business relationships does the seller have that may be used by the buyer in existing operations?

Exceptional or Extraordinary Factors

Summarize any exceptional or extraordinary factors that make the company a desirable acquisition, such as:

1. Financial conditions.
2. Management.
3. Technology or product.
4. Marketing capability, potential, or position.
5. Physical facilities and equipment.
6. Undervalued assets.
7. Earnings potential.

Major Problems

Describe any significant major deficiencies, or things wrong with the company, and the remedial action planned, including a time schedule.

General Management Report

1. How will the acquisition fit into the buyer's organization and management?
2. How much of the buyer's management time will the acquisition require, and from what departments? Who will be involved?
3. Describe the detailed, time-phased plan for integrating the acquisition into the buyer's organization.
4. Evaluate the firm's management and organizational structure. What personnel changes or additions are now contemplated? Prepare a short background summary on the ten most important executives in the company, and the opinion of two buyer's executives of their current performance and potential. Indicate each executive's total compensation and share ownership. What is the probability of each executive remaining with the company if it is acquired? Who will replace any of the five most important executives if they resign? Do any executives have health problems?

5. What steps are being taken or planned to promote a good working relationship between the buyer's management and the acquired company's management? What is being done to encourage key managers to remain?

Management Report—Marketing

1. Describe the markets and the main type of customer. Estimate the size of the potential market and this company's share. What is the condition of these markets? Are they growing, declining, highly competitive?
2. Identify the major competing companies for each product line and compare this company with the major competitors. Will this company's market share grow or decline? Compare the company's products with its competitor's.
3. Describe the method of marketing for each product line, including direct sales, distributors, manufacturer's rep., etc., and comment on the effectiveness of this strategy.
4. Describe any major changes in marketing methods in the past eighteen months.
5. What are the normal terms and discounts given on products or services sold?
6. Identify the major new customers added in the last three years.
7. Identify the major new customers lost in the past three years and circumstances.
8. Describe any seasonal influences to the market and order backlogs.
9. Where are the companies' main geographical markets? How much is sold in each?
10. Advertising.
    a. Describe the advertising program.
    b. Name of agency and its annual fee.
    c. Annual budget.
11. Describe the marketing organization. Prepare an organization chart.
12. Prices.
    a. How are they determined in general?
    b. Who determines the prices?
    c. What are pricing policies?
    d. What cost system is used in pricing?
13. Describe the sales force training program.
14. What product guarantees are normally given? What has been the experience with guarantees?

15. Evaluate the maturity of the products and their growth potential. What is the estimated life of each?
16. Evaluate the quality and diversity of the product line.
17. Evaluate the role and importance of:
    a. Price.
    b. Delivery.
    c. Quality.
    d. Credit, financing.
    e. Post-purchase service.
    f. Installation.
    g. Product customization.
    h. Advertising, product literature, and other communications in the firm's marketing program.
    i. Location.
18. Prepare a sales forecast in a format with which the buyer is familiar.
19. Who sets credit policy? How is it administered in practice?
20. What is the sales cancellation and return policy?

Management Report—Service Companies

(To be completed only for engineering,
consulting, or other service companies)

1. Describe in detail the firm's professional capabilities and actual work experience over the past three years.
2. Describe and identify dollar volumes and relative profitability over the past three years, of each of the firm's kinds of work.
3. Describe how the firm is paid, with details from the past three years of operation.
   a. Fixed price—lump sum contracts.
   b. Cost plus fee.
   c. Front end advance and progress payment terms.
   d. Experience on cash flow on work in progress ahead or behind customers.
4. List the processes licensed to or by the firm, with the associated annual cost or revenue schedule.
5. Describe the kinds of performance guarantees given by the company.
6. Organization.
   a. How many professionals? Describe number in each discipline.
   b. What is the size of each department?

7. Calculate the pertinent billable ratios, both in manhours and in dollars, for the past three years and last six months.
8. What jobs has the company lost in the past three years?
9. What criteria are used to determine the budget for a proposal? What is the annual expenditure? Who decides what jobs to bid and how much is to be spent in preparing the proposal?
10. Who reviews job estimates?
11. What cost control and scheduling procedures are used?
12. How does this firm control, contract for, determine, and calculate escalation for extra work orders?
13. What is the manhours backlog by type of work?
14. What are the firm's hourly billing rates?
15. Describe the firm's R&D program.
    a. Objectives.
    b. Expenditures
    c. Manpower.
    d. Activities.
    e. Results.
    f. Amount spent in each of past five years.
16. List company facilities.
    a. Location.
    b. Use.
    c. Owned or Leased.
    d. Present adequacy.
    e. Age of facility.
    f. Number of employees.
17. Describe any items or services now purchased outside, either being supplied, or could be supplied by the buyer.
18. Describe any critical processes dependent on licenses or other technical contracts.
19. Describe any new facilities under construction or being contemplated within one year.
20. Describe the purchasing function and its actual control over purchasing.
    a. Who is responsible?
    b. Describe any unusual purchase commitments made or soon to be made.
21. List the major and critical suppliers.
    a. Supplier.
    b. Item supplied.
    c. Annual purchase.
    d. Describe any special supplier relationship to the company, its management, or its owners.
22. Describe any sole source supply situations.

Management Report—Manufacturing
(To be completed only for manufacturing companies)

1. List company manufacturing facilities.
   a. Location.
   b. Products manufactured.
   c. Owned or leased.
   d. Age of facility.
   e. Number of employees.
   f. Number of shifts.
   g. Average hourly rate.
   h. Capacity and present percent of utilization.
2. Describe the manufacturing organization and identify responsibilities and functions of each department.
3. Describe any items or services now purchased outside, either being supplied by the buyer's organization, or that could be supplied by the buyer's units.
4. Describe any critical manufacturing processes dependent on licenses or other technical contracts. List any critical tools, dies, or patterns not owned.
5. Describe and evaluate the quality control function.
6. Describe any new facilities either under construction or being contemplated within one year.
7. Describe and evaluate the purchasing function and its actual control over purchasing.
   a. Who is responsible?
   b. Describe any unusual purchase commitments made, or soon to be made.
   c. What are the major items purchased?
8. List the major and critical suppliers.
   a. Supplier.
   b. Item supplied.
   c. Annual purchases.
   d. Describe any special supplier relationship to the company, its management, or its owners.
   e. Describe any unusual payment terms.
9. Describe and evaluate the maintenance and repair program.
10. Describe any sole source supply situations.
11. Are shipments relatively even during month, or are most shipments made near end of month? Are shipments being made on time?
12. Is manufacturing working mainly from sold orders, a sales forecast, or for inventory?

13. Describe and evaluate in general terms the machinery and equipment.
14. What new products were introduced in the past three years, and what was the result?
15. What new products are under development and may be introduced within the next twenty-four months?
16. What is the size of the engineering department? How many graduate engineers?
17. How much engineering is sold to customers as a separate charge?
18. What is the engineering manhours backlog?
19. What is the firm's engineering hourly billing rates, if applicable?
20. Describe and evaluate the firm's R&D program considering:
    a. Objectives.
    b. Expenditures.
    c. Manpower.
    d. Activities
    e. Results.
    f. The R&D expenditures in each of the past five years.
21. Describe and evaluate the manufacturing processes and procedures.
22. Describe and evaluate the plant layout and work flow.
23. Describe and evaluate the use of subcontracting.
24. Describe and evaluate the employee and union relations.
25. Describe and evaluate the production planning and rescheduling systems.
26. Describe and evaluate flexibility to increase or decrease production.
27. Describe and evaluate any environmental problems.
28. Compare labor costs to those of significant competitors.
29. Do the manufacturing locations constitute an advantage or disadvantage compared to competitors?
30. How are the company products normally shipped?
31. Have any locations had difficulty in securing adequate power or fuel, and are any problems anticipated in the future?

Comparison of Acquisition Prospect with Buyer's Policies and Objectives

The acquisition should meet the policies and objectives of the buyer with regard to the following:

1. Type of business or industry.
2. Proprietary products or services.

3. Financial history.
4. Present financial condition.
5. Debt.
6. PE ratio.
7. Return on investment.
8. Minimum pretax profit.
9. Seasonal characteristics.
10. Present state of profitability.
11. Growth potential for sales.
12. Growth potential for earnings.
13. Synergistic effects.
14. Price in relation to buyer's existing PE ratio.
15. Stock dilution.

Literature of Selling Company

1. Annual report of company if public.
2. Product literature.
3. If service or consulting company, government report form 254.

NOTE: If above literature is too voluminous, place in a separate
volume except for annual report.

Part 2–
Contractual Agreements
and Historical
and Statistical Data

This second part of Appendix 1 addresses the original financial data, legal documents, and other documents of the prospect that must be examined. Part 2 also contains extensive questionnaires primarily requiring information on key functions of the prospect either not covered or summarized in Part 1. While Part 1 may be more to the liking of a board of directors wanting a relatively brief overview of the prospect, it is crucial to a successful acquisition that the information requested in this second part be secured. Part 2 covers:

1. Agreements relating to transaction
2. Accounting
3. Cash and cash flow
4. Banking and finance
5. Legal report
6. Personnel, compensation and employee benefit programs
7. Insurance

Agreements Relating to Transaction

1. Copy of the definitive acquisition agreements.
2. Letter of intent or other evidence of initial offer and agreement.
3. Origin of acquisition—How were the buyer and seller introduced? What finder's, broker's, or investment banker's fees are due?

Accounting

1. Published annual reports for the past five years.
2. Annual financial statements (income, balance sheet, funds flow) for the past five years.
3. Tax returns for the past five years.
4. Monthly financial statements (income, balance sheet, funds flow) for the past twelve months.
5. Balance sheet at quarterly intervals for the past eighteen months.
6. Copies of all SEC filings for the past five years.

Accounting Report

1. Describe accounting principles and procedures employed.
   a. Inventories.
   b. Receivables.
   c. Depreciation and amortization.
   d. Reserves.
   e. Capitalization vs. expense.
   f. Deferred charges and credits.
   g. Inclusion or exclusion of subsidiaries or affiliates in consolidated statements.
   h. Revenue and income matching and recognition.
   i. Describe the year-to-year consistency of application of accounting principles and procedures. Note any changes in past five years.
2. Describe any significant or unusual notes to the latest financial statement.
3. Describe any significant differences between financial statements, tax returns, and SEC reports.
4. Describe accounts and notes receivable.
   a. Have they all arisen out of normal sales?
   b. Have they been confirmed?
   c. Classify by age. What is considered "current"?
   d. Identify the major debtors. Make separate list of ten largest.
   e. Describe the method for providing for uncollectibles, including the method for determining when an account is uncollectible and past collection procedures.
   f. Describe the reserve for uncollectible accounts.
   g. Describe any collateralized accounts receivable.
   h. Describe any pledging, factoring, or restrictions.

      i. Describe the credit system and policies, including who has responsibility for extending credit.

      j. Describe how retentions, if any, are accounted for. If appropriate, adjust the A/R aging accordingly.

      k. List all notes receivable, debtor, rate, retirement schedule, collateral, liens, legal status, whether up to date in payment, and reason for note.

      l. Describe the relationship of credit terms to sales prices.

5. Describe other receivables.
   a. Non-trade.
   b. Other, such as "unbilled receivables."
   c. Detailed description of all loans to employees and shareholders.

6. Describe inventories.
   a. Composition by dollar amount and percent of total.
      (i) raw materials
      (ii) components or parts
      (iii) work-in-process
      (iv) spare parts
      (v) finished goods
      (vi) others
      (vii) shelf stock vs. manufactured customer order
      (viii) manufactured vs. purchased
      (ix) on consignment
   b. Calculate turnover for major items.
   c. Describe inventory controls.
   d. Describe the valuation basis.
   e. Frequency of physical inventories and last result vs. book.
   f. Describe the handling of obsolete items.

7. Describe prepayments.
   a. Composition.
   b. Status of current items.
   c. Term of realization.
   d. Company policy of expense vs. prepayment.

8. Describe fixed assets.
   a. Do accurate itemized records exist? When was a physical inventory of fixed assets last conducted?
   b. Valuation method, for book and tax purpose.
   c. Depreciation and amortization method, for book and tax purposes.
   d. Comparison of book values of fixed assets to estimated current appraisal values.
   e. Has there been any recent appraisals? If yes, secure copies.

    f. Prepare a list and description of all owned real estate.

    g. Describe any mortgages, liens, or other financing or encumbrances.

    h. What are maintenance and repair costs?

    i. Describe the history of capital additions in past three years.

    j. What is age of major assets?

    k. Describe any assets held under lease and their terms.

    l. Describe any franchise held and their terms.

9. Intangible assets.
   a. List types and value. (Provide a detailed listing of patents, if any.)
   b. Describe the method of valuation and amortization.
   c. Describe any income produced by these assets.

10. Other assets.
   a. List and describe, including valuation basis.
   b. Identify any unconsolidated subsidiaries and related income.
   c. Describe the search for unrecorded assets and its results.
   d. List of automobiles and trucks.
   e. List of watercraft and aircraft.

11. Describe current liabilities.
   a. Classify accounts payable, notes payable, accruals, current portions of long-term debts, taxes and other.
   b. Classify accounts payable by age.
   c. Describe any advance payments (i.e., advances under contracts).
   d. Any provision for taxes renegotiation or redetermination.
   e. Are payroll, withholding, income, and property taxes current?
   f. Describe warranty exposure and reserves.
   g. Provide details of any other significant liabilities.
   h. Describe the research for unrecorded liabilities and its results.

12. Long-term debt.
   a. Are there any unusual relationships between management and the creditors? Such as warrants, conversion rights, etc.?
   b. Describe the company's plans to meet maturity dates.
   c. Is any debt in default?
   d. Describe the restrictions contained in debt agreements.
   e. Are there any commitments for long or short term revolving lines of credit?
   f. Do any debt agreements contain provisions which could effect control or restrict sale of shares?

13. Describe and analyze minority interests.
    a. Nature and amount.
    b. Sinking funds or other retirement provisions.
    c. Rights and privileges.
14. Describe and analyze net worth.
    a. Composition of owner's equity and any unusual transactions.
    b. Special reserves, origin and disposition planned.
    c. Restrictions upon retained earnings. Secure documents.
    d. Company's dividend history and current policy.
    e. Origin and amount of contributed capital or capital surplus.
    f. What is the actual net worth after exclusion of certain assets with questionable values, such as intangibles? . Include schedule of calculation and justification for exclusion.
15. Sales.
    a. What is the present backlog of unfilled orders? Is this backlog normal, high, low, increasing, or declining? Comment in detail.
    b. Describe the method of recognizing a "sale." When percentage of completed contracts or similar method is used—
       (i) Describe in detail the method of taking up income. If a form or report is used, attach a copy.
       (ii) Describe the contingency reserves established for unknown variables.
       (iii) Is there any profit "hold-back" or deferred profit? If so, where is it taken up?
       (iv) Is "cost to complete" recalculated each month?
       (v) List jobs in-house. Describe status as regards completion, dollar profit taken, and dollar profit remaining. Calculate percentage of total profit to total contract price.
       (vi) Are there any other methods used to book revenue?
       (vii) Describe any unusual contract cost elements.
    c. Reconcile the difference between the gross and net sales.
    d. Classify as to U.S. government vs. non-U.S. government by product lines.
    e. Classify sales volume by product line.
    f. Any material amount of unbooked credit?
    g. Are there any intercompany or interdivision sales or sales to related or affiliated companies? Identify those not eliminated in consolidation.
    h. List the three largest customers and percent of sales for which they account, as well as any customer accounting for over 5% of sales.
    i. If selling through distributors, dealers, or representatives, list the name and the volume for each last year.

    j. List all presently employed salesmen, their sales volume, and compensation for past year. Are salesmen paid straight salary, salary plus bonus, commission, etc. Describe.

16. Cost of goods sold.
    a. What cost systems are used to calculate components of cost of sales?
    b. What are the percentage relationships with respect to material, labor, and overhead?
    c. Describe any over- or under-absorbed overhead, their consistency and causes.
    d. What are the principal elements of cost included in overhead and the method of their calculation and allocation?
    e. If a standard cost system is used, how are variances handled?
    f. What are the non-cash accounts included in cost of sales?
    g. How is cost of sales significantly affected by such matters as quantity buying, discounts on purchases or purchases from related or affiliated companies?

17. Classify gross profit dollars by product line and by type of distribution.

18. Sales expense.
    a. Describe the composition of sales expense.
    b. Classify sales expense by product line and type of distribution.
    c. Which sales expenses vary directly with volume?
    d. What is the relative cost of physical distribution of the products?

19. General and administrative expenses.
    a. Describe the composition of administrative expenses.
    b. Relate these expenses to sales volume on a percentage basis.
    c. Describe the extent of any allocation of expenses or income.
    d. What is the annual lease expense?

20. Describe income and expenses.

21. Net income.
    a. What are the sources of net income by product line and by type of distribution?
    b. What portion of net income resulted from operations? From other income? Is the pattern reoccurring?

22. Adjustments.
    a. Describe any significant audit or year-end adjustments for the past 4 years.
    b. How were foreign exchange differences considered?

23. Review the SEC filings and note any differences with the information maintained at the company.

24. Income, property, sales, and use tax returns.
    a. Status and amount of each.
    b. Date of last audit on each.
    c. List and describe all items in dispute.
25. Describe the circumstances and procedures that give rise to deferred taxes.
26. List all countries in which business is conducted.
27. Annual license income and expense.
28. Annual royalty income and expense.
29. What is the annual value of fabrication or services being subcontracted?
30. List significant commitments of the company, such as capital expenditures, inventory expenditures, currency speculation or hedging, process guarantees, etc.
31. If purchase price is to be allocated to assets, what is buyer's optimum position from a tax standpoint? What is seller's?
32. Prepare a list of all EDP equipment. Indicate its present use, if leased or owned, annual cost, and any plans to change equipment.

Cash and Cash Flow

1. Cash balances.
    a. Bank balances.
        (i) location and account numbers
        (ii) signatories
        (iii) average monthly balances last 12 months
        (iv) confirmation of balances
        (v) reconciliation of bank accounts
        (vi) restrictions
    b. Other cash balances.
2. Securities and other investments.
    a. List and describe.
    b. Valuation basis.
    c. Cost.
    d. Marketability.
    e. Current market price.
    f. Confirmation of securities.
    g. Debt, liabilities, or restrictions applicable to securities.
3. Cash flow.
    a. Cash flow statements for last four years and monthly to date for last twelve months.

b. List any factors materially affecting historical pattern and trend of cash flow.

c. List any factors materially influencing pattern, trend, validity and reliability of forecast cash flow.

Banking and Finance

1. List and description of banking and credit relationships.
2. List and description of all loans and lines of credit.
3. Copies of all debentures and loan agreements, and documents and summary of terms, such as acceleration and prepayment clauses, maturity dates, collateral, interest rates, identity of the creditors, renewal and assignment provisions, restrictions on mergers, acquisitions, etc.
4. List of safe deposit boxes, locations, numbers, and signatures.
5. List of loans and advances to officers, directors and shareholders.

Legal Report

1. Exact corporate name and address.
2. State and date of company's incorporation.
3. List other states in which it is qualified to do business, if any.
4. Exact corporate name, address, and state of incorporation of any subsidiary(ies) of company. List share ownership of each subsidiary.
5. Authorized capital of company.
   a. Class of stock.
   b. Par value.
   c. Shares authorized.
   d. Shares outstanding.
   e. Treasury shares.
   f. Any restrictions on issue, use, repurchase, etc.
   g. Stock options or warrants outstanding.
6. Exact names and permanent mailing addresses of all stockholders of company and number and class of shares owned by:
   a. Class of stock.
   b. Name and address of shareholders.
   c. Number of shares.
7. Counsel for stockholders.
   a. Name and address.
   b. Telephone.

8. Copies and analysis of all contracts by category, including evaluation of contingent liabilities, or other significant and unusual features.
   a. Purchase contracts in excess of $50,000.
   b. Utilities.
   c. Employment.
   d. Union.
   e. Compensation.
   f. Sales agreements with representatives, dealers, etc.
   g. Insurance.
   h. Consulting.
   i. Leases.
   j. Licensing agreements.
   k. Royalty agreements.
   l. Deferred compensation plans.
   m. Patents.
   n. Sales contracts and performance guarantees.
   o. Product liability obligations.
   p. Any agreements with shareholders.
   q. Warranty obligations.
   r. Agreements of obligations to former employees.
9. Relationship to EEOC, OSHA, OFDI, price commissions, SEC, IRS, and other state or federal regulatory agencies.
   a. Copies of reports.
   b. Description of compliance programs.
   c. Previous, existing, or anticipated regulatory problems. List all violations or disputed items.
10. Copies of any judgments against the company and/or officers.
11. History of significant litigation.
12. Description of all existing or anticipated litigation against the company where amount claimed could exceed $5,000.
13. Description of existing or anticipated litigation by the company against others.
14. Annual outside legal expenses (by firm).
15. Description of the review of corporate minutes and its results.
16. Names and addresses of all governmental and private parties (other than stockholders) that must consent to or be notified of the transaction. Are approvals doubtful by any approving bodies?
17. Copies of charters, by-laws, and other corporate documents.
18. Has the company or any of its officers ever been accused of a criminal offense? If yes, describe in detail the events and outcome.

19. Has the company engaged in any kickbacks, political donations, or questionable payments? Is it now in compliance with the law?
20. Has the company complied with government regulations regarding international boycotts?
21. List all management "perks." Would any be considered excessive or unusual, and create liability for executives or company?
22. Do any shareholders, officers, directors, or employees have interests in a business that would represent a conflict of interest?
23. Describe any major restrictions imposed on the mangement as a result of stock provisions or debt instruments.

Personnel, Compensation, and Employee Benefit Programs

1. Employee and Employee Programs Report
   a. List of retirement plans in effect or announced. Indicate who is covered by each plan. Describe the benefits. Describe method of funding and annual cost. Describe in detail amount of unfunded past service liability if any.
   b. Summary of all profit sharing plans in effect and describe in detail.
   c. Describe any bonus or incentive plans in effect and who is covered.
   d. Describe any deferred compensation plans in effect and who is covered.
   e. Describe any stock bonus or option plans in effect, and who is covered.
   f. Describe the company's safety record, program and results of most recent OSHA inspection. Secure copies of all violation reports.
   g. List unions with bargaining rights, location and date contracts expire.
   h. Who negotiates the union contracts?
   i. List any union representation elections held in the past 3 years, and describe results.
   j. What has been the strike history at each location?
   k. List arbitrations held in the past 24 months.
   l. Describe in detail total compensation of each employee who owns more than 5% of the stock in the company, and of officers. Include details of salary, bonus, pension, major fringe benefits, automobiles, club memberships, etc.
   m. Describe any other bonus, profit sharing, incentive or non-monetary compensation plan.

    n. How many graduate engineers or other professionals does the company employ?

    o. Describe any management, sales or other employee training program.

    p. What are the normal hours of work per week at the principal locations?

    q. Describe the employee turnover in the company. How many key employees have been lost in past years?

2. Organization chart.
3. Responsibilities and functions of department/divisions.
4. Total number of employees by geographical location.
5. Copies of incentive, bonus, profit sharing, or stock option plans.
6. Copies of pension plan and government reports.
7. Copies of employee handbooks.
8. Copies of salary administration plans.
9. Copies of EEO reports.
10. List of directors and officers.
11. List of all salaried employees, title, and salaries.
12. Resume information on key employees (officers and department managers).
13. Copies of all company policy manuals.

Insurance

1. Summary schedule of all insurance, showing:
    a. Name of insured.
    b. Type of insurance.
    c. Company.
    d. Policy number.
    e. Limits/deductions.
    f. Expiration date of policy.
    g. Name of broker or agent for each policy.
2. Copies of all policies in force.
3. Provide name, mailing address and telephone number for individuals responsible for insurance matters.
4. The opinion of the insurance department as to the adequacy of insurance coverage.

Appendix 2
Preclosing
Acquisition Checklist

This checklist is for use in the week prior to signing definitive contracts. It is designed to determine if any significant changes have occurred in the prospect since the buyer conducted his initial study and negotiated the agreement about to be signed.

Banking and Finance Checklist

Note changes in banking and financial relationships that have occurred since the pre-acquisition audit was performed.

	Yes	No
1. Compare the actual debt with the forecasted debt for time of acquisition. Is there any difference? If yes, explain in detail.	___	___
2. Has the company received any new loans and/or lines of credit since the acquisition study was prepared? If yes, describe fully and secure copies of all new loan agreements, if any, including documents describing summary of terms such as acceleration and pre-payment clauses, maturity dates, collateral, interest rates, identity of the creditor, renewal and assignment provisions, restrictions on mergers, acquisitions, etc.	___	___
3. Are there any new loans or advances to officers, directors, shareholders, or employees in excess of those listed in the acquisition study? If yes, identify amount of loan or advance, name of recipient, position with the company, and explain fully.	___	___

	Yes	No

4. Have any new safe deposit boxes been rented in the name of the company?
   If yes, give locations, numbers, and signatories.

5. Has the company opened or terminated any bank accounts or bank relationships of any kind?
   If yes, identify by bank, location, account numbers, and signatories.

6. Has the cash balance increased or decreased by more than 15%?
   If yes, identify the major causes of the change.

Legal Checklist

Note any changes in the legal obligations of the company since the preparation of the acquisition study.

	Yes	No

1. Have there been any changes or planned changes in the authorized capital of the company?
   If yes, identify any changes under the categories listed below.
   a. Class of stock.
   b. Par value.
   c. Shares authorized.
   d. Shares outstanding.
   e. Treasury shares.
   f. Any restrictions on issue, use, repurchase, etc.

2. Are there any new stockholders in the company?
   If yes, identify new stockholders by:
   a. Class of stock.
   b. Name and address of shareholders.
   c. Number of shares.

3. Is the company a party to any new contracts or does the company have any existing contracts newly terminated since the date of the pre-acquisition audit?

If yes, attach copies and evaluate, by category, the following items for any contingent liabilities or other significant and unusual features.
  a. Purchase materials, parts, or services in excess of $50,000.
  b. Utilities.
  c. Employment.
  d. Union.
  e. Compensation.
  f. Sales agreements with representatives, dealers, etc.
  g. Insurance.
  h. Consulting.
  i. Leases.
  j. Licensing agreements.
  k. Royalty agreements.
  l. Deferred compensation plans.
  m. Stock option plans.
  n. Group medical plans.
  o. Pension plans.
  p. Profit sharing plans.
  q. Patents.
      (i) existing or anticipated patent litigation.
      (ii) significance of contested patents to company's competitive position.
  r. Sales contracts in excess of $50,000 or with performance guarantees.
  s. Agreements or obligations to former employees.

	Yes	No
4. Are there any new or anticipated regulatory orders from local, state, or federal agencies? If yes, describe nature of order and identify issuing agency.	___	___
5. Has there been any new litigation of judgment against the company? If yes, identify litigants and describe claims, judgments, and intent and/or progress of appeal.	___	___

	Yes	No

6. Is there any new previously undisclosed anticipated litigation against the company or by the company against others?
   If yes, describe nature of anticipated litigation.

7. Are there any newly identified governmental or private parties which must consent or be notified of the transaction?
   If yes, identify and explain.

8. Has the company entered into any joint venture agreements?
   If yes, describe the agreement and explain its impact on the transaction.

9. Describe recent developments on all outstanding litigation with potential losses or recoveries exceeding $10,000.

Cash Flow Checklist

Compare the company's most current cash position with the year-to-date cash flow forecast for the date closest to anticipated closing of the acquisition.

	Yes	No

1. Is there any reason to believe the cash flow forecast is no longer accurate?
   If yes, does the change reflect a favorable or adverse development in the business? If adverse, is the change easily remedied?
   Explain how.
   If yes, explain fully the reason(s) or cause(s) for the change.

2. Does the present cash position as reported on the company's most current cash flow statements exceed $25,000 of forecast levels?
   If yes, explain causes for the changed cash flow and evaluate prospects for meeting year-end net cash forecasts.

3. Have there been any changes in accounting definitions or procedures that result in an understatement or overstatement of the company's working capital position?

If yes, explain in detail, calculate impact and
restate cash position as if reported on a consistent basis.

	Yes	No

4. Have there been any non-business related
   payments reported under such items as legal
   fees, sales commissions, dividends, special
   fees to shareholders, etc., or other items that
   represent a recognizable departure from historical company payments?   ____   ____
   If yes, describe in detail, quantify payments
   and identify payee and relationship to the
   company, stockholders and/or suppliers.
5. Have there been any changes in the com-
   pany's security and investment holdings?   ____   ____
   If yes, describe changes by category includ-
   ing:
   a. Investment or security by name.
   b. Valuation basis.
   c. Cost.
   d. Marketability.
   e. Current market prices.
   f. Debt, liabilities, or restrictions applicable
      to securities.
6. Has there been a decline exceeding 10% in the
   combined value of the securities and investment holdings of the company?   ____   ____
   If yes, enumerate and describe all holdings
   with losses that individually exceed $2,000.
   a. Investment or security by name.
   b. Valuation basis.
   c. Cost.
   d. Marketability.
   e. Current market prices.
   f. Debt, liabilities, or restrictions applicable
      to securities.

Management and Operations Checklist

	Yes	No

1. Have any significant developments occurred
   involving:
   a. Critical or sole-source suppliers.   ____   ____
   b. Sub-contractors.   ____   ____

	Yes	No
c. Processes dependent on licenses.	___	___
d. Company control over tools, dies, patterns.	___	___
e. Company pricing/estimating policies (If yes, describe the success of the changes).	___	___
f. Unsatisfactory relations with or loss of major customers.	___	___
g. Competitive status of the company.	___	___
h. Damage to physical assets.	___	___
i. Actual or threatened union disputes.	___	___

If yes, for any of the above, explain fully by item.

Personnel and Compensation Checklist

Note any significant changes in personnel since the acquisition study was prepared.

	Yes	No
1. Officers.		
a. Have any officers resigned?	___	___
b. Have any new officers been designated?	___	___
c. Have there been any changes in functions or responsibilities among officers?	___	___
d. Have there been any changes in compensation or method of compensating officers?	___	___
e. Have there been any changes in officer accounts payable and receivable?	___	___

If yes, for any of the above items, explain fully.

2. Key Employees.		
a. Have any resignations or terminations occurred among key employees?	___	___
b. Have any key personnel been hired?	___	___
c. Have there been any changes in functions or responsibilities among key personnel?	___	___
d. Have there been any changes in compensation or methods of compensating key personnel including supplementary compensation programs (i.e., bonuses, incentive programs, commissions, fringe benefits, etc.)?	___	___

	Yes	No

e. Have there been any changes in key personnel accounts payable or receivable? ____ ____

f. Have any employees with salaries in excess of $25,000 per year been employed? ____ ____

If yes, for any of the above items, explain fully.

3. Office employees.

   a. Have there been any changes in the total number of employees in excess of 5%? ____ ____

   b. Have there been any increases in compensation other than normal periodic salary adjustments? ____ ____

   c. Have there been increases in total payroll for office employees representing an increase exceeding 2% of total office payroll since the acquisition study was prepared? ____ ____

   d. Have there been any changes in the method of compensating office employees (i.e. incentive programs, fringe benefits, etc.)? ____ ____

   e. Have there been any changes in accounts payable to and receivable from office employees? ____ ____

If yes, for any of the above items, explain fully.

4. Production employees.

   a. Have there been any changes in total number of employees in excess of 5%? ____ ____

   b. Have there been any increases in compensation other than normal periodic wage adjustments or those obligated in advance, such as in union contracts? ____ ____

   c. Have there been increases in total payroll for production employees representing an increase exceeding 2% of total production payroll since the acquisition study was prepared? ____ ____

   d. Have there been any changes in the method of compensating production employees (i.e. incentive programs, fringe benefits, etc.)? ____ ____

   e. Have there been any changes in accounts payable to and receivable from production employees? ____ ____

If yes, for any of the above, explain fully by item.

	Yes	No

5. Marketing employees.
   a. Have any salesmen been terminated? ____ ____
   b. Have any new compensation plans been installed or present plans revised? ____ ____

If yes, for any of the above, explain fully by item.

Backlog and Work-in-Process Checklist

Backlog and work-in-process are among the most critical and potentially illusive of all the items contained in the pre-closing checklists. For these reasons, those conducting pre-closing inquiries are urged to seek in-depth information that will reveal as totally as practicable the real condition of the company in these areas. Accordingly, questions for this section of the report are more open-ended than in other areas.

	Yes	No

1. Backlog.
   a. Does the present backlog indicate the sales forecast can be met? ____ ____
   b. What is the present backlog of unfiled orders?
   c. Is the backlog for each product line normal, high, low, increasing, or declining? Evaluate and comment in detail and depth.
2. New Orders.
   a. Are there any immediate prospects for significant new bookings beyond the acquisition forecast? ____ ____
   b. Evaluate in detail the sales status of each major prospect including client/customer, size and nature of the order or contract, probability that the contract will be let, probability that the company will receive the order?
3. Work-in-process.
   a. List any jobs in-house that exceed 5% of last year's sales volume.
   b. Describe the status of each job as regards percent completed, dollar profit taken, and dollar profit remaining.

    c. Calculate percentage of total profit to total contract price.

    d. Describe any changes in contract cost elements.

    e. What are the prospects for completion on time within the budget?

4. Bids outstanding.

    a. Quantify total order bids outstanding.

    b. Is this figure high, normal, low, increasing, or declining?

    c. Quantify total order bids issued during the last 2 months?

    d. Is this figure normal, high, low, increasing, or declining?

    e. Evaluate against comparable past periods.

    f. Evaluate in detail and depth the prospects for the business.

Sales and Operating Income Checklist

	Yes	No
1. Sales: Do gross revenues, as reported in the company's most recent monthly income statements fail to reach at least 95% of forecast levels?	___	___
If yes, explain fully the reason(s) or cause(s) for lower-than-expected revenues and evaluate prospects for meeting year-end forecast.		
2. Have "sales" been inflated in any manner? (For example, by changing the method for recognizing a "sale.")	___	___
If yes, explain fully, estimate the accounting impact of the change and calculate new revenues and profits as reported on a consistent basis.		
3. When expressed as a percentage of sales, do any of the following items reflect an increase of more that 2% in excess of percentage of sales figures in monthly forecasts?		
a. Costs of goods sold.	___	___
b. Gross profit.	___	___
c. Sales expense.	___	___
d. General and administrative expense.	___	___

	Yes	No

e. Other income (identify).   ____ ____
f. Other expense (identify).   ____ ____
If yes, explain fully citing reasons or causes of
increases and possible remedies.

4. When expressed as a percentage of sales, do
   pretax profits reflect a decrease of more than
   1% from percentage of sales figures in
   monthly forecasts?   ____ ____
   If yes, explain fully the reason(s) or cause(s)
   for lower-than-expected profits and evaluate
   current prospects for meeting year-end forecast.

5. Has there been any change exceeding 5% in
   percentage of total sales volume by any product line compared to the monthly, quarterly
   and/or annual forecast?   ____ ____
   If yes, identify product line, percentage increase and evaluate prospects of retaining this
   type of business on a continuing basis.

6. Has there been any change exceeding $2,000
   in the amount of unbooked credits?   ____ ____
   If yes, explain source and disposition.

7. Have there been any intercompany or inter-
   division sales or sales to related or affiliated
   companies exceeding $10,000?   ____ ____
   If yes, identify company or division, nature of
   sale, and evaluate equitability of the transaction and permanence of this type of business.

8. If selling through distributors, dealers, or
   representatives, have there been any changes
   in representation?   ____ ____
   If yes, identify and explain reasons for
   change(s).

Balance Sheet Checklist

Compare the company's most current balance sheet with balance
sheet forecast for the date closest to anticipated closing of the
acquisition. Note any material changes in the listed item and evaluate
changes with respect to the following:

	Yes	No

1. Is there a change resulting from a change in
   accounting procedures, however minor?   ____ ____
   If yes, explain fully.

	Yes	No

2. Are there any major changes reflecting a favorable or adverse development in the business?

   If yes, explain fully.

3. Evaluate the auditor's statement. Does it employ unusual or unacceptable accounting principles?

   If yes, explain fully.

4. Assets: Are any of the following assets items on the company's most current balance sheet lower than on the balance sheet forecast by more than 5% in dollar terms or by more than 2% when expressed as a percentage of total assets?

   a. Cash and securities.
   b. Accounts receivable.
   c. Retentions receivable
   d. Inventory.
   e. Short-term notes receivable
   f. Pre-payments.
   g. Long-term notes receivable
   h. Fixed assets.
   i. Intangible assets.
   j. Other assets.

   If yes, explain fully by each item.

5. Liabilities: Are any of the following liability items on the company's most current balance sheet higher than on the balance sheet forecast by more than 5% in dollar terms or by more than 2% when expressed as a percentage of total liabilities and equity?

   a. Accounts payable.
   b. Retentions payable.
   c. Short-term notes payable.
   d. Taxes and accrued items.
   e. Long-term debt.

   If yes, explain fully by item.

6. Equity: Is the total of all equity items on the company's most current balance sheet lower than on the balance sheet forecast by more than 2% in dollar terms or by more than 1% when expressed as a percentage of total liabilities and equity?

   If yes, explain fully.

7. Does the company's most recent balance sheet reflect a lower current ratio than the balance sheet forecast exceeding a difference of 0.2 to 1 or a decline to a level below 1.5 to 1?   ____   ____
   If yes, explain fully, cite causes and possible remedies.

8. Since the acquisition study was prepared have any items in the following accounts declined into an older collection or retirement status?
   a. Accounts receivable.   ____   ____
   b. Retentions receivable.   ____   ____
   c. Short-term notes receivable.   ____   ____
   d. Long-term notes receivable.   ____   ____
   If yes, explain fully by item.

9. Since the acquisition study was prepared has any receivable exceeding $5,000 become overdue or questionable as to collection?   ____   ____
   If yes, explain fully.

10. Since the acquisition study was prepared has there been a change of more than 10% in the aging or retirement status of any of the following items?
    a. Accounts payable.   ____   ____
    b. Retentions payable.   ____   ____
    c. Short-term notes payable.   ____   ____
    d. Long-term debt.   ____   ____
    If yes, explain fully by item.

Index

DEC